DESTROYING LIES IN THE CHURCH
LIBERIA

BENJAMIN MARSHALL

© 2020 by Benjamin Marshall
Published by Passion Publications
a division of Tell the Truth International
7005 Woodbine Ave
Sacramento, Ca. 95822
tellthetruthsac@gmail.com
www.tttmi.org

Printed in the United States of America

All rights reserved. No part of this book may be reproduced in whole or part, in any form or by any means, electronic or mechanical, including photocopying, recording or by any information storage and retrieval system without express written permission from the author.

Cover image and design by:
charlyn_designs@fiverr.com

ISBN: 978-0-9729904-2-4

Unless otherwise indicated, all scripture quotations are taken from the New King James Version of the Bible.
Abbreviations of other translations used are as follows:
AMP (Amplified), CEV (Contemporary English Version),
BSB (Berean Study Bible), NASB (New American Standard Bible)
NIV (New International Version), GNT (Good News Translation),
NLT (New Living Translation), ESV (English Standard Version)

DEDICATION

This book is dedicated to every young Liberian dreamer and visionary who believes with God all things are possible.

Those children and youth who refuse to give up hope of having a better Liberia and a better future for themselves and their children.

World changers who will use their faith and gifts to rise above any moral filth and negative influence; pursuing righteousness until they see a positive change in their nation and around the world.

CONTENTS

Foreword 7
Introduction 9
The Authority of Scripture 15
Tradition & Culture 22
The Battle of the Mind 30
Lie #1 Liberia is a Christian Nation 38
Lie #2 We are Naturally Good People 56
Lie #3 Liberia is Independent 68
Lie #4 Liberia Needs International Support 91
Lie #5 Liberians Need More Money 120
Lie #6 Accountability is Not Necessary 144
Lie #7 School is The Key to Success 158
Lie #8 Look Out Only for Yourself 180
Lie #9 Lying is not A Big Deal 192
Lie #10 Sexual Immorality is Normal 209
Lie #11 All Church Leaders are God's Representatives 222
Lie #12 Fatherlessness is Just Another Problem 234
Lie #13 We Understand Blessings and Curses 252
Lie #14 We are Healed from Our Past 269
Lie #15 Some People are Better than Others 286
Epilogue: Do You Want to Get Well? 299
Bibliography 305

FOREWORD

Do you consider yourself to be a part of the church community in Liberia? How about anywhere else in Africa or around the world? Do you believe the Christian community holds the key for positive change around the world? I believe this. Is there hope for Liberia, Africa, and the rest of the world? Yes.

The purpose of writing this book is to help us to see and understand what has really been happening and to do a self- analysis, acknowledge the underlying issues and problems, and take responsibility individually and as a church collectively for these problems.

After my many visits, experiences, and entrepreneurial ventures with Liberian people, what stands out most to me is the spiritual condition of the nation. Despite seeing the effects of poverty, economic underdevelopment, health issues, low accountability, and corruption, I conclude that what is really ailing Liberia and needs to happen for it and other nations to be far less problematic and much more fruitful and productive is more spiritual than anything else. This book challenges the main institution that is responsible to lead this change - the Christian church.

As a church community we must admit our mistakes and make the necessary changes no matter how hard it will be. It is time for this current generation to heal and a new generation of young people to put the past behind them and look forward to experiencing a brighter future.

INTRODUCTION

The goal of this book is about making all Christians better people. However, specifically making Liberia a better place. A better place happens as a result of a better people living in that place.

Why Liberia? How does a Black American man all the way from California, USA next to the Pacific Ocean, find himself with an assignment to go and educate the church and next generation of this particular country, that is sitting next to the Atlantic Ocean in West Africa? Well this was not something I planned at all, or thought that I would ever pursue. This was a call.

In order to get to this place, many extraordinary things had to happen along the way. In 2009 while serving as an associate pastor, I was instructed by God to leave my church and return to a church I had previously attended. I did not completely understand this and actually tried to resist it, but I knew God was leading me back. After having returned for about a month, a video was shown one Sunday about a mission trip to Liberia, Africa. I had never even heard of Liberia up to that point and knew absolutely nothing about the 14 years of civil war that had recently ended and practically destroyed that country's infrastructure.

Immediately I heard the Lord speak to my heart and say, "This is the reason you needed to come back here, you are supposed to go on this trip." A sense of excitement came over me and I began the application process required in order to be a part of this mission team. I prayed and said, "God, if you are truly leading me, I will be picked to go and you will provide the funds."

I was selected as part of the group. My next step in the process was to come up with the amount of $3,000 for my total expenses. After sending support letters, I had raised about $300. I will never forget the day I received the call from the church secretary stating they would not be able to buy my tickets with everyone else because I had not raised enough money. After receiving the call, I was very disappointed and asked God what happened. I remember feeling led to not complain but to thank God for His goodness.

It was during this time of thanksgiving and praise that I received a call to minister and receive more support for my trip. Later that same week, the senior pastor of the church I currently attended found out I was going and was very surprised and glad; asking me to see him. It turned out that he had a health issue that was going to keep him from going on the trip this particular time and he wanted me to take his place teaching the Liberian pastors at the training they scheduled.

After that, the very next day I received a call from a family member who said he had planned to go to Africa and his work schedule wouldn't allow him to go, so he wanted to give me the money he planned to use. The amount was $3,000. God is amazing. This is how I got to Liberia for the first time in 2010. These circumstances and the events that led me there only strengthened my faith that God truly wanted me to visit this place.

Once I arrived, I participated with our mission team, following the leaders and completing all the tasks I was assigned. After teaching pastors and leaders for two days, I visited my first orphanage there. I will never forget that day. As we visited the children that day, it began to occur to me after some time that I had a little hand holding onto me that was constant. Unable to free myself from this little boy's grip, I put him upon my shoulders and he was with me the rest of my time there.

This six-year old boy, that I came to find out later was named Joseph, was not from this orphanage but the village near it. I met his father who wanted to start a school for the many children there who were not attending. I spent a year seeking God's will about this and after receiving miraculous proof with a direct answer to prayer, I later adopted it and my love affair with Liberia was born.

Who would have ever thought as I look on today, that we would have helped launch several schools, assist orphanages, while training teachers and Christian leaders alike over the past nine years there? I have been blessed to visit the country several times in this span.

I have learned so much about the country, culture, and people. I have found through my reading and studying, its history to be fascinating and unlike any other story on the continent of Africa. Liberia has ties to the USA like no other country in Africa. It was the first declared black republic in Africa and was birthed by freed American slaves having been supported initially by the American Colonization Society. Its flag is similar, its governmental foundation set up just like the US; with even its capital Monrovia named after an American president. Maybe it was this relationship that played a part in why God would lead me here.

It was 2004 when I first visited the continent of Africa. I was invited by a pastor I met at a conference in the Northern California area. My wife and I arrived in Malawi with great expectations. We had never imagined we would travel to see the mother of all civilization. We were not disappointed. I had such a fantastic time that I couldn't wait to get back there the next few years. However, in all my efforts I was unable to return. As much as I tried it just wasn't happening for me. I look back now and realize it wasn't meant for me; God had an appointment and assignment for me in a place on the west side of this continent named Liberia.

As I continued to share my gift over the years with Liberia, building many relationships with all types of people and spiritual leaders, I gathered much more insight. As I began to examine how impactful I had really been there, I was forced to admit that it seemed to be very little overall. Where were the results that showed lasting improvement for the betterment of these people and their country?

It was truly hard to think that I had personally raised and spent tens of thousands of dollars, personal time, pouring into many lives through teaching and training, yet after many years nothing seemed to change for the better long term. I could not see it in the children, youth, or adults we supported.

I sought the Lord consistently asking Him was all my labor in vain. What am I doing wrong? What do I need to do in order to help His people and those I love in Liberia? It is the answers with His knowledge, understanding, and wisdom given to me that I pass on to you in the pages of this book. This same message is what I share when I am given the opportunity there.

God shared with me that the solution to Liberia's problems is found in the people who have the truth. Unfortunately, a vast majority of the church there has been a main culprit of disseminating false truth to masses of church going citizens. An intimate personal relationship with Jesus, who is the Truth is necessary and required to see lasting results. Jesus said, I am the way, the Truth and the life (John 14:6). It is His truth that makes us truly free (John 8:32).

When you have the truth and walk in the truth, only then will you be free. The truth lives in people and the people the truth lives in, is the true church. These people walk in the truth. Without this truth in people, there can never be freedom. The truth carries the spirit of Christ and where the spirit of the Lord is, there is freedom. (2 Corinthians 3:17) God's true kingdom is not an organization of religion or a building, it is a group of saints called out of the world.

The only way to keep people in bondage, individually and as a group, is to get them to believe lies. Our enemy attacks us in our mind. He battles against our belief system with human reasoning based off what we see, feel, and hear. This enemy we call the devil, became the ruler of this world by using deception (a lie, a false belief system) to influence the first man and woman to disobey God, passing sin and death to everyone.

We have to debunk the many myths that I believe is preventing the major changes that need to happen for the good of all the people. These lies, as we shall call them, have continually been believed by the masses many years to keep this country in the same place spiritually and physically. The uncovering of these hidden deceptive ideas, are key for the transformation of the nation at large. Only truth can defeat a lie.

Some think we can just fix the problem by physically fighting our way to see needed change and personal independence. How has that worked for Liberia or any other African country thus far? Jesus said, "For all who draw the sword, will die by the sword." (Matt 26:52) He said this when His disciples attempted to fight physically to save him from a certain death. Jesus admonished them saying in so many words, "If I needed help, I could ask my Father to send an army for me, but it would mess up our plan and goal." (Matt 26:53-54)

Physical violence is not and has never been the answer for solving problems long term. We represent a higher kingdom, a kingdom that forcefully advances through the spiritual ammunition we have been given to use that will eventually produce the results outwardly we aim to see if we will endure to the very end.

The weapons of our warfare are not fleshly and our real enemy is not a physical one. What we see happening in the physical is representing what we are up against spiritually. Spiritual transformation must happen first if we want to see social and political change in our countries.

This book is addressed to the faith-based community even though those outside of the faith can benefit as well. The expectation of those who follow the faith is different of course. My former pastor used to say, "Why are we surprised when sinners do wrong? That's what they are supposed to do. It is the Christian believers that are supposed to live righteously." As a fellow believer I am here to challenge my fellow brethren to live according to scripture instead of tradition, culture, and foreign influences. Go back to the word of God and examine why you do what you do and are these practices Biblical. Many times, we are only repeating what we have seen and been told, with no evidence that it is backed by God and His word.

Many people have never examined what God has actually said, relying totally on men who sit in seats of spiritual authority. This is not God's will. Even the scripture admonishes us to study to show ourselves approved unto God (2 Timothy 2:15). He tells us, "My people are destroyed because they lack knowledge." (Hosea 4:6) We will never become what God intended for us to become as long as we are looking to someone else first for anything. We must look to God first for EVERYTHING; especially when it comes to His own words.

Lastly, many things discussed in fixing Liberia can easily be applied to America. I am not the big brother coming in a spirit of pride to beat up the little brother, but rather to protect and save him.

In fact, I would dare say that the powers to be in the country I grew up in is most corrupt and the majority of our churches are even more asleep, divided, and powerless. My hope is in Christ who is able to do much more through us and I believe will, in America and with its relative Liberia, before the end of time.

As someone who loves the Liberian people, having personally invested and participated in so many missionary endeavors, you need to know that I can only share this writing with you because of the love I have for my Lord and Savior and my obedience to His instructions. I pray the church community will receive all that they can and LIBERIA, THIS IS FOR YOU.

THE AUTHORITY OF SCRIPTURE

Your word, O LORD, will last forever; it is eternal in heaven.
Psalms 119:89 (GNT)

We live in a world where most would agree that people should get to decide their own fate without any force. Humanity should have the right to believe whatever they want and live the way they want as long as it doesn't infringe on the rights of others. When someone claims to be speaking the truth, it is usually considered as their truth, not necessarily everybody else's. Our society today seems to mirror the nation of Israel during the time of judges, where it says, "In those days, there was no king; everybody did what seemed right in their own eyes." (Judges 21:25) Everyone seems to have their own set of truths these days; living their lives according to their own beliefs.

There are those who make the choice to believe that there is one God and Jesus Christ is the Son of God and Savior of all mankind. Where does this truth come from? It comes from the Bible. It is also referred to as the Word of God. Born again believers, myself included, believe the Bible is actually from God himself given to mankind. We believe the scriptures that teach us:

> *All Scripture is given by inspiration of God, and is profitable for doctrine, for reproof, for correction, for instruction in righteousness*
>
> *2 Timothy 3:16*

> *Above all, you must understand that no prophecy of Scripture comes from one's own interpretation. For no prophecy was ever*

> *brought forth by the will of man, but men spoke from God as they were carried along by the Holy Spirit.*
>
> 2 Peter 1:21 (BSB)

I think it would be safe and accurate to say, it is IMPOSSIBLE to say you are a Christian (Christ-like) and not believe the Word of God is infallible and the FINAL AUTHORITY on all matters of life.

The same book that tells us how to be a child of God and gives us the assurance of whether we are truly Christian (Christ- like), is the same book that claims all of it is inspired and given by God. If God is the creator of all things, especially us, and He has given us His words to live by, we must OBEY them. If we excuse them, ignore them, or place our own thoughts and ways above them, then we prove we are just fooling ourselves and playing church games.

One thing I love about God is that He is not a God of force. Real love does not force anybody to do anything. It allows each person to make their own decisions and live with the consequences of them. Jesus made this very clear when he said, "Anyone who wants to be my disciple, must first count the cost." (Luke chapter 14) He notified everyone that it would be a cost to pay to be His disciple and wear the Christian name. He said we must deny ourselves, take up our cross, and follow Him. He continued to say family, work, culture, education, or money must not be preferred above Him. (Mark 10:28)

If we are not willing to love Him and prefer Him above ALL else, He said we are not worthy to carry His name and to be a part of His kingdom. He demands total allegiance and commitment to doing things His way. Many think that we can believe on Him to save us, but not follow the way He wants us to live. In other words, He can be my Savior but not my Lord. A lord is someone who is the boss and in charge. Jesus says, He must be Lord of all or He is not Lord at all.

> *Why do you keep on saying that I am your Lord, when you refuse to do what I say?*
>
> *Luke 6:46 (CEV)*

So many people who consider themselves God's children, do not obey Him. Jesus follows this verse by demonstrating the difference between those who hear His words and practice them from those who hear His words and don't practice them. The one who practices them is like a house built on a strong foundation that shall never fall. The one who refuses to practice His words is like one without a strong foundation that the storms of life will knock down and they will be utterly destroyed.

We are warned, but we are still given the choice to say yes, I will or no, I won't. No man has any right to tell another man how he should live his own life. What man can say that his way is better than anybody else's way? However, God the giver of life, has the right to tell us how we should live just by virtue of who He is and what He has done. We are His creation. In Him we live, move, and have our being. (Acts 17:28)

Many things He tells us to do will no doubt go against our tradition, culture, feelings, thoughts, personal ways, and understanding. They will no doubt require us to sacrifice things in this world we have become attached to. Our attention and affection will have to be turned from people and things we cherish more than Him. Our ways will be challenged and He will require more from us. It will come down to whether we will choose to love Him with all our heart, soul, and mind. (Matthew 22:37)

We must be honest enough with ourselves to tell the truth. Is this really what I want? Am I ready to be in a relationship with God? Too many church goers pretend to be connected to God and are actually offended when they are corrected by His Word. We want to still belong to Him, but be free to refuse to follow all His directions.

Some people actually think if they ignore His commandments, they will not be responsible for them. What we don't realize is, we are responsible for everything we know to do. Our conscious bears witness to the truth we already know. In God's love, He always sends a prophet to warn people to repent. We will be held accountable for everything that we have heard.

Our world has begun to use all types of arguments to justify why it is alright to believe some parts of scripture and not to believe other parts. Some cry that there are many ways to interpret the Bible and no one can claim to have the correct one. People say the Bible is a good history book that is mostly outdated and doesn't apply to us today, but this is even contrary to scripture which says:

> *For everything that was written in the past was written for our instruction, so that through endurance and the encouragement of the Scriptures, we might have hope.*
> *Romans 15:4 (BSB)*

> *These things happened to them as a warning to us. All this was written in the Scriptures to teach us who live in these last days.*
> *1 Corinthians 10:11 (CEV)*

Some say that the Old Testament is accurate, but the New Testament has been tampered with. Some say men wrote the Bible so it is filled with mistakes. Some follow the old laws and disregard the new covenant while others do the exact opposite. These are all thoughts and reasons that exalt itself against the knowledge of God. The truth is, if we seek God, we will find Him. If we seek truth, we will find it.

Many people are not really looking for truth, they are looking for excuses to make so they won't have to be accountable to the truth. They want to live their own life without God telling them anything. They want to feel good about their rebellion and disobedience. Therefore, they create a God according to their own imagination. One who is so full of love that He would never judge anyone and just wants everyone to be happy. They put everyone in heaven and dismiss hell as a wild invention by those who are angry and religious; wanting to scare people into following their religion. These become good sounding arguments and debates, but lack any spiritual truth or benefit to its hearers. It's just a way to side step the message of truth and to mislead others.

God's narrative about His love for humanity never changes from Genesis to Revelation. Jesus is seen in every book, in every way, as the one who claims to be God in the flesh and the only way to God in

Heaven. He declares we must believe on Him to receive eternal life. He states we must be born again, dying to ourselves and this world, and living our life for Him. He is unlike any religion. There is no other who has made a claim to be the son of God. There is no other faith that has had its leader claim to be the only way to God. All the rest claim to be prophets who received a word from God. Jesus claimed that He was the Word of God.

> *In the beginning was the Word, the Word was with God, and the **WORD was God**...**The WORD became flesh and dwelt among us**.... full of grace and truth.*
>   *John 1:1,14 (CSB)*

What do you do with this? There is only one thing you can do. Either believe it or reject it, but you can't argue whether it is real or not. We can't even argue about what was said. He makes it very clear throughout scripture what He is saying. All we have is the freedom to respond. What will we do about this?

As you read the pages of this book, you will be challenged with the scriptures to live accordingly. You may uncover you did not know some of these scriptures even existed. You may realize that your leaders used scriptures out of context that would benefit themselves instead of what God intended. You may find some things you regularly do as normal, that God sees as very offensive. As your eyes are enlightened to God's way of doing things, I pray you will surrender to Him and don't get upset and try to fight Him and hold on to what you have always known. He loves us too much to keep us in the dark. He wants us to receive His correction and walk in His light. He came that we might have life and have it more abundantly. (John 10:10) He is not wanting anyone to perish, but for all to come to repentance. (2 Peter 3:9) The day that you hear His voice, harden not your heart. (Hebrews 3:15) God left us His word so we will not be without direction and we would not have an excuse. Let's look at some scriptures that tell us why the Word of God is so important to us:

KEEPS US FROM ERROR

Jesus replied, "You are in error because you do not know the Scriptures or the power of God."
Matthew 22:29 (NIV)

SUSTAINS OUR LIFE

Jesus answered, "It is written: Man shall not live on bread alone, but on every word that comes from the mouth of God."
Matthew 4:4 (NIV)

BRINGS BLESSINGS

But even more blessed are all who hear the word of God and put it into practice.
Luke 11:28 (NLT)

GIVES US GUIDANCE

Your word is a lamp to guide my feet and a light for my path.
Psalm 119:105 (NLT)

BRINGS JOY AND GIVES WISDOM

The commandments of the LORD are right, bringing joy to the heart. The commands of the LORD are clear, giving insight for living.
Psalm 19:8 (NLT)

and how from infancy you have known the Holy Scriptures, which are able to make you wise for salvation through faith in Christ Jesus.
2 Timothy 3:15 (NIV)

SAVES US FROM EVIL

> *Therefore, get rid of all moral filth and the evil that is so prevalent and humbly accept the word planted in you, which can save you.*
>
> *James 1:21 (NIV)*

May the great God that we serve open the eyes of your heart that you may receive His Holy word as you continue to read this book. Man must not live on bread alone, but on every word that comes from the mouth of God. (Matthew 4:4 CSB)

TRADITION & CULTURE

*He answered them, "And why do you break the
commandment of God for the sake of your tradition?"
Matthew 15:3 (NIV)*

When you talk about traditions, culture, customs, and superstitions, we must first attempt to define them and try to understand what they are and how they work. A **tradition** is something that has been inherited after having been established in one generation. It is a social or religious practice. It is a regular pattern of thought and behavior based on a certain belief, continued over some time. A **custom** is a common practice for a certain group of people that regulates what is done socially. **Culture** is a set of shared values and practices featured among a group of people in their regular state of being. A **superstition** is a belief or practice based on the unknown; a life concept believed without having proof.

When I look at what all these words have in common, the word *BELIEFS* come to mind. We are what we believe. Our actions come from what we believe. In our minds, these represent a truth to us and become a standard rule in our life. They have become a part of us and we can't even imagine being separated from them. To lose one's tradition could be like losing one's life and to break away from a culturally held superstition can be like losing one's security. All of these represent a way of doing life. They have been entrenched and embedded into the very fabric of our lifestyle and being.

All of us in the world have been touched by each of these things. In my family, we have a Christmas Eve tradition we do yearly with my mother. At our church we have a certain way we go about doing our services. There are certain behaviors expected by everyone where

I work such as saying excuse me when you walk by, letting someone know when you leave, and saying God bless you when someone sneezes. You may have been taught to always show respect to elders, open the door for ladies, and say a prayer of thanks before each meal.

I guess the question becomes, "Do we have to change any of our culturally accepted traditions, customs, and superstitions to be a Christian? If so, why?" How is either affected? I would first like to state that it is not necessary to change anything except what is in direct conflict with the Christian faith. There will be many things that one is used to doing that is not offensive to God and there will be many things that one is used to doing that is very offensive to God. I tried my very best in the upcoming chapters to deal with the social norms practiced that we need to take a close look at.

The one major topic that will be incredibly hard and almost impossible to coincide with our Christian beliefs are superstitions. Superstitions are beliefs themselves that are unfounded and created by man's imagination in response to solving uncertain problems and issues. This is not uncommon among the people of the world. Its involvement extends way beyond just African traditional religions.

We find examples of groups in the Bible that came to unproven conclusions about life based on their own thoughts. It was the common belief in Jesus day that if a man was born blind or with any other physical ailment, it was because he or his parents had sinned. They believed this was a sign God was punishing them. Man came to this belief and it was the dominant thought taught. The religious leaders used this superstition to control their followers. This is seen in the story of the man born blind. (John 9:2) Jesus said the man's blindness had nothing to do with sin by the parents or him, but the Pharisees rebuked the man born blind, that Jesus healed, as a man steeped in sin because of his condition at birth. **Man wants an answer for everything and when he is not able to get one, he tends to come up with one that he can accept instead of acknowledging I don't know or understand.**

The thing that amuses me most about this story is how they could have this long held community belief since everybody is guilty of sin. Our world is full of sinners. Therefore, everyone should have at least someone in their family physically impaired based off this belief. God would not allow this with one family if all were guilty as well. It doesn't make sense unless they concluded others were worse sinners. Let's list some other superstitions that have been believed recently in different parts of the world:

- Albino people have supernatural powers
- You should wear charms to ward off evil spirits
- The appearance of a black cat means bad luck
- Babies born with a handicap are evil.
- Sex with a virgin will cure you from HIV and Aids.

As we can see, superstitions just aren't error prone ideas and beliefs, but they truly cause harm to people. The results of these false beliefs cause handicap children to be thrown away, unaffected virgins to become infected with life threatening illnesses, and in the case of albinos - to be hunted, body parts chopped off, and killed in certain parts of Africa.

West African peoples are spiritualist of a sort. They believed that there were mysterious forces involved in human affairs. They attributed unexplainable things in life to supernatural forces. They would basically make up beliefs that attached itself to the supernatural and transcendental world. These stories or illusions would connect for them why certain things happen when they couldn't explain it. This is the opening door for ancestral spirits, secret societies, and idol worship which includes rituals. The rituals may even include blood sacrifices and a close tie with the occupation of witchdoctors, voodoo priests, and sorcerers.

Today, people are the accumulation of what they have learned, believed, and practiced in all of their previous years of existence. Change is very hard, but not impossible. When change does happen, it doesn't usually happen overnight. The greatest challenge to any nation of people is to try to change their mindset to a belief system and culture they are not accustomed to.

One thing that the African traditional religionist got right was that the physical realm was affected by the spiritual world. They just didn't know how. When the Apostle Paul visited Athens in Acts chapter 17, he was disturbed because he was surrounded by idols. He even noticed one of them was dedicated to an unknown god. He told the people of Athens, that they were **very superstitious**. He said, "I am trying to tell you about this God you are searching for. He is more than some spiritual force. He doesn't live in temples or idols made of stones and gold. **There are no devices in the mind of men that bring Him to you**. He is near and can be sought after." Look at what Paul says to them after this:

> ***"God overlooked people's ignorance*** *about these things* ***in earlier times****, but* ***now he commands everyone*** *everywhere* ***to repent of their sins and turn to him.*** *For he has set a day for judging the world with justice by* ***the man he has appointed****, and* ***he proved to everyone*** *who this is* ***by raising him from the dead."***
>
> *Acts 17:30-31*

Paul had his work cut out for him to try to convince a whole city, that was passionate about their beliefs in the Greek gods and goddesses, that Jesus was the one and only God they were searching for. He was telling them, "Now is the acceptable time; today is the day of salvation." (2 Corinthians 6:2) John the Baptist told the people, "Repent for the Kingdom of God is here." (Matthew 3:2) Jesus understood this challenge of changing your belief system and said that with men, this heart and mind change would be impossible, but with God all things are possible. (Matthew 19:26)

Superstitions must give way to God's truth. We can't have both if we will follow Him. The Word of God overrides all customs, traditions, and rituals that oppose Him. We can't hold on to what once was or where we came from. We must examine it next to God's word and choose which one we want to obey.

Much of the superstitions we have come to believe is fear based. People do things to avoid what they call bad luck or being cursed. This tormenting spirit convinces them that certain harsh and extensive sacrificial conduct must happen to have peace, break a curse, or keep oneself and their family safe. However, these things that we do out of fear instead of faith, does not come from God.

There is a practice in some West Africa countries called trokosi. It means "slave of a fetish." This is where a virgin daughter is taken from her family to become a shrine prostitute to keep bad things from happening to the family. It is like making restitution to gods who will protect you and your family from evil. It is another form of sacrifice or paying for sins. Once again it is generated by a spirit of fear.

As I am writing this book, I received a call from my Godson in Liberia who shared with me that it was now a common practice for many to follow the directions of a so called spiritual leader who told everyone to grab a Bible, turn the pages, find your hair on the pages, put them in a glass of water and drink the water to save yourself from getting sick with the coronavirus. These dreamed up superstitious beliefs are steeped in witchcraft and are contrary to God's word. This was only one of many so-called antidotes to be safe from this disease. It is amazing to me how people will just believe what they hear and do this stuff because they are so afraid. **Superstitions will flourish where ignorance lives.**

Anytime we believe something physical and spiritual will happen to us outside of our control unless we do certain extreme and harmful things, we are being driven by FEAR. God has not given us the spirit of fear (2 Timothy 1:7), so this SPIRIT is not from God. This is an evil spirit. Evil spirits are defeated by the Holy Spirit of God, not by blood sacrifice, dances, or giving things to appease a spirit. These beliefs are contrary to God's Word. We must leave these practices of fearing false gods. God commands all men everywhere to repent from creating and following their own false idols and ideas. (Acts 17:30) We have been set free from all this if we have Jesus Christ living in us and by our faith and decree of Jesus, nothing has any power over us to do anything. When we are living in God's perfect will, He has given us power and authority.

> *Listen!* ***I have given you authority****, so that you can walk on snakes and scorpions and **overcome all the power of the enemy, and nothing will hurt you.***
>
> *Luke 10:19 (GNT)*

Many people feel forced to lie, steal, sell their body, and operate with greed and harshness in order to survive. Others seek out witchcraft and sorcery for help or rely and live on superstitious beliefs. They are living trying to control their own life and do not realize that God doesn't need this type of help from them to take care of them. They are afraid that they won't be able to survive any other way. When you begin to operate like this, you become in bondage to this way of life. We seem to survive this way though we don't like it, but we are afraid to stop and just submit our life to God. We seem to have more faith in our backward ways than in God's promise to take care of us His way. The Bible tells us to taste and see that the Lord is good. (Psalms 34:8) He wants us to trust in Him and do it His way. If we never try His way, we will never know how much He will do for us.

Somehow the message of Christ has been received by many without them understanding that it means you have to give up everything of your culture and tradition that goes against this new culture called the Kingdom of God. This is what accepting Jesus is all about. This includes American culture as well, but most of the time God's kingdom has been mixed in with the dominating ideas, norms, and values along with authority structures present in this world. These don't agree, but instead compete, affecting the potency of God's power to change our lives. This poses a huge problem and Biblical answers for everyday life take a backseat to the prevailing world cultures.

We must put family traditions and superstitions that contradict God's word out of our life for good. The power of these stronghold beliefs, imaginations, and practices created in our minds must be broken off our life. This mixture of Christian faith and traditional beliefs is harmful. It nullifies our faith in God. We can't have faith in God and faith in superstitious beliefs that contradict His word at the same time. How can two walk together unless they be agreed? (Amos 3:3) We can only belong to God if we are in complete agreement with Him. All tradition based in fear and man's own thoughts must surrender to God's Holy Word. Here are more scriptures that make this clear to us:

But now that you know God - or, I should say, now that God knows you - how is it that you want to turn back to those weak and pitiful ruling spirits? Why do you want to become their slaves all over again?
Galatians 4:9 (GNT)

You have died with Christ, and he has set you free from the spiritual powers of this world. So why do you keep on following the rules of the world, such as, "Don't handle! Don't taste! Don't touch!"? Such rules are mere human teachings about things that deteriorate as we use them.
Colossians 2:20-22 (NLT)

You disobey God's commands in order to obey what humans have taught.
Mark 7:8 (CEV)

Don't let anyone capture you with empty philosophies and high-sounding nonsense that come from human thinking and from the spiritual powers of this world, rather than from Christ.
Colossians 2:8 (NLT)

Put all things to the test: keep what is good
1 Thessalonians 5:21 (GNT)

I was in Kenya, shopping in a market a year ago. While in the store, I decided to buy some muffins for the children with me. As we left the store and I preceded to hand them out, a young man, who had appeared to have a strong faith in God, that had adopted me as his spiritual grandfather, told me that the kids could not eat treats walking around the market because if a witch sees them eating it, she could put a spell on them and they would get really sick. I thought he was kidding, but you could see the great fear on his face. I realized he wasn't joking.

At some point growing up as a young boy, he was told this lie and believed it. **WHEN YOU BELIEVE A LIE, THAT IS WHEN IT HAS POWER OVER YOU.** It was necessary for me to show him God's word and what Jesus blood, death, and resurrection did for us. He sets us free from what the enemy uses to torment us. No weapon from the enemy formed against us can work (Isaiah 54:17) and the plans of hell can't overcome God's people (Matthew 16:18). My spiritual grandson had put his faith in God while still holding on to some of the superstitions he received from childhood.

No matter what we have believed and become used to, when we hear the voice of truth and we see the words of God in scripture that may challenge our customs and superstitions, we must decide whose side we will be on. I will always take the Lord's side. I pray that you will do the same.

Dear God,

Whatever your word says, I will do. Whatever your perfect will is, that is what I want. Whatever cost I must pay to please you Lord, I am willing to pay it. Amen

THE BATTLE OF THE MIND

As a man thinks in his heart, so is he....
Proverbs 23:7

Man's greatness lies in the power of his thought.
Blaine Pascal

Your future begins with your next thought.
Bryant McGill

Everything starts and ends with a belief system. Never underestimate the power of your thought life. The way you see yourself will determine the way others will see you and whether you are able to accomplish your God given destiny. Some of the most powerful verses in the Bible show us this:

Jesus said to him, "If you can believe, all things are possible to him that believes."

Mark 9:23

But without faith it is impossible to please him, for he who comes to God must believe that he is and that he is a rewarder of those who diligently seek him.

Hebrews 11:6

...It shall be done to you, according to your faith
Matthew 9:29b (NASB)

> *Then we saw the giants; and **we were like** grasshoppers **in our own sight** and **so we were in their sight.***
>
> *Numbers 13:33*

You are what you think. You have what you believe. You are the product of your faith. There are those rare exceptions, but in almost all cases; people are in the condition they are in because of their regular actions and behaviors based off their thoughts and beliefs. We many times see ourselves less than what God has created us as because we base our value and potential off of what we physically see, by comparing ourselves to others, and by looking at what has already happened to us.

Jesus said, "According to your faith, it will be done unto you." We attract what we believe. Our beliefs end up becoming the reality we will forever live in. People have all kind of deep hidden beliefs such as: White people are better. Asians are smarter. Americans are rich. Africa is poor. Liberia is too difficult a place to have a great life. While it is not wrong to notice patterns or state our opinions, we must be careful not to conclude these things as facts. It could just be a faulty belief system and a lack of faith on our part.

For example, if we say Liberia is a hard place to live in, are we saying it to acknowledge that even though it will be tough, we are going to overcome? Or do we say it to convince ourselves and others that it's almost impossible to be able to live, let alone survive, so we don't expect to have or do much without a miracle or man's help. Our reason for saying it determines whether we have God's mindset and are able to thrive regardless or if we have a negative and faithless, worldly mindset that will end in our defeat.

Be careful of living with a survival mindset. God never created us to survive, but to live. A survival mindset leaves a person defeated. Defeated people have given up and accepted what is happening around them, feeling powerless to do anything about it. They have no expectation for more or to see their situation different. Defeated people have convinced themselves of certain outcomes based on experience and have settled for a subpar existence. They become comfortable to less than ideal circumstances. They get tired of fighting and say, "Well it's not that bad, it could be worse." They give up on God because it is Him who is calling all of us to be better and do greater.

Like anyone else in the world, most Liberians are a product of their environment. It is stinking thinking that causes the majority of problems in people's life; keeping them in a perpetual cycle of dysfunction. Unfortunately, our major goal in life, which is what we base our daily decisions on, can become SURVIVAL. We have learned to survive instead of live. We focus on feeling happy, eating, and being respected. In our pursuit to have just some pleasure, we abandon living a life of PURPOSE. A life of purpose is the actual reason for our existence.

How do we come to believe correctly about our life and live out God's original plan for us? Our thought life is the key to this. How did we come to think the way we do about our life? I once read a statistic years ago that stated about **70% of the way someone thinks about life has already been determined by the age of twelve.** Thought life gets passed down from previous generations through what is said to the child and observed by them.

One time during a visit to Liberia, there was this seven-year old boy in a class I was talking to. I asked all the children if they ever wanted to fly in an airplane. Many raised their hands and I told them then one day you can. This little boy, after our class, went around telling everyone don't believe me. He said I was lying and that I wouldn't be able to help them fly in an airplane. He was already convinced that it could never happen for him, but he was also convinced that it wasn't going to happen for anybody like him that lived where he lived. It was very sad.

This is opposite to hearing a story about a man who came from the U.S. and adopted a kid from an orphanage in a country near Russia. It took a lot to get this little boy. It took many years and lots of money. After visiting the boy for the first time in this crowded home of abandoned children, the man's heart became attached to him and he was willing to go through the difficult process to make him apart of his family.

When the dust had settled and this dream had become a reality, this adopted boy was sitting on the airplane next to his new father on his way to his new home. The happy boy told his new dad, "I have always known you were coming for me." The new father looked at him and said, "How did you know?" The boy answered, "Growing up living in that place; I would pray every day and I believed God heard my prayer and I would say to myself, "My father is coming for me." I just didn't know how, who, or when, but I believed it."

The greatest asset we have is our ability to believe in something beyond what we can see, feel, or hear. Life attempts to strip us of this at an early age so that we will always live a defeated life. You must believe. Use the faith that you were created with. Everyone has it, even those who say they don't. Some place their faith in God, some in man, money, science, and some in believing the worst possible things will always happen to them.

Our belief system is the key element behind whether we will overcome and become the person we were meant to become. By changing our old way of thinking and changing our behavior as a result, we will prove our faith in the God we say we trust in.

The evil one has declared war on every human being. His greatest tool is deception. This trick of the enemy has been used on countless numbers that live on the African continent. **The greatest type of war waged against Africa and people of African ancestry is psychological warfare.** The battle against them is the weapon to destroy a people's true identity spiritually and nationally starting with the mind.

One of the strategies used in this battle is to do this without them realizing what was done and who did it. How is this accomplished? There is nothing accomplished in this earth without man. God gave humans the earth to rule. Everything is done through human beings here. Even though we know that Satan, the devil, is our spiritual enemy behind all the evil that is happening, we must also ask ourselves, what is he using and who is he using? In order for him to accomplish his work here, he needs willing yielded people who carry out his work and promote his lies. Our goal is to identify these. How can we defeat an enemy we are not aware of? The Bible tells us we are not to be unaware of his schemes (Ephesians 5:13).

We find in 2 Corinthians 10:4-5 an explanation of the battle we are dealing with. This passage will unveil to us the major way our enemy works against us. It will probably not be what you think it is.

> *The weapons of our warfare are not carnal (fleshly/physical) but mighty through God to the pulling down of strongholds; casting down every vain imagination and taking captive every thought that exalts itself against the knowledge of God.*
> *2 Corinthians 10:4-5*

Weapons are instruments or tools used during warfare. Warfare is a campaign of service where there is fighting. To be carnal is to display behavior that is typical of human nature with a focus on one's physical desires. This behavior is not what our weapon should be like, says God. This type of fleshly, external fighting is powerless to change anything permanently. However, with the might that proceed from God, we have the power within and without to influence and construct or build what is needed for change. This mighty power from God is made available to us because we are fighting for Him and His purpose.

What are strongholds and where are the strongholds? Strongholds are VAIN IMAGINATIONS and THOUGHTS in our mind THAT EXALT itself against the knowledge of God. Our spiritual battle we must fight daily is about pulling down false ideas. The word for pulling down is to demolish, destroy, and tear down a strong defense. It is like a demolition, where dynamite is needed on each level and at every layer and an explosion occurs bringing it down from the top to the very bottom. We must use God's powerful word to topple every evil thought we have, before they become our defenses and bind us.

These defenses described are likened to a fortified wall. This was a fort of safety and strength where fighters could hide. It was very hard to go against a fort and be victorious. The advantage was on the side of the defense. In this passage, it is used figuratively. A heavily fortified containment in this case is a false argument which a person uses to shelter himself. A truth has been twisted and the twisting has become a reality in place of the truth. A person has come to the place of hiding with this false belief, not to face what is really right.

As we can see from this passage, the fight is indeed not against flesh and blood. This is not where the real fight exists. It is not the fight the church of Jesus Christ fights. So many of us do what the world does because we don't understand the Word of God. We place worldly ideas above Gods. We ignore God's ways and thoughts and we lose because the real battle between good and evil, righteousness and wickedness, and right and wrong is not here between me and you, it is instead in our minds between ourselves and the whispers, suggestions of the enemy of our souls. **Our spiritual battle is in our mind. If we win in our minds, we win in our bodies.**

The vain imaginations and thoughts that go against God come from Satan. The plan and strategy of the demonic kingdom against us understands whoever controls the mind, controls the body. If you can convince someone of something in their mind, it will dictate the actions that they take. The mind controls the body. If we want the body to do something, we must convince the mind.

If Satan wants us to disobey God and behave in a certain way, he must have control of our mind. He understands where the control tower is, the center of command and what makes the operation work. If someone wanted to attack a country, they would strategically focus to hit the bases of command and to weaken everything from the inside out. They would target the heads of operation. The enemy is headed straight for our head. He knows how to topple us.

Just like he did with Eve in the Garden at the beginning, he brings imaginations, thoughts, and ideas to get you to believe. Once you believe them, they become your stronghold beliefs. These beliefs now control what you do and become. That's why the Bible says what you think in your heart becomes who you are. Our beliefs get saved to our heart drive, the heart base of our being. This is the core or center of everything. This is why we must guard our heart, because what gets saved or downloaded in our heart becomes the thing that impacts all of our life's issues. (Proverbs 4:23)

Let's go deeper in our understanding. Where do these thoughts from Satan, that he passes on to people, come from? He doesn't originate anything, so how does he come up with these things that come out of Him? He is a copier. He can only copy God. He can only use what God has already created. Satan takes from what is God's and he perverts it.

Every sin is a perversion of the mind first. It is contrary to what God said. Every sin is thinking of doing a right thing wrong and following through on it. Every sin is a twisting and bending of what was right into what is not right. You can't have a lie until you have a truth. You can't have darkness unless you had light first and it was removed. If we look at the sin of sexual immorality, we can see it is the changing of its original intention. If we look at lying, this is also a changing from its original intention. It is a form of deception. The same with pride, it is us making ourselves the center of worship instead of making God the center of worship. It is us placing our will above His.

There is a word in the Bible that is used interchangeably with sin but many of us may not understand why it was used. However, I believe it is very important for us to understand it. The word is ***iniquity***. The very first non-perfect act in heaven and earth is referred to as iniquity. This is the very first sin ever. You can't have sin without iniquity. When we read the history of Satan, we find in Ezekiel 28:15 these words, "You were perfect in your ways from the day you were created until *iniquity* was found in you."

What is iniquity? While sin and iniquity are both used interchangeably, they are distinguishable in description. Sin is missing the target God set. We aim but miss. Initially our aim was to do right, but we don't. We are disobeying God, not doing what He wants us to do. Sin is focused on the act done. However, when we look at the word iniquity, it is the thought and character of wrong. It's the forming of thoughts in your mind that have been bent and led you away from doing the right thing. So, you can't commit sin without iniquity. It is the changing in your thoughts of how you see right and wrong. It is to see what God says is right, wrong.

Here is what God acknowledges for us to do in order to fix this problem in our mind:

> *Let the wicked **change their ways** and **banish the very thought of doing wrong**. Let them **turn to the Lord**, that*

> *he may have mercy on them.... For **my thoughts are not your thoughts** and my ways are not your ways. For **as high as the heavens are above the earth so are my thoughts above yours** and my ways above yours.*
>
> Isaiah 55:7-8 (NLT)

God is speaking to His people here and yet He refers to them as wicked and unrighteous. Remember, I said sin is missing the mark God set. After a long time, God's people stopped even aiming for this mark. At this point they are not even trying to do right. There is no effort. At this point it is wickedness. This is beyond being ungodly, unrighteous, and committing sin. They are depraved in their mind and understanding. At this stage, it takes the power of the Holy Spirit to get them back on track. I believe this is where we are at today. He that hath an ear to hear, let him hear what the spirit is saying to the church (Revelations 7:3).

We must acknowledge when the way we are going is wrong. We must change our direction. **The problem is THE WAY OUR MIND WORKS.** We must leave our thoughts. God says change the way you are thinking and return to thinking like the Lord. Turn around and return to Him and His thoughts. God doesn't think like we do and doesn't see it the way we see it. We must now make a choice. Will we think like God does and live? or Will we think our own thoughts and die? The rest of this book will be one challenge after another to provoke change in your thoughts and action. **We can never truly be the Body of Christ without the MIND of Christ.**

> *And so, dear brothers and sisters, I plead with you to **give your bodies to God** because of all he has done for you. Let them **be a living and holy sacrifice—the kind he will find acceptable. This is** truly **the way to worship him**. Don't copy the behavior and customs of this world, but let God transform you into a new person by **CHANGING THE WAY YOU THINK**. Then you will learn to know God's will for you, which is good and pleasing and perfect.*
>
> Romans 12:1-2 (NLT)

LIE #1
LIBERIA IS A CHRISTIAN NATION

These people honor me with their lips,
but their hearts are far from me. They worship me in vain;
they teach as doctrines the precepts of men.
Matthew 15:8-9

The latest statistics show that over 80% of Liberia's population identified themselves as Christian. If this statistic is anywhere close to the truth, then the country, that has one of the highest percent of Christians, is one of the poorest in the world.

God doesn't guarantee every Christian will be or should be rich, but when we hear about the struggling condition so many people find themselves in, the corruption throughout the society, treatment of the poor, and hopelessness that prevails among so many- especially the youth; it gives reason for one to wonder, How could this be with so many having confirmed a faith in God and Jesus Christ?

Why does it seem as if on a mass level, these Christians are so seemingly powerless to do anything about their life and country? How come the church doesn't seem to have any answers for the ever, present problems their nation faces? Did God lie when He said, "The gates of Hell shall not prevail against my church?" Yet it seems like evil is winning the battle inside and outside the majority of the church community.

I believe we are able to solve this perplexing dilemma by asking and answering the question: How do the majority of people define what a Christian is? Our personal understanding of what a Christian is and does will be the most significant clue as to what is wrong with this picture. By getting an accurate description, we will be able to figure this out.

In order to separate the truth from the false, I must first define what Christian actually means. A Christian, according to scripture, means a follower of Christ. Christians, a name given by outsiders, were referred to in scripture as the "anointed ones" because they resembled their leader Jesus Christ, in their love and actions. A Christian, according to the truth in scripture, is seen as a righteous person who is in right standing with God. It is to be morally right in your present state or condition.

The challenge is many people don't understand what it really means to be a Christian. They never had it explained. They just come in and do what everyone else does. They may sing, serve, and attend service. They become a part of a church structure, but not a part of Jesus Christ. This means they never became part of the body of Christ. This is the real Christian church. They never have what we call a "born again" experience. Jesus said, "you must be born again." (John 3:3) You must have a true, personal, intimate encounter with God.

In order to truly be a Christian, you must believe that Jesus Christ came to earth, lived a sinless life, died on the cross to cleanse you from your sins, and resurrected so you can enjoy a new life in Him. You must surrender your whole life to Him and allow Him to take full control and live His life through you. **There must be true repentance, confession, and submission that leads to a transformation**. This causes a real change to happen to a person, that is noticeable to all. Their whole life is impacted. **If anyone is in Christ, he is a new creation, the old things are gone and behold all things are new**. (2 Corinthians 5:17)

Immediately afterward, they began to impact their world as a witness for God. The Bible refers to these new followers and children of God as the "Light of the World" and the "Salt of the Earth." They shine in its darkness. They preserve it for the good, so it doesn't go completely bad.

So, in the Biblical sense of the word, to be a Christian person is to be a righteous person and to be a Christian nation, you must be a righteous nation. You can't have the name Christian from scripture without the ingredients holy, righteous, just, and set apart from this world. These are characteristics of Christ and to be expected of His church that carries His name. However, righteous and Christian, does not go together for many in churches around the world, and Liberia is no exception.

Is Liberia a Christian, righteous nation according to God's definition? We would have to look at the nation from its beginning up to where it stands today. We must also observe the influence of the church in its society. Is it positive? How is it impacting the people of the country? Does the leadership in the departments of government and overall general population exemplify these Christian characteristics wholly as it governs this society's affairs? If not, does this mean that Liberia does not have any righteous leaders and people within its country?

I have elected to go with the word "righteous" in place of Christian, because this is the difference maker and the issue at hand. This helps separate the many people who are Christian by name only. Without understanding that being a Christian, according to the Bible, is impossible without righteous living, it makes sense why many believe they are Christian, even if they are not. As we will see by looking at its beginning and where it stands today, Liberia could only be a Christian nation according to a diluted version.

This false assumption by many Liberians is not theirs alone but found in many other nations as well. It is the case especially with the United States of America where this belief has been in place since its inception by a majority. It has been a believed lie, rarely questioned from time to time by fearless dissidents who were willing to be criticized and to die to uncover the wrongs of this false, ideal image to the public.

By using righteous it causes the average person to think twice. Is Liberia a righteous nation? Well, I can't really say that so quick. Is Liberia a Christian nation? Well yes, of course we are. We have so many churches, so many preachers, revivals, crusades, prayer meetings, and conferences. Most of our people attend church and many have business names that include God. We credit God for all good things. We believe He exist. We believe in Jesus and that He was crucified and resurrected. We sing Christian songs. We volunteer our time in church, so therefore we must be Christian.

This is what is called the religion of Christianity. Now righteous is different because it starts zeroing in on one's character, behavior, lifestyle, and everyday actions rather than on religious activities and what we profess.

Let's look deeper at this and take the "Fruit of a Christian" challenge. Do you know Christ? Do you know what the scriptures actually say? Do you read and study the word of God? Are you a Liberian who calls yourself a Christian by following what others have done in the church? Do you know if your church leaders' behavior is consistent with the Biblical pattern? Are you led by your own feelings, thoughts, and experiences or by the Spirit of God, His will, and purpose?

Let's take inventory of those Christians around you. How many people do you know who spend personal quality time with God and you truly experience the love of God when you come around them? They make Him the first priority in their lives. They can be trusted. They would never cheat you. They share with everybody and are willing to give their last to anybody. They love their enemies. They are very humble and willing to serve rather than be served. They exemplify peace and joy almost always.

They can pray for you and it makes a difference. They truly care. They forgive. They trust only God for their basic needs. They make decisions that benefit others and has everybody else's best interest in mind before their own. They make sacrifices to do the right thing. They will meet other people needs before their own. They don't speak against others or talk about them. They don't pretend. They are not hypocritical. They confess their sins and acknowledge when they are wrong.

The scriptures are not just memorized verses quoted from their head, but they are lived out regularly in their life. They don't have a form of God but truly love him. This is demonstrated to those outside of church as much as with those inside. They love people and use things, instead of loving things and using people. If they borrow, they pay it back because this is what a righteous man does. A man's word is accomplished even at his harm because a righteous man's word can be trusted. Do you know Christians like this?

Do the professing Christian leaders in the community and government make choices for the best of the people they are supposed to be serving? Do they refuse to take bribes? Are they careful not to lord over God's people like the unrighteous are characterized for doing? Do they show compassion and mercy to others? Are they not focused on money and material possessions? Do they care less about money than people? Do you know Christian leaders like this?

I have found very few people who carry the Spirit of God and represent what the Bible defines as a Christian well. Liberia may not be a wholly Christian nation, but it is a nation that has some righteous Christians living in it. There are some believers and churches that truly understand God's heart, but unfortunately, they represent a small remnant. They are the exceptions to the mass church community.

Of course, nobody is perfect, but even when we fail, a righteous man is humble, repenting and quick to make things right. This is the major problem. The word humility is lost among many adults who claim to be a Christian. I have met many church leaders from the continent of Africa in America and more so in Africa and only in a very small percent, native to this continent, have I seen such humility and love displayed authentically and continually at home, on the streets, and with whoever was around.

There are few that have a testimony of great Godly character that precedes them. Upon meeting the few, I knew without a doubt that they were connected to God, they really knew him, and being in right standing with Him was more important to them than anything else.

How does one become a Christian nation? Was Liberia ever a Christian nation? How effective has the Christian church been in influencing the nation as a whole? I have read where the religion of Christianity in Liberia has its roots from the founding of the nation. In order to understand this kind of Christianity, we must go back and look at the transition of what was once a Biblical, righteous, and Godly entity to what it has unfortunately become around the world today.

Most of what we refer to as Christian practice today was changed from the Biblical pattern where there were people following the life and teachings of Jesus to a religious European Christianity seen in American Christianity which passed down to Liberian Christianity.

The two significant events that happened to bring this European style of Christianity into Liberia's foundation, making it what it is today, is first: After many years of persecuting the early authentic Christian believers, Constantine, the emperor of Rome, declared Rome to be a Christian empire in AD313. He declared everyone under his influence a Christian. They became a religious state overnight. This is where the Roman Catholic Church started. This was a new and very different brand of what Christ real followers were. It was now European Christianity. A religion of political, social, and economical domination. That which is from the Bible is nothing like this, doesn't happen like this, and doesn't follow this. Christian living can't be forced by a man, because no man, organization, or government body can make you righteous or God fearing.

Once this was put in place, history shows that anyone who did not align itself to Rome's new religious Christianity was seen as a threat. This is a huge contrast from before, where those who professed to be Christ followers were persecuted and killed. In this new state, you would confess to be a follower of Christianity according to what the Roman Catholic Church taught you.

This is the beginning of where a relationship with Jesus Christ was ignored and the focus turned to a religious and political organization under the name of Christ. Under this now false Christian religious state, history showed they killed innocent nations in their religious zeal, they stole other nations land and resources under this banner, they enslaved inhumanely others in this name, and they abused others around the world in the name of God. They made money their God while using God's name to steal it.

History reveals one of the most corrupt spiritual leaders of the papacy, bought his position as pope. During his reign, he introduced and promoted the picture of Jesus Christ, which was actually a portrait of his son, a homosexual. Even today, when I travel around the world this picture of a white, European savior, representing the Son of God, is hanging on the walls of homes and churches due to false teaching and our ignorance of the truth.

Several people through the centuries dared to go against this universal church. It was a man by the name of Martin Luther in 1517, a former catholic priest and reformer, who was responsible for the founding of the Lutheran Church, who God used to start a spiritual revolution. Others followed in his steps, John Wesley of the Methodist, the Baptist, Episcopalians, etc. This time period was called the Protestant Reformation because of the protest against this universal, corrupt church.

During this time, the focus returned to the actual teachings of the Bible and drifted away from the traditions and beliefs of the universal (Catholic) church. Unfortunately, the seeds had been planted and even in the protestant churches who rebelled, many of them still copied the Catholic mindset in their churches and organizations. For so many, God and church had become a religion where man controlled their worship experience and less about men being led by God and His spirit while following closely to the teachings of its Lord and Savior Jesus Christ.

Passed down now through many generations we have been given this traditional religion of Christianity from our forefathers. With the removal of the true reason for our faith, and the focus becoming something God never intended, man has become the center instead of God. We have become just like this unproductive man-made religion called Christianity instead of righteous living disciples of Jesus Christ after the Biblical pattern.

The second reason, which is huge, is white supremacy. The belief that white people are superior to people of other nationalities and therefore should be dominant over them. This belief has been the determining reason for the perpetuation and maintenance of social, political, economic, and institutional dominance by European people. It is where the white color of the skin has been set up as the basis for structural, privileged systems over other ethnic groups throughout the world. This has been seen in slavery, colonialism, apartheid, and the Native American massacres to name a few.

It's been said that these European groups landed initially on all these lands offering the religion Christianity with the goal of civilizing what they saw as barbaric, heathen people and tribes, but while the natives were receiving their religion and goods, the Europeans were stripping them of their land and natural resources. **This type of religious Christianity did not benefit anybody but themselves at the expense of everybody.** Their supremist attitude and imperialistic belief system caused them to legitimize the exclusion of basic human rights and equality for their fellow man. This led to many lands, tribes, and nations being conquered, followed by a denial of social and political freedom while men were susceptible to all kinds of abusive behaviors and crimes without any protection.

The U.S. showed its hypocrisy as a nation supposedly founded on Christian principles, by also believing others God created equal were less than them. The Native Americans, original people of the North America territory were slaughtered off their own land while Africans were captured, enslaved, bought, and brought to the new world to provide free labor. They were treated horribly while making the so called "Christians" rich. Yet, while all this was going on, the founders and people of this new land continued to promote the religion of Christianity at home and abroad. Even today much of what is called Christianity is actually controlled, organized religion; motivated by political power and financial gain. It is totally absent of God's Holy Spirit and void of any real spiritual transformational power.

America's constitution was written for white Americans, not Indians or Blacks who lived there. Justice and the right to conquer was based on the definitions they made. Non-whites are the minority in the world and people of color have the greatest wealth of national resources on the planet, but yet are the most impoverished. The strategy of divide and conquer was put in place by European powers during the Africa scramble in 1884 to insure they would remain in a privileged state while people of color stay subservient and poor.

Why is this important to Liberia? What does this have to do with Liberia? Liberia is the nation birthed by freed American slaves. These slaves carried this Christianity religion they learned from their European teachers and put into effect the same exact thing after becoming the leaders of their own government. The institution of the church was a major force in this society but it was not from the Biblical pattern.

The mirror image was seen in a government that ruled over the indigenous people and that separated people by class. Everything done to these Liberian founding fathers by the Europeans who called themselves Christians in America, they did to the native people in Liberia. The idea that all people are created equal by God was not practiced as such from its beginning.

How can we say the nation was founded on Christian principles when the principles stayed on a piece of paper and never became the reality for everyone living in the society? The founders of Liberia produced a declaration filled with great promise, hope, and future, but not meant for all and accompanied by ugly deeds. This is a repeat of the founding of America.

I am sure, despite this general application, there were righteous Christians who followed God and not a man-made system. Unfortunately, these were the minority while those that proclaimed the religion Christianity, which was a false form of godliness, led the nation and received all the recognition throughout the world. This historical account of all that has happened in the past, has made a profound impact on the way masses view God and what a Christian is today.

What the religious system of Christianity doesn't get is: God is not interested in building beautiful church buildings. He is not impressed with large church organizations. He is only interested in saving people and having them experience His abundant life here on their way to eternity. God's focus is on helping the poor and outcast, while religion is focused on structure and power.

Our spiritual enemy is behind all the evil happening. He is influencing willing humanity. His cunning shrewd plan was put into effect as He saw he was losing the fight against a persecuted church who were willing to give up their lives for their faith in the first century. The enemy decided to become a false version, joining himself to the church to kill it from the inside out. His goal has worked in deceiving as many as he can who are sincerely looking for God by giving them a religion dressed up as the real thing.

His false church and religion can be spotted by the fruit that is produced. You can always tell what kind of tree it is by looking at its fruit. You can tell what type of people you are dealing with by the results you are getting from them.

RELIGION IS THE WORSHIP OF MAN IN THE NAME OF GOD. REAL CHRISTIANS HAVE A RELATIONSHIP WITH AND WORSHIP JESUS CHRIST AS GOD ACCOMPANIED BY RIGHTEOUS DEEDS.

God is holy, and man is not. However, the scriptures teach us that God wants us to be holy as He is holy. (1 Peter 1:16) Jesus was holy and we are instructed to imitate anyone that follows Him. (1 Corinthians 11:1) Jesus told the crowd and His disciples **do not follow the example of the religious leaders** because they don't practice what they teach. (Matthew 23:3) God requires His people to produce good fruit in line with repentance from bad deeds. This doesn't mean we live a perfect life, but that we have no desire to break God's laws and when we fall short of doing the right thing, we confess, repent, and do the right works because our greatest desire is to please God. **Christians are not perfect people, but people who strive for perfection. This means correcting faults immediately and walking in truth.** The following verse of scripture reminds us of what God requires of us:

> *But the solid foundation that God has laid cannot be shaken; and on it are written these words: "The Lord knows those who are his" and **"Those who say that they belong to the Lord must turn away from wrongdoing."***
>
> 2 Timothy 2:19 (GNT)

The Bible also says,

> ***Righteousness, makes a nation great; sin is a disgrace to any nation.***
>
> *Proverbs 14:34 (GNT)*

This is the first step of change with any society, the pursuit of righteousness. God promises a nation can be changed if the following happens:

> *If my people, who are called by my name, would humble themselves and pray; seek my face and turn from their wicked ways. Then will I hear from heaven, forgive their sin, and heal their land.*
>
> *2 Chronicles 7:14*

It is amazing that God said He will do this not based on the government or society but if those who claim to belong to Him would make the necessary change, they could see transformation of their country. The answers to our problems are sitting right in front of us, but since it's not what we want to hear, we keep looking to other sources for answers. We haven't found anything else that will work and we won't. The problem will always be getting people to believe God and obey Him.

There will be no hope and future with sustained positive growth in Liberia until the pastors, leaders, and believers in Jesus Christ continually repent and turn from their sins and wicked ways and truly turn their hearts fully to God. As long as everyone keeps doing what they are doing, we shouldn't expect anything to change. Remember, one definition of insanity is doing the same thing over and over and expecting to get a different result one day.

Spiritual transformation in communities, cities, nations, and around the world always began with **prayer and repentance** which produced positive change. **This is the formula for progress in Liberia** as well. Everything starts here. Becoming a righteous nation is the foundation for a people rising above a disgraced and shameful state.

As long as Liberia's church community keeps repeating the same things that they have done in the past, expect the same things to happen. There is no change outside until we change inside starting with our thoughts. God will hear the cries of the righteous only. The righteous ways of righteous people will produce Godly results.

When the true church is pure and cleansed from its sin, the prayer then becomes powerful and change begins to happen. The Bible tells us,

> *When the righteous are in authority, the people rejoice: but when the wicked have rule, the people mourn.*
> *Proverbs 29:2 (KJV)*

Our prayers become powerful enough to affect the political voting process where just men are placed in authority. We would not be encouraged in scripture to pray for this, if our prayers could never make a difference:

> *Pray for kings and others in power, so we may live quiet and peaceful lives as we worship and honor God. This kind of prayer is good, and it pleases God our Savior.*
> *1 Timothy 2:2-3 (CEV)*

Liberia has an example of what can happen with sincere prayer. During the last years of its notorious civil war that killed so many of its citizens, destroying and disrupting life in a terrible way, the story is told about the women who banded together across denominations and even faiths and interceded daily for over five years asking for God's help to end this war. They committed daily to prayer followed by actions to stop this war, even putting themselves in harm way at times. They prayed continually and God moved through them. Today, small political groups protest to change what is happening but nothing good happens, it only gets worse because real change doesn't happen by force, but through prayer, repentance, and obedience. We are shown from the praying women, what is possible if we respond to adversity God's way. I have no doubt that these women's formation and involvement was a key component to stopping the war and seeing physical peace.

Now, I want you to see the connection between a country of mainly false Christians who have been deceived by religion and true Bible Christians that follow the teachings of Jesus Christ.

Those that are false Christians; Christians in name only, have these characteristics:

- ❖ Only look out for themselves and their own
- ❖ Are divided among themselves.
- ❖ Do not trust or work with each other.
- ❖ Put temporary needs before future.
- ❖ Put immediate money before growth.
- ❖ Put their pride before morals.
- ❖ Practice pretense and focus on image before honesty.
- ❖ Tell lies before truth.
- ❖ Lead from their head not God's heart.
- ❖ Put education before knowledge.
- ❖ Put tradition before wisdom.
- ❖ Put programs before practicality.
- ❖ Live a lifestyle of worldliness before spirituality.
- ❖ Practice sensuality before self-control.
- ❖ Operate impulsively before patience.
- ❖ Practice judgement before understanding.
- ❖ Being led by flesh instead of spirit.
- ❖ Carnal minded instead of spiritual minded.
- ❖ Focused on worldly cares before the Kingdom of God

The specific problems seen in this church are:

- ➢ Lies are told, the truth is covered and its perfectly fine and defended.
- ➢ Infidelity is rampant and money is used in exchange for sexual favors.
- ➢ Leaders worship themselves and the people worship the leadership.
- ➢ Prayer is a monologue and there is the absence of hearing the voice of God.
- ➢ Church servants and workers are given positions without being Biblically qualified.

- Leaders have a spirit of rebellion and a spirit of lording over others.
- Leaders have a lack of humility and are full of pride.
- Preferences are made of oneself above another and another above someone else.
- People look to other people to help them more than God.
- There is never apologizing and making things right with God and others. There is never taking full responsibility for ungodly behavior.
- People speak treacherously behind others backs.
- Jealousy against someone else for what they have or who they know.
- Focusing on building one's personal image than on having the character of God.
- Following superstitions and mixing traditional customs with the Bible.
- Take bribes, expecting bribes, and stealing property.
- Living in a broken, unhealed, undelivered state where real feelings along with hurt and pain from the past have been ignored and covered up.
- Focused on buildings for church, over discipling converts who are the real church.

This description of what false Christians look like is unfortunately all too common in the majority of churches in Liberia and around the world. How do we change this? **God's word must first become the final authority in all matters. God's word must not only be on our lips and copied into our memory, but must be in our heart.**

I want you to ask yourself this question, "If everybody was the kind of Christian I was, what kind of country would we have? The signs of true Biblical Christians are seen in a righteous church characterized in a powerful way by those who actually follow the footsteps of Christ. These characteristics are found in Acts 4:31-35; Acts 5:13-16; and John 13:35. They are:

- ✓ A life of prayer
- ✓ Being filled with the Holy Spirit
- ✓ Boldness and power in sharing God's truth.
- ✓ Sharing your possessions with those in need.
- ✓ Being one in heart with other believers
- ✓ Experiencing God's abundant grace
- ✓ Each member having all their basic needs met
- ✓ All gifts and donations given to the leaders were distributed to meet people's needs in the church.
- ✓ Believers gathered with one mind and purpose
- ✓ Signs and wonders were done by the leaders
- ✓ Many people were brought to the Lord (they received salvation)
- ✓ The sick are healed and unclean spirits driven out.
- ✓ Love is demonstrated from one to another.

This is what the true church looks like. You will notice everything starts with continual prayer. It is in prayer that His church was filled with His Spirit and given power to destroy the works of the devil. It is very important to receive the Holy Spirit of God. Many do not have the Holy Spirit. ***Since God's spirit is holy, if you really belong to Him you can't live unholy***, because you will feel the grieving in your heart when you do wrong. ***If you can do wrong and not feel any conviction in your heart, the Holy Spirit is not living inside you.***

God only comes to live in a vessel that is clean. You must allow your life to be cleansed by placing your total faith in Jesus Christ and giving up **ALL** sin, humbling yourself, and completely giving Him total control as the only one who can save you and lead you.

God is looking for worshippers who worship in spirit and in truth. (John 4:4) Those who appear to be worshipping but refuse to obey God's word are not really worshipping. We can fool people but you can't fool God. True worshippers obey God. **If you do not obey God, your worship means nothing.** Churches spend more time taking offerings and making announcements and just singing songs rather than having actual worship which is an act of submission of oneself and their desires to God.

Those who worship and practice lying, sexual favors, cheating, and other ungodly behavior are playing with God and God knows who is serious. I'm praying for Gods mercy to lead them to repentance because they don't believe that when they breathe their last breath, they will open up their eyes in hell.

His mercy today makes it appear to them that nothing will happen and they are getting away. No one gets away with sin, God's wrath is being reserved to be poured out unless there is repentance. We must use this time on earth to repent.

Christian living must go beyond church attendance and activities to be for real. There must be a focus on loving God with everything, denying ourselves, pouring our heart out to God, and spending quality time in prayer and in His Word. This quality time with God is where you have a personal encounter not just church experience. **We can't love church and ministry activities, but not be in love with God. This is the lie that most are living that must be changed.**

The latest statistic in America says 7 out of 10 of those who say they are Christian very seldom pray, read their Bible, or attend church in any given month. What I noticed in Liberia is, many more attend church and pray, but since it is out of religious duty and mostly absent from an intimate personal relationship with God, it does nothing and has the **same results** as those who don't pray or go to church at all.

If we continue to embrace the religion of Christianity, that lacks no power to change us and make a difference, as the real one; we are left more hopeless than anyone else in the world. If the religion of Christianity we have come to know is the maximum experience that we think can be had, we will look for nothing more and settle for this limited, dead, and false version of God.

However, I have come to let you know that a better, supernatural, and true version of Christian living exists. The religion of Christianity you have come to know is not the one Jesus is the head of. It is not the real one. It is not the life giving, life altering, spirit filled, heavenly speaking, power packed, and miracle working abundant life He has provided. What we have now in most churches is this weak experience of what is supposed to be a real thing. God has made the real version available for you to experience fully. Do you want it?

Our worship must be sincere, and surpass all man-made programs. It must go beyond just having a religious experience. It must include a transforming heart change encounter with the Most-High God. When true repentance is tied to revival in the land and works its way throughout the churches and ultimately in the nation, hope can then be restored. It is our only chance if we want to turn this believed lie into a true reality.

> *Dear Father God,*
>
> *There are so many people in the church who don't really know you. Use those who have truly given you their lives to reach as many of these as possible. I know there are many people who really don't want to change and know you in a very real way, but I also know there are many who do. There are those you have pre-determined and ordained to receive eternal life. Bring them in. In Jesus Name, Amen.*

If you have never truly asked Jesus Christ to come into your heart and make Him your Lord and Savior, please do this now. Pray this prayer from your heart:

Dear God,

I come to you. I know I am a sinner in need of a Savior. I repent of my sins. I believe your testimony Father God, that you sent your only son Jesus Christ to the earth, He shed His blood and died for my sins and rose again to give me new life. I accept Jesus as my Savior and Lord. Thank you, Lord; for saving my soul. Now Lord God, fill me with your Holy Spirit that I may have the power to live for you. Amen.

The Bible says, "If you confess with your mouth the Lord Jesus and believe in your heart that God has raised him from the dead, you shall be saved." (Romans 10:9) Find a Bible believing church to attend that teaches the word of God. Be baptized as a witness of your new life. Pray and read His word daily so you will know Him and grow into His purpose for your life.

LIE #2
WE ARE NATURALLY GOOD PEOPLE

*"Why do you call me good?
No one is good except God alone."
Mark 10:18*

I would like to make you aware of three truths about mankind I have found from reading the scriptures. **We are created by God.** (Genesis 1:27; Psalms 139:13; Colossians 1:16) **We are loved by God.** (John 3:16; Romans 5:8; 1 John 4:19) **We are valued by God.** (Jeremiah 29:11; 1 Peter 2:19; Matthew 6:26) I am fully convinced of these truths and believe that God wanted us to know their importance. They explain to me where I came from and how my Creator feels about me. They help me to know I have worth and there is a reason for me being on the earth.

These are the things everyone should know. They should make anyone who hears them, feel really good. What a wonderful thought that God loves me, and made me, and sees value in me. We should readily accept these truths. However, with these also come other truths that are for our benefit that don't necessarily make us feel so great.

We are also taught in scripture that we are not good and God is the only one that is good. Jesus said, "***No one is good but God alone.***" (Luke 18:18) God tells us throughout His word that no person is good by himself. There is no such thing as a nice, moral person without God. God is the good one and every good and perfect gift comes from Him. (James 1:17)

The Bible does not teach humans are naturally good people. It does not teach Christians are good people. It teaches the opposite of this. In our current human condition, **ALL** of us are sinful. We are born into this world as creatures that have received a sinful nature passed down from our parent's bloodline. Paul said, "I know that nothing good dwells in me, that is in my flesh." (Romans 7:18) Sin came into the world through one man's disobedience and death through sin; but redemption and life came through the man, Jesus Christ. (Romans 5:12) We do wrong because our human nature is to do wrong. Even our seemingly good deeds many times is done with wrong motives, thereby making it wrong.

The world, on the other hand, teaches us that we are good. Humanism teaches we are gods and we don't need a supreme being called God to live. We are told we are wise, smart, and capable of doing anything on our own. Some refer to themselves as atheist, suggesting God never existed and the world formed from a big bang and evolved without any help. In their mind, chaos accidently came into order. I think it's harder to believe this than to believe in an all supreme being. Globally, people are being indoctrinated with this idea of no God. It is being presented as a scientific fact without the presentation of any other beliefs in schools and colleges around the world.

Without realizing it, the so-called Christian has, in some ways, adopted an anti-God rhetoric. Many now believe that man is inherently good without God; that we can be good and do good without Him. If the Bible tell us differently, who will we believe? The Bible says out of the mouth of two or three witnesses let every word be established. (2 Corinthians 13:1) We have an abundant amount of scripture passages to prove the fact that we in and of ourselves are not good people.

If you say,

"I am a good person naturally."

The Bible says,

***For all have sinned** and fall short of the glory of God.*
Romans 3:23

If you say,

I have a good heart.

The Bible says,

*The **human heart is** the most **deceitful** of all things, and desperately **wicked** - who really knows how bad it is.*
                                              Jeremiah 17:9 (NLT)

If you say,

I am not an evil person.

The Bible says,

***If you then, being evil,** know how to give good gifts to your children, how much more will your heavenly Father give the Holy Spirit to those who ask him!*
                                              Luke 11:13

The truth pill is not always easy to swallow, especially when we are informed in the Bible that our righteousness is as filthy rags before God and there is no one righteous, no not one. (Isaiah 64:6; Romans 3:10) We are told our hearts are desperately sick. The Christian Standard Bible version says, "incurable or beyond cure." The Berean Bible breaks it down as our hearts being hard to understand, change, heal, or know what's deep inside. We know God knows what's really going on down in there. David told God to search his heart, to see if there be any wrong and lead him in the right way. (Psalms 139:23-24) This is what God wants us to do regularly. This is why I believe David was referred to by God as a man after His own heart. He wanted to please God. He wanted to be good in God's sight. He gave God all his heart.

We have an evil, wicked condition that we inherited. We are more than capable of surrendering to our sinful fleshly desires and being influenced by the evil one at any moment. The truth about our condition is: God is perfect and we are not. We were made after His image to begin with. We were not great, good, average, or poor; but perfect. However, sin entered the world through man's disobedience. It marred our humanity which reflected the divine and we became separated from that which is all good. We became exposed to the natural elements, serving it instead of God and began to deteriorate and fade away spiritually and physically.

The fact is, there are people who appear to be good and do good things by our definition and who don't know God. In these cases, it is because the good you see in us, we got from Him. We still have some residue from the original creation, we resemble some, but not much. Could it be that God, who is all good still knows how to get imperfect humans to accomplish His purpose? The good they do is not of them. He puts it in them to do of His perfect will. Anything that can be associated with good comes from Him, not them.

In other words, like a perfect car that has been in a wreck, but still has areas not completely destroyed, you can still see some resemblance to what once was. Something good appears out of something that has become messed up. God still uses this. God will use someone who is evil to do things that he doesn't know why he is doing it. God knows how to get that person to do what He wants.

Could it be that when we were created good and perfect in the beginning, being made in the image of God and when sin came into the world and corrupted it, as we became more and more depraved, yet in our lower and lowest condition we still remembered how to do some good. There is still some good stuff in us which initially came from God and can still be seen, but whatever good you find is the residue of the good God first put in man. You can't depend on that good alone because that good is not good enough since it has now been mixed with our evil. Like the tree of the knowledge of good and evil which was forbidden by God for man to eat, having both is not good enough.

ALL good we see, will come from God. It is impossible to experience any good without Him. **It is possible for you to do something from God without having Him.** You can do a good thing and it doesn't necessarily mean you have God, although the good through you comes from Him. You will need to be totally submitted to experience God's perfect goodness, wisdom, and purpose. Only what is done for Christ will have any lasting value. God's goodness includes the best timing with all taken into consideration, including the future. In His goodness, all factors are considered for the benefit of all involved and can be seen as the good that can only come from Him. Anything done that is independent of God, as good as it looks, results in sin.

OUR GOOD VS GOD'S GOOD

For some, in their opinion, if we do good things that outweigh the bad things then we are good people. If we have good intentions to do good things whether we do them or not, we are good people. We like to say God knows my heart. We like to see ourselves always in a positive light and never in a negative way. We see our strengths and we ignore our weaknesses, even when we are well aware of them.

The vast majority of us like to judge what is good according to our ideas, but we are evil compared to the divine. The truth is bad people do good things just like so-called good people do bad things. A lot of our good is only good from our natural view or perception but not from an eternal perspective.

We, in our fallen human condition, have the tendency to see our faults as not as big as others. We are blind to our faults and we are quick to judge others when they do wrong. We compare wrongs to each other, forming categories of what is serious and what is minor. For example: lying is bad, but murder is really bad. When we believe these things then our comparison makes us look good. In God's eyes one sin is never above another. God does not judge people on their wrongs compared to somebody else. He never excuses wrongs based on categories. All sin is bad and grievous to God, regardless of what it is.

Also, our believed good many times does not lead us to the best results. Sometimes our good is for good sakes, but not for God's sake. **Every good thing is not a God thing.** We should make it our goal to fulfill God's perfect will. Is what God wants being accomplished by my good works? For example: If I give a man money on a street corner who says he is hungry, but he uses it to support his alcohol addiction; did my good benefit him? If I let a family member continue to borrow money when they keep making bad financial decisions and they refuse to change; is it still a good thing I am doing?

Some people help people so they can look good or they want to receive something back later. What appears to be good is not always good in God's eyes. God's good is perfect always, that is why our good always comes up short unless it is His good actually working through us.

There is a universal belief by many that babies are perfect. That all children are born good and are only molded into bad characters by external influences. However, this is not what the scripture teaches. Let's look at a few scriptures:

> *Behold, I was brought forth in iniquity and **in sin did my mother conceive me.***
> *Psalm 51:5*

> *…even though **every inclination of the human heart is evil from childhood**….*
> *Genesis 8:21 (NIV)*

> *You have done wrong and lied **from the day you were born.***
> *Psalm 58:3 (CEV)*

Amazing!! We thought that beautiful, wonderful, precious little baby we were holding in our arms was just as perfect and pure as they could be. We may have thought that they were incapable of doing anything wrong, because they are just too little to know better. This is not true however. I see babies manipulate their parents all the time, it doesn't take many months for a child to learn what to do to get what they want. No one has to teach a child to lie, it comes naturally.

God's word reminds us that they were born of the flesh and have their parent's humanity and inclination to do wrong living within them. Just like we wash them up on the outside to make them clean, they will need to accept God's cleaning for their dirty insides as well at the time of accountability God has set. We were all born this way. We all need a cleaning.

HOW DO I BECOME GOOD?

As you can see from scripture and our previous discussion, it is impossible for you to be good without God. Anyone who desires to become good must follow God's way. He has provided only one way for any of us to be good. He is creator and judge, so His requirement is the only one that really matters.

The key to meeting God's requirement of righteousness is to see yourself from His perspective. I am no good. I need a Savior. Lord I ask you to save me. We need His forgiveness. We need Him to cleanse us. We have to understand that we are not doing God a favor, rather we need His favor. He doesn't need us, we need Him. We need Him to work His work in us and live His life through us. We need His heart and to operate according to His purpose.

Jesus did all the good things He did because God was in Him and in control of His life. He submitted His life and will to His Father God. We may seemingly do good things, but we can only become righteous if God lives in us. We must submit ourselves to God to become the good He accepts. **God doesn't want us to do good without being good.** This is possible when we become a believer who has submitted their life to Him. After we have become a true disciple of His, the good He sees in us is His good, not ours. There is one scripture that says,

> *A good man out of the good treasure of his heart brings forth good things, and an evil man out of the evil treasure brings forth evil things.*
>
> *Matthew 12:35*

Looking at this verse, it may appear that God is calling an ordinary man good. However, His definition of a good man here is a man who has received God and He is at work in him. In the previous passage, Jesus lectures the religious leaders by telling them to make the tree good. (Matthew 12:33) The tree He was referring to, was their lives. How were they to do this? They would need to receive His message of repentance. They would have to change their mindset and place their faith in God's salvation. They would have to decide to follow His commands and obey His words. Only after they did this, would their tree (life) become good.

Noah was known as a blameless man and righteous in his generation. He heard God's voice and obeyed, which was a testimony that God could be heard and obeyed. Those during his generation could not be excused as Noah was a witness that God was near and at work. **A good man really is a God man, which is a man that has God working in Him to accomplish His good.** God declared Noah righteous because of his faith in Him that was demonstrated by him building the ark.

Abraham was a man of faith and was considered righteous by God because of it. He believed God and his righteousness came from Him. He left everything that was dear to him in this life to follow God. He risked he and his son's life that he might attain the righteousness that could only be given by God.

You can never become righteous and good in God's sight until you can admit you are a sinner. You must acknowledge you are not good. You must agree with God and what He says about you and what you must do to be saved. Here are some scriptures about mankind and sin:

- There is not a righteous man on earth who continually does good and who never sins. *Ecclesiastes 7:20*
- There is none righteous, not even one. *Romans 3:10*
- There is no one who does good, not even one. *Psalms 14:1, 3*
- For in your sight no man living is righteous. *Ps 143:2*
- How much less one who is detestable and corrupt, man who drinks iniquity like water. *Job 15:16*
- Without God in Christ, you are a slave to sin. *Romans 6:17*

The only human being that lived a perfect life without sin was Jesus. He was God in the flesh. Every man has sinned. Only someone who is sinless can help you; someone who has overcome sin. **One of the greatest lies and deception of mankind is the idea that I am a good person.** Only in God through Christ can we be the good He intended and requires.

Only people who don't see themselves from God's point of view, but from their own point of view believe in their own goodness. Man can't see everything, but God can. From God's view, we miss the mark. This is the definition of sin. It means to miss the target God set for man. It means to not meet his standard and if we were honest with ourselves, we would admit this. I know it's hard to say, but **if you want to be free and clean, you must open up your mouth and say: I AM NOT A GOOD PERSON.** When you say this, you are saying what God says.

Why is this important? Until we humble ourselves realizing who we really are without God, we won't see ourselves in truth. We won't see our real need. We can't really appreciate the gift He has provided for us in His son Jesus. Without acknowledging our guilt and what He did for us, we are lost forever. We can never receive Him and apply His goodness to our life, making us good for the first time. Everything good is in Christ alone.

The danger of this lie is if we believe we are good people and are already fine, then we don't see our need to change. We won't make an effort to adjust in the areas we need to. The church will continue to believe this lie and it will keep it from repenting and from seeing its true, broken, spiritual condition. An evil stronghold will stay in place as a result. This is dangerous like the first lie I mentioned. If I believe I am a Christian, there is nothing else more I will do. If I see myself as a good person, there is no need for me to confess my sins. Everything remains the same because we believe falsely. The best thing to do is to acknowledge God's truth. God sent a warning to us through the church of Laodicea in the third chapter of Revelations. This church saw themselves as fine, but God said,

You say, I am rich; I have acquired wealth and do not need a thing. But you do not realize that you are wretched, pitiful, poor, blind, and naked.
Revelations 3:17 (NIV)

This church was in a lukewarm state and didn't realize how deceived they were. God sent this message to get their attention. There is a way that seems right unto a man but it ends in death. (Proverbs 14:12) Don't believe this lie. Realize only God is good and God determines whether you are righteous or not. A Christian nation must be righteous and understand its righteousness comes from God's goodness, not its own. Although we have missed it, it is an easy fix if we acknowledge the truth.

Some people will say God is love, God is understanding, and God judges mercifully. They don't believe their wrongs can overcome His grace. They believe you do not have to be good; God accepts you as you are and His good is enough to cover all your bad. They do not realize that when a person stays in their sins, God's grace is ignored and is not allowed to do its job. God came to destroy the work of the devil, which is sin. How can He be fine with it, when it cost Him His life to remove it?

We can never fix what we refuse to admit. And if we won't ever admit the problem and fix it, it will eventually destroy us and our children. If we want to be justified in God's sight, we must humble ourselves.

I'm a good person, you insist. The gospel has come to bring us to the realization we are not. This is hard for religious people to accept. This is hard for pastors and those who feel they must portray themselves as someone great and better than others. They don't want to see themselves for who they really are, but God is the one who they must answer to. He could care less what title we call ourselves. He is not impressed with us because He knows who we really are. We are impressed with ourselves and our glory only comes from another man, but not from God. People like this have already received their reward and it is a temporary one.

In Luke 18, Jesus shares a story to teach us a lesson. The lesson is that those who rely on their own goodness would never be justified. We are told about an ordinary tax collector who recognized his need for forgiveness and a religious church leader. Let's look at how God responded to each one of their prayers to Him. The Bible says these two men went to the temple to pray and the religious man stood at a distance bragging about how great he was, mentioning all the good works he had done. He characterized himself as not greedy, dishonest, or a womanizer like others. He condemned the working tax collector across from him. He saw himself as a better person. However, Jesus makes a point of who got His attention:

> *But the tax collector stood at a distance and would not even raise his face to heaven, but beat on his breast and said, 'God, have pity on me, a sinner!' I tell you," said Jesus, "the tax collector, and **not the Pharisee**, was in the right with God when he went home. **For those who make themselves great will be humbled**, and those who humble themselves will be made great."*
>
> Luke 18:13-14 (GNT)

God could care less about the religious leader's good works. They were never mentioned and he was judged as someone who was not in right standing with God. He made himself great in his own eyes and couldn't see how much of a sinner he actually was.

We are told in scripture that we are all sinners in need of a Savior. Ephesians 2:8-9 says, "**By grace** are we **saved through faith** and **this is not of ourselves, it is the gift of God, lest any man should boast**." We are incapable of saving ourselves by anything we do. We can only use the faith God gives us and place it where He tells us if we want to be saved from our sins becoming His children and receiving eternal life.

Lastly, John says, "If we say as his children, we have no sin, we are deceiving ourselves and we call him a liar and his truth is not in us." (1 John 1:8) Agree with God and pray this prayer right now:

Dear God,

I am so sorry. I am a sinner. I am not worthy of your love, grace, and mercy. In me is no good thing. I need you to be good. Forgive me for thinking more of myself. Forgive me for seeing myself as better than others. You don't have favorites. You are just and require all men to repent of their sins. Accept my confession. I now realize how much I needed your son Jesus to die on the cross for my sins. It was an ugly death because of my ugly sins. Cleanse me and make me whole. In Jesus Name.

Amen

LIE #3
LIBERIA IS INDEPENDENT

Poor people are slaves of the rich.
Borrow money and you are the lender's slave.
Proverbs 22:7 (GNT)

Yes, Liberia is recognized as the first African republic to proclaim their independence. It is a legally recognized country, just like any other country with its own governmental body. It has the power to make decisions and run its affairs without involvement from outside governments. Based off all these descriptions, it would only seem right to call Liberia an independent nation.

However, the reality of truth is found in the definition of independent. **Independence means to be free from outside control and influence.** It is not to be dependent on another's authority. It means you do not need someone else for your livelihood. If I am independent, I can support myself and live on my own without needing another's help.

From its inception, historical records reveal Liberia has always been dependent on other countries, organizations, and foreign citizens in some way for its general welfare. After 172 years since its declaration of independence, it is even more dependent today than ever before. How did this happen?

It was the United States through the American Colonization Society that introduced the conversation of sending freed slaves somewhere else other than America. Many slaves free or not, were plainly against it while others believed it was the only solution to ever have complete freedom for themselves and their families. They couldn't see this possibility in a racist America. The initial voyages would be financed by the Society who would send governors with the free blacks to govern them. It was to be a colony ran by white governors over the free blacks and former slaves.

These black immigrants would look to the American Colonization Society and its governors for protection, supplies, housing, and food. They would be under their direction in building the new land. After a brief stop in French controlled Sierra Leone, they had to find their own space. It is in what was known as Camp Mesurado, after a gun to the head of a local chief king named Peter and combats with the natives, that land was secured for them.

The creation of Liberia was not easy. The earliest settlers had several battles with the natives who did not want them there. This resulted in loss of life, kidnappings, and lootings of possessions. Firearms helped the settlers to prevail as this caused never before seen damage to the native tribes and instilled a fear of this weaponry. The new settlers also struggled to adapt to their new home due to unfamiliar climate and diseases such as malaria. Almost half of these new immigrants lost their lives in the first years due to sickness. As early as 1821, a few years after the initial landing, letters were written by the former slaves to former white owners back in America about the rough conditions. These letters included pleas for support. Many of these new immigrants couldn't see survival without this support. The provisions by the ACS to care for people until they could get on their feet turned out to be insufficient for what was needed in those beginning years.

Those that endured and stuck with the plan, especially the determined free blacks who had skills, built their power and wealth as builders and merchant traders. In 1847, Liberia became a republic governed solely by its own black leaders, yet it still relied heavily and expected financial assistance from the U.S. for its survival. In 1870, after they were acknowledged as their own nation, Liberia accepted high interest government loans from Europe and the U.S. This officially started their debt and financial, economic dependence on other nations.

So, the truth is that Liberia as a country and in every aspect of the societal community, even in the church, has for decades been heavily dependent on others for its survival. How much aid has been given to Liberia over the years? Let's take a look at some figures:

- President Doe received over 500 million in direct and indirect assistance from U.S. Overseas development assistance which includes money, food, supplies and services.
- Under President Tubman, the US poured in 280 million to Liberia.
- Foreign aid increased its money from 748 million in 2003 to 3.3 billion in 2017.
- Liberia received an average of 776 million in aid from 2010 to 2017. This accounted for a quarter to almost half of its income as a nation.
- Aid from the US was 86 million in 2018.
- In 2007 foreign aid paid for 75% of Liberia's health care.
- Liberia received 172 million in aid in 2009 from US.
- It has been estimated and reported that about 35% or almost one-third of Liberia's gross national income comes in from personal support sent in from different parts of the world. A huge percent of Liberia's citizens, depend on family and friends from other countries to live.
- Currently United Nations, NGO's, and missionaries provide dependent, humanitarian aid through social services like education, medical, housing, and more.

If we removed all these outside agencies and their support, what kind of condition would Liberia be in? What kind of debt does the nation of Liberia have? Liberia exports over 1 billion in products with the main being iron ore and rubber and imports twice that much in products. This means that Liberia's output of resources to other nations is less than half of what it receives from around the world to function. This means it needs more than it can offer anyone as a nation. This is a nation of debt. If we look where Liberia is on the wealth index today, it is #225 out of 228 countries; one of the poorest countries in the entire world according to a developed country's studies.

How can we get out of this condition before it gets any worse? This idea of dependence affects every part of society. The church community is no exception. Many churches receive their support from outside of Liberia through traditional church organizations. Many others are referred to as missionary churches and receive mission support from the states. Monies sent to family members are passed on so that church offering baskets, local stores, shops, and community businesses are impacted by this support.

Church buildings and schools receive benefits from outside support. Since a good percentage of families don't have the income to pay school fees outright, the schools which usually run solely on tuition and registration fees, are able to increase student body numbers and afford to pay teacher salaries because of families who are able to pay from support received from the states and elsewhere.

These facts about the country's current condition are not pretty, but they paint the true picture of where our dear Liberia is. It is very far from being independent. There will have to be a major adjustment in the way people think and act in order for it to be turned around. I believe it can happen. It would be nothing short of a miracle, but it is possible.

A whole country doesn't get turned around all at once. It doesn't happen overnight. It took a lot of years to get into this condition and will take some time to get out of it. Like a big ship, it will take some careful steering and wide round turns, but as long as it can agree on the destination God has determined and use His ways and methods on how to get there, it will be alright. It feels overwhelming, but a movement can begin to change the trajectory of a lifetime of dependence. Like eating a big animal, we must take one bite at a time in order to finish it.

This book was written primarily to the people of faith because these are the type of opportunities needed for God to show His power through us. We need to see ourselves in the role God has called us to. We are ambassadors on the earth with authority from heaven to address these issues and belief systems in our world, starting in our own church community.

> *For the eyes of the LORD run to and fro throughout the whole earth, to show Himself strong on behalf of those whose heart is loyal to Him.*
>
> 2 Chronicles 16:9

> *…but the people who know their God shall be strong, and carry out great exploits.*
>
> Daniel 11:32

Let's see what God's word has to say about this whole idea of dependence. God's word tells us:

> **Rest in God alone**, my soul, for **my hope comes from him**. **He alone** is my rock and my salvation, my stronghold; I will not be shaken. **My salvation** and glory **depend on God**, my strong rock. **My refuge is in God. Trust in him at all times**, you people; **pour out your hearts before him**. God is our refuge (protection).
>
> Psalms 62:5-8 (CSB)

> *Woe to those who go down to Egypt for help, and rely on horses, who trust in chariots because they are many, and in horsemen because they are very strong,* **but who do not look to the Holy One of Israel, or seek the LORD!**
>
> Isaiah 31:1

God gets very upset when His people look everywhere else for their help and they do not seek God. It's like treating the almighty God with contempt. We are saying to God, either you are not able to help me or I do not trust you to help me. Either way, it is a slap in the face of a great God for us to look to other men and nations to do for us, when God has already told us who He was and promised us what He will do for His children that trust Him.

> *And my* **God will supply all your needs** *according to* **his riches** *and glory in Christ Jesus.*
>
> Philippians 4:19

This passage of scripture is regularly quoted by Christians here in the states, but what does it mean? The author is Paul, the apostle and missionary. He reminds the church that God is the supplier of all your needs. That **God does not have limited resources**, and He has already demonstrated this through what we gained by knowing Jesus Christ as our Lord. God does not want anyone else to be our provider because He says He is.

The Heavenly Father doesn't only take care of other people so they can take care of you. **He wants to take care of you directly.** He may use them to give you what He wants you to have sometimes, but He deals directly with His children. We must first stop looking to God's other creation to take care of what is His. Every time He does use someone, we must realize it's Him behind it and not look to the person He is using. If you really are His child, God will eventually make things uncomfortable to show you your faith needs to be in Him. He never wants help from others to become permanent, but only at the moment He needs to fulfill His purpose. He wants us to be in a place of independence, not for us to be dependent on somebody else. God is jealous. Our reliance can't be on anyone else but Him.

> *Now this is the confidence that we have in Him, that if we ask anything according to His will, He hears us.*
>
> *1 John 5:14*

The word of God tells us when we come to our Heavenly Father in prayer, we know that He will hear us as His children. We are to have confidence that He will answer us positively. The next verse says if we know He hears us, then we know what we ask we have. There is only one condition that can prevent our answer from being yes; if we ask anything outside of His will for our life. God reserves the right as Father to say no to us. He knows what is best. Many of the things we say we need, are really wants that have nothing to do with accomplishing His purpose in and through our lives. **Many people don't even ask or wait for God's answer.** They know what they want and do whatever they can to get it regardless if the ways are wrong and regardless of how God may feel about it.

> *Seek first **the kingdom of God** and **his righteousness** and all of these things **shall be added unto you**.*
> *Matthew 6:33*

    We are told by Jesus himself the order we are to go after anything in this life. He says, first of all seek after the things that have to do with building God's kingdom and being in right standing with Him. If we make this our focus, then He promises to take care of all our other needs. If we read the previous verses, we understand this has to do with clothing, food, and shelter. We are told we never have to worry about these things. In fact, Jesus commands us saying, "**DO NOT WORRY.**" Worry does not bring these things into your life, seeking God does.

> ***Trust in the Lord with all your heart, lean not to your own understanding, in all your ways acknowledge God** and **he will direct your paths**.*
> *Proverbs 3:5-6*

    David, the man after God's own heart, encourages us all through the book of Psalms to put our total trust in God. In Psalms 118:8 he says, "put no confidence in man." In Psalms 143:8 he says, "Cause me Lord to hear your lovingkindness in the morning and cause me to know the way I should walk because I trust you." In Psalms 62:8 he tells us to trust in our God at ALL times. In Psalms 23 he tells us the Lord is our Shepherd and we shall not be in want. One of the most asked questions by God to man on the earth is, "Where is your faith?" In other words, "Why don't you trust me?" We are supposed to trust God with ALL our heart. We are not supposed to live according to our own understanding, but instead ask for God's knowledge in everything so He can lead us regarding what to do and where to go.

    We are to be dependent on God. We are to be independent of man. We are to be interdependent on each other. This means we are to understand that we are here to give help to each other as needed without becoming a burden. God's desire is that man would be able to help one another as needed. **He never intended that one group of people will ALWAYS need to receive help from the other group. There is something wrong with this picture.**

He also did not intend for anyone who receives help in their time of need to make this a permanent thing. We are not to receive welfare aid on a regular basis. This is no longer called *HELP*; it is now called *PROVISION* and no one is supposed to be our provider but God. Widows, children, and orphans are to be cared for because they are either too young or too old to work and need to be cared for physically. This is why God provides supervision from the parents for children. He provides family members and the church to assist in the process for widows and orphans. God looks out for people who can't look out for themselves.

> *Give them these instructions, so that no one will find fault with them. But if any do not take care of their relatives, especially the members of their own family, they have denied the faith and are worse than an unbeliever. Do not add any widow to the list of widows unless she is over sixty years of age. In addition, she must have been married only once.*
>
> *1 Timothy 5:8-9 (GNB)*

Widows and orphans must be looked after, because they do not have anyone to care for them. You won't find anyone else in scripture who He wants us to regularly look after. This scripture refers to how the early church received directions to look after these groups. It stated if you were a family member of this group, you should do the Christ like action and care for them so the church can focus on those who had no family at all. **This was not an instruction for family members to take care of healthy relatives who don't have a job.**

Now, God instructs us throughout the word to **<u>help</u> the poor, not <u>provide</u> for the poor**. We are to help others with wisdom as God leads for His will to be done only and not provide for others lifestyles and wants. The best way to help someone meet their needs is to go beyond giving them what they need now and show them how to trust in God and provide for themselves. We are to teach them how to fish and explain to them not to look at the hard, difficult, and corrupt things in the way and convince themselves that they can't do what God says. We can do all things through Christ who strengthens us, (Philippians 4:19) even against all odds. If God can feed a bird every day who does not store up food, how much more valuable are you? The scripture is clear that, "If a man does not work, he should not eat." (2 Thessalonians 3:10) A man was created by God to work. He must work. He must work even if it's for free. He must find something productive to do. In doing this, at least he is learning a skill and contributing. While we are obedient to work and trust God, He is faithful to fulfill His word in our life.

> ***Make it your goal*** *to live a quiet life, minding your own business and **working with your hands**, just as we instructed you before.* ***Then people*** *who are not believers **will respect** the way **you** live, and **you will not need to depend on others**.*
> *1 Thessalonians 4:11-12 (NLT)*

We have people in the states who have complete health, all their body parts function, and they are smart enough to commit crimes and get away with it. However, they have convinced themselves that the odds are stacked against them and they are helpless to do anything in a good way to care for themselves. The only thing wrong with them is a disease in the mind. I call it poverty mindset. They look to be taken care of by others. There are many inspirational stories out there of people who have many physical limitations and handicaps, but provide well for themselves. The only difference between them and others is they refuse to make excuses and feel sorry for themselves and their condition. If you look for a reason to not be what God intended, you will find one. If you believe you can be what God wants regardless of what you face, you will. For every excuse and reason, a man gives for why he can't succeed, there are thousands around him with similar or worse challenges that succeeded against all odds. Where is our faith?

God has given us the ability to manage our life and resources. God trusts us to handle our business. We don't have any excuses.

God would not give us a healthy body and a healthy brain, unless He thought we could start anywhere and become a success.

We are to use the tools He gave us. We are to look at Him and stop looking at everything and everybody else. Everybody has been given different circumstances to work through. Our focus as His child has to be on Him not everybody else. **God doesn't feel sorry for anybody.** He is compassionate, loving, caring, and concerned, but He knows feeling sorry for all the bad things happening around us and to us is not going to help us get where we need to go. Instead He asks us, do we have faith in Him? He doesn't ask us to have faith in man, the church, the system, our friends, or our associations in this world. He wants to see us be independent from other men and countries so that we can live a life of true freedom found in Him.

In regards to man's relationship, we are interdependent. This means we were not created to live alone but for the benefit of each other, to add to one another. This is what community is all about. God blesses a man to be a blessing to someone else. Man is not to use his talents and gifts God gives him to hoard for himself, provide comfort for himself, and to supply all his meaningless wants. He should rather minister to his fellow man. Interdependent means we give to each other. If you are in a relationship where one person is looking to you to repeatedly give, while they offer nothing back to you or anybody else, this is not interdependent but DEPENDENCE. This is the state where a majority of Liberians are.

I am dependent on God when I look to Him **alone** to provide all I need. He knows my needs and uses whomever and whatever He chooses at times. God brings the blessings into my life. He chooses how He wants to do this. I do not choose or tell God how to bless me. **I do not have to ask or beg anybody to help me.** If I was to ever do so, it would be to look to them as the supplier of my need and be my personal helper.

If you are following God, He may speak to someone to bless you or choose someone to do something so you can accomplish His purpose in your life. **Anytime we are regularly receiving from people and they are not requiring any accountability from us for completing the purposes of God with it, it is unscriptural.** It is not a blessing but a hinderance. It creates dependency and unrealistic expectation. It reduces respect for self and respect by others.

When God speaks to your heart and tells you to be a blessing to someone. You should do it. God will no doubt use people to bless you. They can be a source of God's provision in your life. I do not negate this. Unfortunately, **many of those getting needs met by others is not set up this way; a lot is out of expectation, guilt, faulty belief systems, and begging.** Ask yourself these questions:

1. Did someone make the decision to help you, not because they felt led by God to be a blessing to you? Did you approach them requesting help?
2. Are you manipulating someone by your actions making them feel responsible for helping you?
3. Do you make someone believe they are your only help and rescue and you will be in a worse condition without their personal help?

First for the recipient, if you answered honestly YES to any of these questions, your trust has not been in God. Anything that someone is doing for you that is not a God directive and not led by Him, is based on human emotion and the personal desire of one's own heart to help. It is not a horrible thing to want to help others. It is a good thing, but our understanding of help and Gods understanding of help is not the same. What appears in a natural state of helping is not always helping. God knows what is best and we don't always understand. **Remember, the more one does for others, the less most are willing to do for themselves;** so, you are not helping others in the long run.

There is something beneficial about pain, toil, and struggle. It produces patience and character in the end. This is what we have a short of more than anything; CHARACTER. Hard times should make us run and depend on God and wait for Him to help us His way. Something strong is built inside us when this happens. Anytime we pay people without God's leading and without holding them accountable for their actions, we hurt them and are probably getting in God's way of working out some heart issues in their lives.

God's church is not to be dependent on man or the world. The disciples received gifts from the church. The gifts were spread out to help everyone who had a need. These were not used on building buildings or buying excessive materials for the leaders. Most buildings are about the organization or the man leading it and not so much about the people lives attending. The people in desperate need are not crying, "Please help us, we need a nice place to worship." They are rather thinking about how they are going to pay for food, shelter, and clothing.

The church is supposed to show you how to trust God and take care of yourself and be independent. Instead, we are guilty of using our leadership to make people in our church dependent on us instead of God and using their God given giftings and monies for our own personal purposes. We have been guilty of having them depend on us so we can get what we need and want from them: like sex, property, labor, favors, position, and their worship. The church for the most part is not independent, but dependent on organizations and people. Since the church leaders don't really trust in God as their provision, but put their faith in the people who attend, we see many of them manipulate church attenders into giving. I see more offerings and fundraising at churches than I see people giving their lives to Jesus as Savior, repenting from their sins, and living a holy life as God intended for His children. God will move on people's heart to give automatically when they receive His Word in truth, not when they are constantly being targeted with words and scriptures used to try to get them to give money. This is not from God.

When I arrive from America, there are people who expect to receive money from me when I come. Our relationship means to them, I will support them. A large portion of people in this country have turned their attention entirely on dependence from outsiders for survival or anything they can get. It has become an expected way of life for way too many. **Liberia will never be financially independent as long as it is dependent and looking to others.** As long as she keeps saying, "What do you have for me?" "What did you bring me?" "Are you going to help me?" "I have a request." This is from a mindset that says, it's the only way I can get ahead or survive. This can't any longer be embedded in our mind. When we feel desperate, we don't care how we get our needs met. This desperate feeling is called anxiety. This is another word for worry. This is the opposite of faith. How does God tell us to deal with anxiety?

> ***Do not be anxious about anything,*** *but **in every situation, by prayer and petition, with thanksgiving, present your requests to God*** *and the peace of God which transcends all understanding, will guard your hearts and your minds in Christ Jesus.*
>
> *Philippians 4:6-7 (NIV)*

DEPENDENCY IMPACT

How does being dependent on others affect people? I believe there are three areas of our life that are influenced: Our enthusiasm, esteem, and expectation.

Enthusiasm – Dependence hurts a person's drive and ambition to do the thing God has created them to do. There is not as much incentive. We now have a tendency to look to others and don't work as hard. The necessary life and character skills are not being built in us. This happens when we seek God and fight through the battles and attacks that try to hinder our call and destiny. It is only during this process that we are able to build the necessary skills we need for our life. We are never able to take ownership of our lives as long as somebody else is doing the providing for us. We lower our standards and goals because we are comfortable, but we will never maximize our potential if we stay in this place. **Comfortable people never become great.**

Esteem – Dependence affects how we see ourselves, how we think God sees us, and how others see us. It reduces one's self-respect because you know deep within, you have taken the easy road and not tapped into the resources God has put inside of you. This is amazing in itself because Liberians crave respect from each other, but it appears too many have settled for looking the part to have respect. People may have respect from one another in their small sphere of influence, but not from God. Also, many outside the nation find it hard to respect and esteem people who do not look to care for themselves, but always need their help.

Expectation – Dependency teaches a habit of getting without the work. It's the quick way. This means people are willing to have without putting in the work necessary to earn it. It has convinced itself that the best way is to wait for somebody else to do for us when we have the ability to make it happen for ourselves. The expectation has become less on what we can do together and become more about what we can't do and our need for others to do for us. The more that is done, the more the expectation increases and becomes solidified. This has led to a dangerous belief system now passed down to the youth, our future.

Many years of dependence, aid, and bail outs have hurt my brothers and sisters in the long run instead of helping them. **To be dependent on God is to look to Him first and His word first** and apply it to our life in an effort to resolve any problems. This is the practice of Biblical Christians. We have seen from looking at what the Bible says and the daily practice of many, that dependence on man and dependence on God, at the same time, do not go together. **The church community should show the rest of society what dependency on God looks like and its benefit**, but the culture has had more influence and is allowed to override what God has spoken. Many of those in the church are doing what everyone else does. This has to change.

REBUTTALS ABOUT DEPENDENCY

Let's deal with 4 rebuttals given by dependent church members about not depending on man:

1. *If you don't ask, how can you receive? Doesn't the Bible say, "Ask and it shall be given?"*

This question and response assume that the main way God works for you to get anything in life is that you must ask people for it. "A closed mouth, don't get fed" is what people have said. Another common phrase shared is, "You have to speak up if you want people to help you." I agree with both statements, I just think we need to be talking to the right person. This passage of scripture is referring to God's children coming to Him. **The Bible response is that you ask God.** The Bible never directs us to ask another person to meet our need. It *always* refers us as His children to pray to our Father in Heaven for anything we need and expect Him to respond. If we understand the meaning of this text, we know that this asking and praying is continual until we see the results of our request.

The only time I'm led to ask people to do something is if God has told me *after* I came to Him in prayer. He will make it clear if this is the way He has decided to accomplish His purpose. God will always confirm it in the heart of those who give. The focus should never be on my needs and wants, but on God accomplishing His will. God does indeed use man to give and accomplish His purposes. God may have you share your needs with someone else, but it is usually when people ask you. This is not the same as you asking people outright. If you are sharing your needs with certain people to try to get them to meet them, your motive is wrong. If you happen to share casually about something God is wanting you to do, this is not a problem. God may speak to their heart to help you and you will know. **Let it be God.** You should always leave it open to God to direct people. If we are asking outright or secretly hoping for that person to do things for us, more and likely God is not going to be behind it. He is truly looking at our hearts intention in everything we do. He wants us to bring everything to Him first. He wants to see whether we trust Him or a man.

2. *The Bible says an earthly father gives good gifts to his children and our Heavenly Father gives us good gifts.*

I am a dad for so many around the world. On more than one occasion, I have had one of my God children call me. In the phone call, they were frustrated because they didn't believe I was doing enough to help them. They say a father is supposed to give to their children. About half of my children are young adults and these are the ones that seem to call me on this. I explain to them, I agree that a father should give good gifts to his child. Now let's understand what God is actually saying here. If you fully read the whole text (Matthew 7:11) it says, "If he asks for bread would he give him a stone and if he asks for fish, will he give him a serpent?" The answer to this rhetorical question would be NO! The idea here is a child looks to and trust his father to not give him anything that will harm him, but rather provide for these legitimate needs. This is true he provides, but it is also true that this child is totally dependent on His father because he is too small and unable to make the bread himself or fish for himself. In most places and the culture Jesus grew up in, a grown mature man didn't expect his father to get him bread or go catch a fish for him. He could do this himself. **So, it is not talking about an earthly father taking care of an adult child.** 1 Corinthians chapter 13 tells us, "when we become a man, we think and act like a man and put away childish ways."

I explain to them, the best gift I can give you as a father is to show you as a man what you need to do to meet your needs. Afterward I expect you to do likewise. The best gift God wants us to have, is the Holy Spirit. He knows this is what we need most. **He gives gifts according to our needs, not our wants.** He knows this gift will lead us every step of the way in what we are supposed to be doing.

3. *God uses man to give and be a blessing.*

This is true. I have been the recipient of this many times and I have been even more blessed to be the one giving other times. Christians help one another. God will use unbelievers also to give to accomplish His work and purpose. There is a scripture that says when we give, God will give back to us good measure, pressed down, and shaken together *men* will give unto our bosoms. (Luke 6:38) We have to ask, what am I giving? God has given you something to give first, whether you realize it or not. We must also ask, **Is God using**

somebody to bless me or am I looking to use somebody to help me? How do we know the difference? When is it God and when is it us? The answer is, where is your focus? God knows our hearts. He knows when we are looking and expecting from people. He also knows when we are not looking at people, but entirely up to Him. We are usually caught off guard with God because He doesn't always tell us what He is doing. He will usually use different people and different ways because He knows how we tend to start looking to particular people who have helped us before.

Where are your eyes looking? **Are you a man using God's name to get to another man?** We will find that God doesn't need us to reach out to connections, family, and associations to bless us. He doesn't need us to ask man repeatedly to help us. We know it is really Him when He leads the process. Jesus fed over five thousand after preaching to them one day and they came looking for Him on the next day. They made it seem like they wanted Him and what He offered, but He got on their case because He knew they were only looking for Him to get fed again and He revealed to them that He knew what was in their hearts. (John 6:26-27)

Jesus never asked anyone for anything. He prayed to His Father and gave commands based off what God spoke. When He needed the donkey to ride on, He just told his disciples to get it. He told the lady at the well to give him a drink. He told Peter to fish and get the coin out of the fish mouth to pay their taxes. He was always in control. This practice continued with Christ disciples when you read throughout the early church and New Testament letters. We need to spend more time in the presence of God and trusting Him like they did and stop looking and asking repeatedly from our family members, organizations, and connections.

4. *How am I supposed to live without outside support?*

This is a great question especially if you have been supported as an adult for some time. You have become accustomed to living your life according to what you regularly receive from others. **First, you must reject the lie you have believed that this is the only way**

that you can live. You must believe there are other possible ways for you even if you can't see them. Next, you must **be honest enough to confess to God that your trust is in someone other than Him** and you don't want that to be the case. Ask Him to help you and show you what He wants you to do. He will make clear what He will have you to do. He will show you how to better manage your money. He will show you what skills you can use for Him to bless you. He will bless you in other ways you least expected and show you how He can supply your needs if you totally trust Him. Like the widow in the Bible who needed money and thought she had nothing, God used the little oil she had in her house to bless her abundantly. (2 Kings 4:1-7) Little becomes much in God's hands. What are you doing with your ability?

Overall, many Liberians are some of the hardest working people I have ever seen. Many are grateful and thankful for any opportunities given to them while fully taking advantage of them. Unfortunately, there are also a vast number of opportunistic people that are looking for a handout. They may have no moral foundation, seeking whatever they can get and as much as they can get with doing the least amount they can.

One of the first development projects I supported and assisted with in Liberia, was a Christian school for children. After several years of support, we put a plan into action for them to become self-sufficient. I made efforts to provide a way for them to support themselves and they agreed. When the money was spent and the plan was put into action, they refused to implement it and regularly contacted me to continue to send money instead. They made many excuses why they couldn't do it. They were upset because we refused to continue to provide financial assistance. This was a necessary and unfortunate lesson for me. They also believed that my heart for the children and their many needs we were helping with, would override the principle of personal independence.

They are convinced still today that they were dependent on God when they had depended on me all along. No matter what I said and they supposedly agreed, they didn't quite get it. I learned as well by this experience that **most people do not listen to what you say,**

they follow what they believe in their mind. What you say most of the time goes in one ear and totally out the other ear because it is not what they want to hear. I have learned when you are discussing and talking with many about God and His provision, they don't hear what you say, they hear what they believe. What did they believe? What did they hear? We are depending on you and need money from you, that's all there is.

I learned the more I do, the more I am expected to do and be responsible for. Even after agreeing to plans that end with self-sustaining projects, I found an unwillingness for my Liberian peers to run the business. Some of those who became accustomed to our support became hostile when it ended. They expected the support to last a lifetime. All I could do was shake my head. For many, who I and others had helped go to school, finish college, and start a business, it seemed no matter how much was given, it was never enough and at the end nothing usually had ultimately changed. Of course, there were always a few exceptions.

I spoke recently with a government official there who talked about an agricultural program in Liberia sponsored by another country. The program ran for five years providing for the students while teaching and training them. The goal was for those trained to take over the program providing expertise and multiplication of agriculture around the country. However, those trained only stayed a part of the program as long as they were having their needs taken care of. When the program ended and it came time for them to take over and continue on their own for the good of them, their family, and their country – they abandoned the project because they were not getting paid anymore from the outsiders.

In the states we call it a welfare mentality. I call it a feeling of obligation, entitlement, and requiring someone to do a duty. This is a mindset that is not from God, but from the evil one. Some believe based on relationship I should receive help from you or just because you are American, but I believe most of this thought process in people has happened because after helping people for so long, some start to believe it is your responsibility to take care of them. In America, when you don't prepare your adult children to leave home and take care of themselves, they start to feel entitled, like it is your job to take care of them even as grownups. We along with them are responsible because we have been a deterrence to their own progress.

Ask yourself these questions to make sure you are on the track to being independent: As an adult do you live without someone else supporting you? Are you dependent on someone else work? Should someone else work for you, a healthy adult, to eat? Should you not do everything you can to feed yourself? Are you looking for others to provide for you?

Statements I hear include: We are starving. What did you bring me? What will you get for me? We need this and that. We have no water. The children are hungry. I lost my phone. I need school fees. I need to go to the doctor. Can you bring me a computer? Some people have become professional beggars, but I understand that much of this was passed down as one of the only ways to get the things you need and want. This has been taught from the inception to many. They have been told to make a connection and take advantage of others who you believe have. I heard one Liberian say, "Everybody is looking for a white man to help take care of them." This is not true, but to some of us, it sure seems that way.

How you get something is just as important as what you get. For example: You may have a teacher's certificate, but if you paid for it without putting in the work to actually know the information and have the expertise to do the job, this is nothing to be proud of. Please hear me and my heart. I understand that life can be difficult. Jesus told us Himself, "In this world you will have trouble." People have real needs. I get it. I am sensitive to this, but there is a way to go about this. Jesus also continuing said, "But be of good cheer, for I have overcome the world." (John 16:33) If He overcame and you are connected to Him, that means you can overcome.

DEPENDENT CHURCHES

As we have seen from scripture, God is not glorified when His people are dependent on other people beside Him. If the church believes like the rest of its society, that Liberia is already independent, then it won't address those things that keeps it so dependent on charities, foreign government aid, and family and friends outside the country to keep it going and build its future. What discussion and plan implementation does the local church have to address its own independence from organizations outside?

Churches are building bigger and better edifices and creating schools, yet its communities are filled with problems and members are dependent on outsiders for help. We must stop blaming government officials and anybody else solely for the problems we are facing in our own communities and nation. We must stop ignoring the real issues, because we don't want to do what we need to address them. We must stop pretending everything is fine when it's not. We must take responsibility for our part. **People are perishing because the church is not implementing God's vision.** God has been trying to give His vision to the churches but they have preferred to follow man's. We know when it is God's vision because first, it will only be something He can accomplish through us. Secondly, it will impact and benefit EVERYONE in a practical way.

It was necessary to relay these facts and truth that affect most Liberians and the false belief system in the culture that has accepted a dependent way of life from its inception. Without acknowledging this truth, the church can't see the stronghold lie that is in the way of progress. It is the lie that most hold to be true. Like most of the rest of the country, the Liberian church community doesn't see where it truly is. Most will claim to you that they are dependent on God. The truth is that too many are dependent on man and their confidence is more in what a human being or another nation can do for them than in what God is able to do. They are not independent from others. Most would only be dependent on God if they have been left to die and all other options in life were gone. If you have to come to a place where you have no other choice, then this is not true faith and dependence on God. **God can't be your last resort. He has to be the first**; otherwise it is a slap in the face of His greatness. The church community has been slapping God in the face. They have been telling Him that they trust Him, while focusing and depending on everything and everybody else to help them out.

I have put together a list of what we can start doing to change this culture of dependence:

TEN COMMANDMENTS FOR AFRICAN ADULTS
WHO DESIRE INDEPENDENCE AND HAVE
FRIENDS AND RELATIVES LIVING ELSEWHERE

1. DO NOT ASK THEM TO BUY YOU A PHONE
2. DO NOT ASK THEM TO BUY YOU A LAPTOP COMPUTER
3. DO NOT ASK THEM TO PAY YOUR TRANSPORTATION COST TO GO SEE THEM OR LEAVE THEM WHILE THEY VISIT YOU
4. DO NOT EXPECT THEM TO HELP YOU PAY YOUR SCHOOL TUITION OR REGISTRATION FEES
5. DO NOT EXPECT THEM TO FEED YOU EVERY TIME YOU ARE HUNGRY.
6. DO NOT EXPECT THEM TO PAY YOUR MEDICAL FEES WHEN YOU ARE IN NEED OF MEDICAL CARE
7. DO NOT EXPECT THEM TO PAY FOR REPAIRS OR REPLACEMENT TO WHATEVER YOU HAVE BROKEN OR LOST.
8. DO NOT EXPECT THEM TO BRING YOU A GIFT WHEN THEY COME TO VISIT YOU (INCLUDES BIRTHDAY, WEDDING, GRADUATION)
9. DO NOT EXPECT THEM TO PAY YOUR FAMILY FUNERAL COST TO BURY A LOVED ONE
10. DO NOT EXPECT THEM TO SEND MONEY REGULARLY OR TO PAY FOR ANY OF YOUR LIVING EXPENSES.

Does Liberia want to do for itself? Can Liberia live independently from help? So many already do. What does God want? Yes. It's clear what the Bible teaches us. Let's therefore practice using these phrases:

- *No thank you, I want to try to do it myself.*
- *I want to earn my own living.*
- *I don't want anything regularly that doesn't cost me.*
- *I don't always need your handout.*
- *I don't need you to feel sorry for me.*
- *God will take care of me.*

Wherever you go, you will have a part of the population (including in the USA) who expect others to take care of them. Some expect the government to make sure they have what they need. This is not Biblical or acceptable for us who say we are Christians. God is responsible for taking care of us.

I'm not saying this mentality is the main cause of poverty throughout Liberia, Africa, and the world. I understand that a lot of the problems that nations face, were created by outside forces. However, I'm convinced continued years of expectations has helped in keeping our communities impoverished. We must take some responsibility and the fact that we could do much more to empower ourselves. Let us follow the principles in scripture as believers, uniting together, putting our trust in God's word, praying His will, and doing the actions He wants from us.

Dear God,

Thank you for showing me what I have allowed to enter my heart and mind regarding dependence. Forgive me for trusting other people and things besides you. Help me to return to looking to you alone as my provider. In Jesus name. Amen.

LIE #4
LIBERIA NEEDS INTERNATIONAL SUPPORT

Stop trusting other people to save you.
Do not think too highly of them;
they are only humans who have not stopped breathing yet.
Isaiah 2:22 (ERV)

Liberian people are a proud people. They love their country and love their culture. They share the heritage of Liberian dishes, family traditions, and colloquial language. It is the life they have become accustomed to. Despite the tough life, people find reasons to smile and the children love to play. They are great at making the best of their life. You will commonly hear them say, "We thank God for life."

What most common Liberians I know don't love is what Liberia has become. They don't like what they refer to as a hard and difficult life in their country. Some of the challenges include finding a job, dealing with corruption, and a high cost of living.

Liberia is considered by developed nations to be one of the poorest countries on earth. Based on their statistics, over 50 percent of the population lives in what they call extreme poverty and the life expectancy is about 60 years. The illiteracy rate is about 60 percent. Liberia is ranked by the United Nations at the bottom, being placed on the international's global corruption barometer as low as you can go. I can think of lots of European nations that are not mentioned that are lower, but that's another story for another time.

For a vast majority of Liberia's citizens, they are convinced that leaving Liberia is the best thing for a good life. A man I have been working with for many years, when I told him about my desire to help his son with college in Liberia, he stated to me that the best thing that I could do for him was to take him out of Liberia to the states. In his mind, what good is a college degree in Liberia if he can't find a good paying job. Getting help from someone in another country, particularly America, is more preferable. It is hard for many people to believe they can take care of themselves well in Liberia or become anything great without outside help or leaving the country.

Minnesota has one of the largest communities of native Liberians in the USA. Many found refuge there while fleeing Liberia during the civil war. They received a special residency visa. Recently, many were told they would be deported if they did not have citizenship; as their special status was about to expire and would not be renewed. U.S. government proponents stated their homeland is safe enough for them to return. The response to this potential order of returning native Liberians to their home in Liberia was an immediate outcry; as they fought viciously to retain their right to stay in the USA. They did not want to return to their homeland. They gave many reasons why, but it basically came down to the fact, they saw no hope or future for themselves or their children in this place. Based on my own personal survey, almost 90 percent of Liberians I know would leave their country to live in the US or Europe if they had the opportunity. There are numerous citizens who play the diversity visa lottery yearly with the hope of leaving.

Looking at the difficulties most face and their continual search for a better life, it is not surprising that most Liberians feel they need help from outside with the International community to survive. This belief does not exclude the government and the church community. They both gladly accept any help they can get. I'm not suggesting this is a totally bad thing, however I truly believe that Liberia should and could have an awesome existence without handouts from the international community if it wanted. They would be much better off.

I also believe this is the way God would have it and I will show you scriptures to support this point. I will also proceed to explain why I believe constant international support is not necessary? Why it doesn't work? How it has not helped? What could Liberia do instead?

and How the church community is supposed to lead in helping Liberia become independent from outsiders?

Let me first establish that support care is different from emergency help. Is Liberia receiving help or regular consistent care from outsiders? There is a beneficial help and there is a help that hurts. We all need and receive help from time to time from each other and that is fine, but the majority of aid and support that has been given internationally over the years, has been clearly regular supportive care. Unfortunately, this is the kind that hurts and is debilitating to a person and country.

The real question is, does Liberia really want to provide for itself? I believe they want to, but too many don't believe they can. The lie is that Liberia as a nation does not have the ability to support itself and it needs others outside to help it. This is a wrong belief, but since it is a widely held common belief, it holds power over the nation. Can we stop believing we are helpless to be self-sufficient without international help? Can we stop believing the lie that only those who live well are able to do so because of outside help only. This type of thinking has become one's personal truth and hinders them from any further progress.

As seen in the previous chapter, aid given would come to an astronomical total if added up just in the last ten years. This is international aid through loans and grants. Aid also has come in the form of social welfare, education, and medical aid supplies by non-governmental organizations and agencies. They have played such a huge role in Liberia, that the country is totally dependent on it. This does not even include the grants and monies from donors with religious organizations and personal contributions from individual donors. Dependency is bred throughout without a system in place for the country to replace this help.

Why regular aid doesn't work?

How has international aid helped Liberia? Has it worked or not? President Sirleaf Johnson wrote a letter of thanks to America for coming to their aid immediately after the civil war. She stated that

Americans can rest assured that generous aid provided to her country is paying off in saved lives, increased productivity, and political stability. She said, with continued support during their transition, she was confident that Liberia within a decade would be able to sustain its own development and end its need for foreign aid. She said America aid is helping us get there and Liberia aspires to outgrow the need for aid. It was a wonderful letter but after the ten years, Liberia was still dependent on international help.

More aid does not make an economy or nation healthier. Foreign aid seems to help out a lot in the short run but hurts in the long run stability of a country. It doesn't grow or stabilize an economy in the long term. It is only a short-term fix. When you rely on foreign cash aid to keep your economy going, it deceives people into thinking things are getting better. The aid keeps Liberia from dying, but never helps it get healthy. Why? There is nothing internally being invested, built, or growing to replace or increase those monies received.

Under these circumstances, it is now actually dangerous for the foreign aid to be withdrawn, because a crisis will develop. So, what has been started is continually needed to keep things going. If foreign support, which is depended on, is all of a sudden lost, you will have economic instability followed by political instability. Economy struggles usually lead to protest, violence, more political unrest, and potentially war. It's as if we are a puppet and someone else is pulling our strings (controlling things). All they have to do is pull a string here or there and everything shifts and it is felt by everyone negatively. This is not a good place to be in. What is being built to replace the aid? How much time will it take so that Liberia can be strengthened?

The goal of Aid

The ultimate goal of international aid is really not to help Liberia develop. I believe it doesn't work because it is not supposed to work. If that was truly the goal by those outside, it would have worked by now. The reason I say this is the first aid was given to Liberia over 100 years ago and it has been continual ever since. Today, everywhere around the world, money seems to keep disappearing that is given as international aid. Why do we see money given without seeing the benefits received for the people supposedly being helped? Who gives money like this continually without making sure the money is being used effectively? This is the worst case of stewardship and accountability I have ever seen. Why does international aid continue to pour money into a country without accountability, where money can't be traced and accounted for, but yet continue to give more and more money? Maybe there is another agenda or agreement involved. If that is the case, money is not the issue anymore, the agenda of getting what they want is. Why would you care how much money is being wasted if your purpose is being accomplished? If the money is only given in exchange for favors or to keep control, this would make more sense of what is going on. I believe the bottom-line goal of almost all international aid from governments has to do with their own benefit, not the other country.

Could it be that they don't really care what happens to the people of the country they give it to? Perhaps, the goal is to make people more dependent. Could it be to keep the domination and control against Africans? The International community which includes the USA – once they get you in debt and you have no money to pay it back, you become slaves. Loans are given with agreements that benefit the loan giver. Grants are given with restrictions and directions that promote the grantors interest. Overall, the United Nations helps you in ways that promote their agenda, not yours. All exchanges of resources and goods have policies that benefit them, not us.

It is a problem when somebody else controls all your resources, so you have no other options except to turn to them. If you stop doing what powers in place tell you, they can make it hard for you to get what you need. This is what control does. **Whoever has the money, uses the money to influence, influence is used to gain power, and power is used to control.** In this case, the world's resources and the right to determine how those resources are used.

When millions of dollars in aid are given to a few people on the top, it stays there. When all the money, law enforcement, and rules are in the hands of a few, the nations will continue to suffer. All other nations fear a multitude of average people waking up and being empowered. They never fear a group of people they can control sitting on the top.

The fact is, resources are not getting to the people. Many countries, including Liberia, would be better off not receiving any aid to government officials, non-government organizations, or religious institutions and all money going to the common people. Unfortunately, these entities are very quick to receive money. The money received is made to appear that it benefits everyone, but it's really hard to see how the people of a nation benefit. It too often appears to many that a certain group of leaders, because of greed and personal interest share the spoils and it never reaches the common citizens.

Wouldn't it be wonderful if the common people got to decide how to use the money? Who they want to pay? What they want to build? At least it would give them control over their own existence. What would we lose? It couldn't be any worse than it is now. Might as well give it to the people on the bottom and let them decide what they want to do with it to build their own life. I want to see this dream become a reality. This may seem impossible for the world, but this was the norm for the New Testament church. (Acts 4:35) I pray our churches today would show our world what Christ and His love for mankind looks like.

God is looking for servant's like David, a man after His own heart and those who follow our Lord and Savior Jesus, loving the people and caring about what happens to them more than a love for themselves, a fear of other men, and a unwillingness to understand the danger for a nation that stays dependent. Liberia will continue to suffer if we don't get free from outsider's control as a whole nation.

Where can this control further take us? We get a picture of this when average citizens are being forced to accept policies they don't want; such as same sex relationships which international agencies tried to push on Africa as a human rights issue. How about future mandatory vaccinations? How about future electronic devices required in our bodies? Will an organization say one day unless you accept this, we will no longer provide aid?

Will our countries be able to respond to other nations they are dependent on for support and say we don't have to accept your policy because we can live without you? NO, not at this moment and there will be no change in the future unless we are building our own infrastructure, managing our own resources, creating our own goods, and growing our own food, while finding other countries to trade with within our own continent. This would be the best response in my opinion.

International partners can't have this type of control over Liberia and other African nations without the cooperation from some of its leaders. African leaders and representatives shouldn't be able to be bought and bullied.

Friend or Foe

I just read a report from the U.S. Department of State that says: U.S. assistance and engagement is critical to Liberia's long-term development. Really? After 172 years of their help, where is Liberia today? How much longer will Liberia need this type of support from the U.S. for its development? Maybe another 172 years? What will Liberia look like then? There have been many questionable activities and decisions made throughout Liberia's history by the U.S. that goes contrary to their support of its development. I will not divert from the purpose of this book to go into the specifics, but I plan to address it sufficiently at a later date. Does Liberia really know and understand who their friends are and who their foes are?

A friend or an ally is a mutual joining of forces in some area for a mutual benefit. I haven't quite seen the mutual benefit where Liberia has been concerned in many policies with the international community. We have to stop believing since a few people are doing well, that it is good for everyone. This is the furthest from the truth. Liberians have been made to believe this first by its supposed greatest ally America. America wants Liberia to believe that they need them if they are to fix their problems. They are also supposed to believe that the government of America and other nations have their best interest in mind. Liberians are supposed to believe their organizations, trade policies, and everything else they do is helping them. In the short run, it appears to be a mutual benefit, but in the long run it is created to be one sided and assist outsiders in their overall agenda of controlling everything and everybody.

We have to ask, what does the other country really want? What is the worst-case scenario? How can we protect ourselves? If we continue to accept these plans, we are placing faith in others and keeping them in positions above us. When we put our trust in others to do for us what we need to do to live, we allow others to gain the right to control us. This is dangerous.

Does anybody owe Liberia anything? No. Does Liberia owe anybody anything? Yes. As long as this is the case, they will continue to bankrupt Liberia. Liberia should not be a social welfare program to other countries. There are powers to be that will do everything they can to keep Liberia from being truly independent and without need of them. I am praying for the day when Liberia and all its leaders will join forces on an agenda that it no longer wants to be controlled and dependent on others and are willing to do everything possible to make that dream come to pass. I pray the same for all of Africa.

The world is always happy to give foreign aid and loans to Liberia in exchange for its resources. The contracts and deals provide temporary relief in exchange for long term raping and suffering of the nation at large. A great example of this process was seen when the U.S. company named Firestone took advantage of Liberia's vulnerability after WWI, knowing their need for assistance and its need for the natural resource of rubber due to the invention of the automobile. The deal saw Firestone get one million acres for ninety-nine years at six cents per acre with any gold found belonging to them. Liberia also accepted a new five-million-dollar loan over forty years to settle previous loans. This agreement to contract also included outsiders controlling and managing the governments money to insure repayment. Firestone financial records show more money made from their Liberia plant in one given year of operation than Liberia received for a total of ninety-nine years. Today, the contract is a little better than this, but this is an example of what is still going on today in our beloved country and other African nations around it. The colonizers still run the African countries through the World Bank,

United Nations, World Health Organization, and other agencies and in other ways.

China is another benefactor of Liberia. How has China benefitted Liberia? All we have to do is look at where the average Liberian citizen is today and where they were before China started investing money and building here. How has it made Liberia more independent? **Progress without independence only leads to a more beautiful looking slavery.** Is there even such a thing? Liberia will continue to look outside itself until it wakes up and sees what it is doing to its people or until it is too late to do anything at all and it has been completely overtaken by others. Our willingness of looking to others and letting them provide for us without a goal of independence and investing these monies that will lead us there is truly hurting us.

CHURCH

The reason for this book was to challenge the thinking of the church community to lead in the transformation of a whole nation. It has always been God's desire for the church to be the salt and light of the world. I can use many scriptures that talk about where our help should ultimately come from as God's people and where we go when we need help and how this help looks. I have chosen to use the ones regarding God fighting against nations on behalf of His people. Israel was His chosen nation to display to the world, the salvation of the Lord. God wants to do the same with Liberia.

We need to know how God would have us to think. We must make the changes in our thinking so we can change. After we change, we will have the belief system in place to help change the nation. What does God's word tell us about what He expects from His church? We know without faith it is impossible to please God. (Hebrews 11:6) We are sometimes guilty of having our faith in everything else but God alone. Where is your faith? Where is the church community's faith? I pray the church will completely be released from its dependence on man so it can be used by God.

God teaches us it is not good to make alliance with other nations to accomplish our mission. We can't make an alliance with evil either to accomplish God's purpose. Israel, being God's people, was not to trust in Egypt or anywhere else. They were not to look for help from anybody else. These other countries were practicing wickedness and God had called His own people and separated them to be a holy nation unto Him. The other nations did not serve the same God they did. To allow other nations to live in their land without driving them out, caused them to be thorns in their sides; leading them to false worship and being enslaved in their own land.

> *At that time Hanani the seer came to King Asa of Judah and told him,* **"Because you have relied on the king of Aram and not on the LORD your God,** *the army of the king of Aram has escaped from your hand. Were not the Cushites and Libyans a vast army with many chariots and horsemen?* **Yet because you relied on the LORD, He delivered them into your hand. For the eyes of the LORD roam to and fro over all the earth, to show Himself strong on behalf of those whose heart is fully devoted to Him.** *You have acted foolishly in this matter. From now on, therefore, you will be at war."*
>
> 2 *Chronicles 16:7-9 (NIV)*

We as God's people are guilty of looking elsewhere instead of at God. We have replaced God as our main source. We have abandoned, forgotten, rejected, ignored, and removed the Lord from our daily affairs. It cost us nothing to just give Him church time but God doesn't want this. God wants a personal relationship. He doesn't want your church building, organization, or ministry. This is not for God. This is for man. If He is not the object of our love, time, and devotion, He is not a part of our ministry. We can't continually make our requests to other men to help us with our needs and wants if we want to live according to God's way. God wants us in regular fellowship and meetings with Him to receive His direction.

How can Christian leaders influence government leaders with truths that they don't even live by? We have two choices, we will either look to God as our source; praying and seeing His word as our cure or we will look to man. Whoever we look to becomes the ultimate authority we are under. **Will Liberia put its complete trust in God or will it continue to be ruled by other nation's monies?**

We will use Biblical references to discuss the key issues concerning obstacles and hinderances in being loosed from demonic strongholds through ungodly alliances to becoming totally free from international dependency. These major issues to consider are: identity, vision, disunity, idolatry, and corruption. We would not need international support if we functioned according to these powerful and practical principles outlined in the scriptures.

IDENTITY - SELLING OUR BIRTHRIGHT

Esau and Jacob were the sons of Isaac and the grandsons of Abraham, the father of the faith. Esau, being the firstborn, held the birthright - the inheritance from his father which carried the privilege of an everlasting covenant with God as well as a double portion of the estate. In the story, Esau was very hungry one day and asked his younger brother Jacob to give him some of the food he had prepared. Jacob, who desired the right to the inheritance and blessing of his father, took this opportunity to ask Esau to sell it to him in exchange for the food he wanted. Esau reasoned to himself, this birthright is not going to do me any good right now because I am hungry. So, he traded it for a bowl of stew. (Genesis 25:29-34)

This may not have seemed like much, but in actuality Esau had given up his destined future for the immediate satisfaction to eat. This story shows us that he despised the birthright that was given to him by God. Did he really understand it represented the inheritance and blessing that would be passed down to his next generation? If he really thought about what he was doing and treasured its importance, he would not have given up something so valuable for something so temporal. The fact is that he actually traded away what God had planned for him and God was very much displeased.

Liberia keeps trading their future for a quick meal. Liberia and other nations like her must stop selling her birthright for immediate gratification. There is much more to life than food and possessions.

The greed of getting money causes her to trade away her land and people. Fear of not trusting in God and what will happen in the future causes her to trust in someone else whose ultimate plan is to starve everyone who will not allow them to control them. Esau would not have starved of course, he just wasn't willing to wait, plan, and prepare a meal that would allow him to keep his future blessings as well. He allowed his immediate appetite and feelings to rule what was in the best interest for him and his children's future. He didn't value what God had planned for him and as a result, he and his descendants would serve others.

We can't allow ourselves to be deceived about what matters most. We must stop exchanging a few moments, months, and years of temporary momentary relief and comfort for our future. Let's not sell the control of our nation and future. Those who allow this don't realize they are jeopardizing everything. Our posterity will suffer. It's something much bigger at stake than you growing rich while the population stays poor. You may go down in history as the leaders who allowed evil to take down Liberia and Africa. It is our future demise at stake, as others use you to get control. They will harm you as well when they are in complete control. You have to say, "OUR FUTURE IS NOT FOR SALE!"

Liberia has despised what God has said and as a result had its blessing stolen. When you don't know or understand your purpose and what you were destined for, you will destroy yourself and others without care. When you don't know your identity and the purpose God has given you, you will abuse and misuse it. Liberia, fight for your birthright, fight for your identity, fulfill your purpose, and save your nation and those around you.

WHO ARE YOU?

Israel was a nation at one time to be envied by the rest of the nations because they had a God that literally carried them out of Egypt with a mighty hand. They saw miracles the world could have never imagined. All were awestruck and feared the God of Israel. He provided for His people miraculously and brought them into the prosperous land of Canaan for a possession like he had promised Abraham many hundreds of years before. They had a God who fought for them and delivered them repeatedly out of their enemy's hands when they repented and cried out to Him.

They had an established worship system and supernatural commandments written by God himself, delivered by His servant Moses. They had the ark of the Covenant where the very presence of God would come and rest in their midst. They had the other nations attention as the only nation that worshiped one God, for most other nations were polytheistic, worshipping many gods. The other nations believed they needed to worship all those gods to live. Israel only needed one God to be and do everything they needed.

Despite their legacy, heritage, and glorious history, and despite their unique commandments, laws, and worship that set them apart from all the other nations, they preferred to be like everyone else. This is so sad. God blessed them so that they could be different from everyone else to be a blessing to everyone else and they didn't want it. They longed for the identity of other nations. They wanted a government set up like all the other nations had. They longed for the foods and materials and buildings all the other nations had at the expense of their God given identity.

When all the people came to God's prophet Samuel and said, "We don't want your sons to lead us, instead we want a king like the rest of the world has." Samuel went to God and God said, "It is not you and your family they are rejecting; it is me." (1 Samuel 8:5-7) **When you want to take on the identity of other nations, God says you are rejecting Him.** Is Liberia rejecting God and His plan for them? It certainly appears this way.

God has created Liberia to be who He wants her to be as a nation. This is not to follow the same pattern as the United States, United Kingdom, China, or anyone else. Liberia must find its own identity in God. It must find its own purpose on the world stage. Samuel explained to the people what would happen if they followed the pattern of the other nations. The leader would abuse them. He will use them. He will take their best and give it to those he preferred. He will make them his servants. Their response was they didn't care.

We just want to be like them. God knowing everything, gave them what they asked for.

How much are we willing to lose as a country to be like those around us? Let's follow God's plan instead and let everyone know that we are not copy cats and our unique identity is not for sale either.

VISION - WITHOUT A VISION PEOPLE PERISH

The Bible says without a vision, the people perish. (Proverbs 29:18) Another version says without revelation, the people cast off restraint. What vision does Liberia have that is keeping it together so it does not fall apart? There has been no lack of candidates seeking the office of leadership in government who did not have passion about something they wanted to see happen for their country. There are slogans and promises made and shared concerning various issues that interest people. Many of our visions for what we see for a better country are good. **A major problem is our visions exclude the qualities that are needed to see them happen**. Better schools, better roads, more business, and more jobs are all great things but if these things are pursued on a foundation that is without character, integrity, accountability, love, and unity; they make these simple external goals almost impossible to accomplish. Everyone wants to see physical change but we won't until we are willing to correct our character issues. **Spiritual and mental change must precede physical change in order for there to be any change.** This is why everything is at a standstill. We must resolve the issues that are the real culprits to our progress.

Having a vision doesn't guarantee people will still not perish. The scripture only tells us that without one, they will perish for sure. The vision mentioned here is a revelation that comes from God. The vision that comes from a man alone is like building a house on sand. It may look good on the outside but every time adversity comes, it will not be able to hold up at all. Man's vision is not God's, in fact most of the time it is the complete opposite. It may even compete against what He desires. God's vision leads to life for everyone. It is a sure foundation that can weather any storm. If our vision and methods go against sound Biblical laws, precepts, and commands and they are absent from His foundational structure, we can expect to fail.

WHAT'S IN OUR HOUSE?

Lastly, our vision along with who we are is closely tied to what God has given us. When we find ourselves seemingly without, we must not get anxious and cry out in desperation to others to save us. Every time we do this, we get in trouble. If our identity is truly from God and in Him, then we must cry out to Him and He will give us our answers.

We find encouragement in the story (2 Kings 4:1-7) of the widow and her two sons who faced a crisis that threatened to leave the family hungry and separated. The husband had died and the family had debts in which creditors would come, take the sons, and make them slaves to work off what they owed. They seemingly had nothing in the house to live off of. The first thing the widow did right was call the true prophet of God. After telling him her dilemma, the prophet asked her, "What do you have in the house?" She said nothing but a little oil. She couldn't see how much value she had with that oil. The man of God could see. He told her to gather as many jars as she could and pour the oil in them. She obeyed and God did a miracle filling everyone. The oil kept going until there were no more jars to fill. He then told her to go and sell the oil, pay the debts with the money, and live off the rest.

God says to Liberia, what do you have in your house? What is in your own country that He can use to take care of you, pay off your debts, and live good with? What has He already given you? Are we like the widow who could not see that what she had was an abundant resource which could take care of her problems? **Vision is being able to see what God sees and obeying what He leads you to do.** He never asks who you know because when you put the focus on people, you take the focus off where it should be, God. God looks at what He has already given us. This is how He plans to bless us. What He has given us in our own house is part of our identity as a nation. Hold on to your identity and do not let others take it away from you. Like the widow, you have enough resources to pour into your neighbors (other nations) containers and sell it to them, so your debts are paid, and you can live the life God has called you to live.

DISUNITY - A NATION DIVIDED WILL FALL

A people divided against itself, can't stand. A church divided against itself, can't stand. A nation divided against itself, can't stand. We are in trouble when we allow so many things to divide us. We are divided in so many ways. People don't work together based on social status. Tribes don't work together due to mistrust. Governments don't work with people based on prejudices. The worst of this is the church is more divided than anything. Each leader is building his own kingdom. Leaders are trying to see who can plant the most churches and schools throughout the country. Things are so hard because instead of trying to come together to accomplish something great for the whole nation, people rather be great as individuals. **We are divided when Liberians trust and treat whites better than each other.** We are divided with Africans against other Africans. We have African Americans against African Americans. Africans and people of African descent all over the world must become united for a common goal. We must learn to love each other and sacrifice for each other or else we will all fall. There is no safe place, except through the unity we have been given with each other. **All the other families of the earth have identified with where they come from, who they belong to, and what they believe their manifest destiny is, except for black people.**

A nation can't survive and defend itself against outside enemies when it is fighting itself. We must open our eyes and see that divide and conquer is the game that has been used against us since time began over and over because it works, it is effective. I am waiting for Africans to awake and say we will not be divided and we will not fall. God commands a blessing when there is complete unity. The spirit of God fell on the day of Pentecost when they were in complete unity. The tower of Babel was going to be built and the builders were going to accomplish their goal because of complete unity. Haitian slaves overthrew France dignitaries because they were unified. When there is unity, there is a supernatural power that is at work. **When there is disunity, defeat is inevitable.** A divided group can't stand against a united front and a united front will pose a real threat to any enemy.

We are not going to agree on everything, but as Christians especially, we must come together as one on the fundamental elementary teachings of the faith. We must as the Church of Jesus Christ and answer to the world, lead by example and pave the way to national unity. I like the quote by St. Augustine:

> *"In essentials, unity; in non-essentials, liberty; in all things, charity."*

We must come into unity and agreement as individuals who represent the church of Jesus Christ so we can build unity as a nation who will follow our righteous example.

We can't stand if we are against our own land. A nation that shuts down its own plants and production in order to buy the same supplies from another country won't stand. It is more than putting its own people out of work and not developing its own food and living off of its own land; it is fighting against itself. It is ruining its own future. It is allowing outside forces to control it and keep it dependent. So, what if it is cheaper, it is still not worth killing one's own society. We also can't allow other countries to come in with their own police, to set up shops, and disrespect our people. We can't survive if we are divided against our own self. We are divided when a minority group of governmental leaders are receiving perks and dividing up the wealth between themselves while working in collusion with outside world organizations who don't have the best interest of the future of their country. In God's name, let us stand together.

IDOLATRY - THE CYCLE OF A CURSE

Have you ever felt stuck in the same old pattern? Have you ever felt like you were going in circles? The children of Israel had at one time wandered around in the wilderness for forty years. During this period, they were never able to progress any further. In the time of the judges, God's people would operate according to a repetitive pattern. They would enjoy a time of peace, followed by sinning, which would lead to them to being enslaved, and after crying about their condition, God would deliver them. They would then enjoy a time of peace again before falling back into sin again.

They could only blame themselves for their slavery by their enemies. It was their sinful behavior which caused their problems. The enemies were always around them, but could not overtake them as long as they were in right standing with God. It happened to Israel over and over again. This itself is key for our churches. **If we practice evil, we will be oppressed by evil.** They did evil and they were oppressed by evil.

I am reminded previously, before this time period, God's people were given orders by God to remove all the enemies out of their land when they were taking possession of it. However, the people did not obey this charge. God said because they did not follow His orders, the other nations left would be a thorn in their sides. This means they will always be a temptation and problem to them. God would use these temptations to test His people's allegiance to Him. The other nation's lifestyles, sinful practices, and pagan worship would prove very tempting to Israel. Israel, before they knew it, found themselves abandoning their faith in God and doing sinful things. Following after the false gods, committing wicked acts, and living the lifestyle of their ungodly neighbors, brought a curse of slavery eventually into their lives.

Idolatry always leads to slavery. Anything we put before God is an idol. Whatever, we give our time, attention, and affection to, is our god. We have been guilty as a nation of craving and desiring money, material possessions, sex, positions of power, college degrees, and entertainment. We have become lovers of pleasures more than lovers of God. This is idolatry and these things have begun to control us. We are addicted to all this stuff and are led by it.

When we don't seek God and follow His way, we compound our problems and allow the enemy's plan to thrive. The enemy's plan is to hurt man and kill a nation. Once the enemy has distracted people through media, material possessions, and other people, he gets them to live in disobedience to God by having them pursue the things of the world. After we are caught in the trap of this worldly system, we are left destroyed.

God calls a deliverer such as He did Gideon, who is hiding with his produce where the enemy can't see it and steal it. At this moment, God's people are being taken over by their enemy who has stolen all the work of their labor. **We end up working for others when we abandon Gods purpose.** It leaves us in fear and helpless to do anything about it. God is looking for Gideons to use, to battle the enemy. The enemy would come and destroy the sustenance and food the people needed. Israel was greatly impoverished because their production was being destroyed. Israel had to hide in caves and mountains to have anything. **Someone else was reaping all the benefits from their hard work.** Doesn't it appear that outside nations are reaping all the benefits of our African nation's resources? This doesn't happen when God is fighting for you. God reminded the people through His servant that He told them, "Do not fear other nations and their gods, but you wouldn't listen." Let's not follow Israel's example. Let's start listening to God.

CORRUPTION - FROM LEADERS TO FOLLOWERS

In the first few chapters of the book of 1 Samuel, we read the story of God training up a prophet to help Israel get back on track with Him. At the present time, the priest in charge is a man by the name of Eli. Eli and his two sons are representing God to His people. They are offering the sacrifices He requires for the nation. However, there is a problem. Eli's sons, the clergy of the nation, are corrupt and wicked. The Bible says they did not know the Lord. They would sleep with the women who came to worship at the tabernacle. They would steal the sacrifices that people made to God and take them for themselves even by force sometimes. They would use God's sacrifices to feed themselves and they would share these offerings with their father, who in turn would not stop them from sinning against the Lord. As a result of the spiritual leaders' behaviors they would cause the rest of the nation to sin against the Lord.

Leadership influences those they lead to be righteous or follow in the footsteps of doing evil. **What leaders do moderately, the followers will do in excess. What leaders will allow; they actually encourage.** This is unfortunately the state of many of our churches. Spiritual leaders are corrupt infecting the whole church and darkening the whole community. Our churches and leaders are supposed to pray for the government leaders so there can be righteousness and peace in our nation. How can God work in our nations if those who say they represent Him are corrupt?

Corruption can't be dealt with in a nation until the church stops being corrupt. When the church lives a life without corruption, God can do something about the national problem. As long as the churches are as corrupt as everybody else, don't expect anything to change. Paul says to the church:

> *and we are ready to punish all disobedience, whenever your obedience is complete.*
>
> 2 Corinthians 10:6 (NASB)

As Paul is talking about spiritual warfare, he explains that every spirit of disobedience that is at work around the church can be dealt with, once the church has come into complete obedience first. Let's deal with nepotism in the church. Let's deal with injustice in our churches. Let's deal with corruption in the house of worship including bribery, stealing people's money, and using people. Only after that, can we challenge our governmental leaders to do what is right.

The misuse and embezzling of funds supplied to Liberia over the years by its own leaders across all sectors of society has only added to Liberia's currently poor situation, the poor conditions with infrastructure, the education system, and more. **Corruption is one of the greatest hinderances to progress and development of a nation.** In every industry of its societal structure, I am reading articles on corruption, from government to churches, from the airports to the hospitals, and from the banks to the ports. We hear everything from bribes, money missing, embezzlement accusations, followed by investigations that lead to very little justice and nothing seemingly in place to prevent it from happening again. Everyone has now come to expect it and think if they were in the situation, they would do the same thing.

Like in Samuel's day, God has once again sent His prophets to His church to bring the word of the Lord as Samuel did and restore His people to righteous judgement and prepare them to receive and follow the righteous King.

BECOMING INDEPENDENT AS A NATION

Only after a spiritual cleansing in the land, can we then begin to become God's nation. How does Liberia get away from government aid, foreign aid, and assistance? How are problems with unemployment, consumer prices, education, healthcare, political repression, social exclusion, and high corruption going to be dealt with? The problems of expectation, entitlement, not taking responsibility, jealousy and envy, and dependence are things that we can no longer allow to prevent our progress.

There must be a vision, plan, action, and goals with target dates for self-dependency. There must be no further borrowing. There must be an end in corruption. The leadership must understand the goal of aid and its eventual impact on the whole nation. I cover the *six* areas that one should consider. These are suggested ideas that may have never been considered and may go against the norm. Liberia should form a government that works for her, put the people first, develop her human resources, grow her own food, build her own economy, and manufacture her own goods. Here are my practical ideas to help:

#1 FORM OF GOVERNMENT

Before Africa was divided into small countries, not by her own choosing, but by others who invaded it, it was a continent of kingdoms. The amazing thing is, a kingdom is the form of government talked about in scripture. Thousands of years before Jesus arrived on the scene, God's people were a kingdom of kings and priest unto

Him and are called to be that today as well. Queen Sheba in Africa traveled to visit King Solomon during his reign. Queen Candace of Ethiopia was ruling when her treasurer came to Jerusalem to worship during the first century church. On a side note, based on this evidence, let's not believe the lie that European missionaries brought Christ to Africa during their invasion and conquests in the fifteenth through nineteenth centuries. The real gospel was already in Africa during the first century church. The man-made version was brought later on.

Jesus is the King of kings and He proclaimed His Kingdom had come here to earth. Citizenship to His kingdom was first made available to His chosen people Israel and then to everybody else. Those that live according to the Kingdom of God follow Him and those that don't, live according to the kingdom of darkness. Satan is the god of this world, the prince of this earth, and the ruler of this age. All countries operating without God as king is under Satan's domain. All people operating without God through Christ is operating within the system that is set up from this dark kingdom.

The key, for the Kingdom God created for man to help rule, is having a Godly king. If there is a righteous ruler, the kingdom works the way God has planned. God is righteous. It's hard to find righteous men, but they are around. There is nobody like King Jesus, but there are people who follow Him who can lead.

Man has created countries and within those countries, a system of government that is contrary to God's kingdom set up. In kingdoms, the King makes the rules for the life of the people that live in the kingdom he rules. There is order, security, and respect for life, land, and for others. Kings and chiefs are usually elders' who have much wisdom, passed down from previous generations. Royalty was always based on the family line, not chosen by the people.

Africa at one time was ruled by Kings, Queens, and chiefs throughout its land. Each tribe and people lived and operated respecting each other's sovereignty. Of course, there was tribal wars and kidnapping at times, but there was a lot more chiefs and kings recognizing each other, coming together, and making pacts so they could live peaceably.

Africa is not Europe. Africa is not America. I thank God it is not. The beautiful land has unlimited natural resources, a natural habitat, a distinct animal kingdom, rain forests, beaches and lakes, and tropical paradise with abundant fruits and plants. It has everything you need and more. There are so many things that can't be found anywhere else in the world. It is the oldest occupied place in the world. The mother of all civilization. The apex of man's beginnings and his works throughout the earth.

Democracy is being celebrated as the best form of government for these people. I disagree. I believe democracy is a cover for elected representatives to use an agenda where they make laws and decisions for people without their best interest, without their knowledge, and without their ability to fight it. The only balance of power is between those at the top. There is no balance from the top to the bottom. Even those elected and supported are pre-selected and made visible with monies usually from influential people behind the scenes. It is almost impossible for a new representative with a heart for the people and fresh ideas to do much against an already established governing network of men and women set in their corrupt ways.

Does Capitalism work here? Should our population run according to a system of business production? I love free enterprise where anybody can start a business and grow. This is where dreams can be fulfilled. The only problem is regulations must be set where businesses do not become so big that they can control everything and everybody. The more they make, the more they should be required to give for the benefit of the nation at large. Does Socialism work here? Should everything be divided up and set up without regard to peoples dreams and giftings, potentials, and growth? Should the population be assigned where to work and be given everything they need in the society? I think everybody should be able to enjoy natural resources such as water, land, air, and plants without anyone paying for it. These things should never be controlled by a few. At the same time, people should never be forced to work for a state system, but have the freedom to do the work God has given them to do.

Man's forms of government give us the appearance of freedom but many of these when practiced as a daily function have rather suppressed our freedoms. While other African countries were fighting to be free from colonial rulers and masters, Liberia didn't realize how much it was under one. Only in image does it appear to run its own country fully, but truly under the powers and influence of another country in practice.

Freed blacks attempted to bring a European born concept of government into a black nation of Africa where indigenous mindset was different. The chiefs and other main leaders in the land ended up having no say so. It was truly a mindset of superiority that prevented a coming together and learning from each other. This hurt this country and the effects are still seen today.

We must free ourselves from a borrowed system of government that keeps us entangled in a web of poverty. The best form of government, in my opinion, is a King over a kingdom, where judges oversee different areas of free people who are not limited by anything but righteous rules. Everyone should be able to have life, liberty, and the pursuit of happiness in a kingdom where they can care for themselves; becoming whatever they choose.

#2 PUT AFRICA PEOPLE FIRST

Our country is only as good as its youth. When our education system is not our priority and our teachers go months without pay, and students attend schools where teachers have not shown up, we have failed miserably. All this, along with our facilities being in bad shape, is telling our children and the nation they are not a priority to us. When our healthcare is poor and people are unable to get the medical care they need, we are telling our nation we don't value them. When the lowest parts of our society are neglected, we are letting them know they are not important. When we think money is the main need and we make deals to obtain it that don't put our people first, our future is placed in grave danger.

Liberia and Africa must live under the conviction of the golden rule: DO UNTO OTHERS AS YOU WOULD WANT THEM TO DO UNTO YOU. The great commandment to LOVE YOUR NEIGHBOR AS YOURSELF is given to us as well to follow. We must ask the question as leaders, what is in the best interest for us as a nation? What will happen to most of our people if I make this decision today? Where will we be five years from now if I don't do a certain thing? We have to start thinking about the long-term impact of other peoples lives. We have to care about what is happening with others. **What happens to others, will in the end happen to us.** Remember, God will not be mocked, whatever a man sows, he will reap (Galatians 6:7). We always get back more than we plant. It may take some time, but count on it; it will come.

#3 DEVELOP HUMAN RESOURCES

Liberia has a wealth of natural resources but with inadequate human resources, it will never be able to develop them. **The quality of the people, not quantity of material, makes the biggest difference.** We don't lack a human workforce, but we do lack human resourcefulness. This means most of our workforce do not have the mentality or professional skills to put us in position to function where we need to. In order to build systems and infrastructure for a large amount of people, we will need progressive minds, leadership skills, and gifted workers.

The majority of our nation only knows how to work hard to survive, instead of working smart to thrive. We have to change our thinking. We can do this through effective training. Even those with limited educational skills have no excuse. We live in the age of technology with the world wide web. We have access to knowledge at our fingertips. We must use this tool to train our mind to take in the right things, develop the right habits, and practice the right vocation. We must do everything to excel at our profession. We must think like someone independent and instead of focusing on limited employment opportunities, we have to build skills and create favorable circumstances that will make work for us even when there is none available by others. We must tap into our gifts and become excellent at them. We need everyone to focus on their purpose.

One main area we must change that hinders the growth needed in all levels of society is what is called "Nepotism." This is when those who are in power or have influence, favor relatives or friends to perform work over others. What people fail to understand about nepotism is, it hurts the whole country. When you give jobs to people who are not the best qualified for a position, that industry does not have the proper people in place to advance the technology or work for greater growth. There can be no excellence or expansion where the best workers for the job are not at. I understand people do it for family support and trust reasons, but we sacrifice our nation's economy and overall growth. We sacrifice a whole nations advancement and development for one person's salary. Let's be wise stewards and do things the right way. This is another example of us trusting in man's ways instead of in God.

#4 GROW ITS OWN FOOD

Too long has Liberia depended on imported products it needs, like rice to survive. A nation whose main food source comes from without is not feeding itself. Liberia spends 130 million to have rice imported in from places like India. Did you know in the 1940's, rice producers were forced from the land and sent to Firestone to work in slave like conditions while Firestone supplied the rice imported from the U.S. making it available for Liberians to buy and once they developed the taste for that rice, they abandoned the naturally grown rice?

In April of 1979 under President Tolbert, Liberia had its famous rice riot. The minister of agriculture gave three reasons for the hike in price which led to it. They wanted to encourage and jump-start the abundant production of local rice for domestic consumption and export, minimize or stop the importation of imported rice, and to discourage the preference for imported rice over that which is locally produced.

The stated reasons envision national independence, which I believe was fantastic. Unfortunately, the method of implementation during this time was not wise and the way protesters were handled was even worse. What if the leaders instead of raising the price, actually lowered the price? What if they put in place projects of rice production for the nation? It would have cost the citizens who needed it most less, produced more locally grown rice, and provided jobs and incentives for workers in the agricultural field. After this, they could increase the price to export to other countries while making the cost of imported rice cost more to the locals, causing people to move toward buying, eating, and preferring the local rice which would be less. This would have met the goals they were seeking, while satisfying the people. They may have made little money personally in the beginning, but for years to come they would have put the country and themselves in a better place.

This is an example of what could happen when leaders place their people and nation first versus being greedy for personal gain. **Selfishness is killing us**. This is happening all over the world, this conflict of interest where government leaders are able to use their positions to cash in personally. This is part of the reason we see so much corruption. We must learn how to sacrifice now to reap more benefits later. Church leaders listen up. This is what Christ leadership does. He sacrificed His own life for the people. It prefers others. This is the heart of God.

Agriculture projects and farming is the best way to feed oneself. The original settlers from America detested farming upon coming to Liberia because it was the work they did as slaves. Some areas did embrace agriculture. Many preferred to live in the city and make money as merchants. I understood why many did not want to farm, while as a slave you did not own it, but as a free person you would have directly benefited from it.

We have to eat to live. Communities must start taking food production into their own hand and work together to grow food and not look to outside sources and stores so much to provide what they need. Let's develop our own food sources. Let us also stop supporting foreign owned stores where people don't respect us. Let us rather support our brothers and sisters who own businesses.

#5 BUILD THEIR OWN ECONOMY

Liberia needs new thinkers who think on a much higher level. Faith sees beyond what has been and what is. In order for you to become independent you must think independent. We must dream with vision and faith. It is important for a country to support everything and everyone in its own house. It is essential to build one's own economy. We must protect our natural resources. We must place a value on these resources and trade receiving fair prices and compensation. We must build through our own personal investment before making investment opportunity available to outsiders. Liberia has farms, rubber, mining, manufacturing, passenger and cargo ships, gold, diamonds, timber, iron, coffee, cocoa, and palm oil. We must set up policies that protect what we have. We must learn to develop these resources ourselves. We must use them in a way that provides for our needs and future plans as a country.

We must look at what we are trading for and getting from other countries to see how we can develop these things in our own country. Our trade works best when we have what others need and want. We must provide what other countries need and our commerce will no longer be driven by products from other nations. We seek too much from those outside.

Liberia people have inventions and creativity within them. It is said, "Necessity is the mother of invention." We have the potential to create something that has not been made before and do things that have never been done before. We must utilize these gifts and make them available to our world. This is one way to compete on the world stage.

We must also set up Liberian owned stores, factories, and businesses that will employ others. Our work and money must be applied to those who have a vision to build a system of help to accomplish our goals of being independent. This has not been a focus, but must become a focus. Liberia is oversaturated with people selling goods not made in Liberia. We must think out of the box and build something bigger. We don't want to follow in someone else steps, but we can learn what they did and develop our own.

#6 MANUFACTURE OWN GOODS

People do work hard to sell and trade and make money, but like I mentioned, almost all of them are materials that belong to those outside its own country. There is very little that Liberia produces in Liberia. If Liberia can grow, make, and sell its own rice, cloth, bottled water, and plastic ware, what a better shape it would be in. People already sell their fruits, vegetation, and fishermen their catch. Give people vision like this and put a plan together with action steps and it may surprise you what can happen. This lack of higher thinking with a limited mindset that only does what is already been done, impedes human resourcefulness. This along with no monetary investments, has hurt us.

Liberia has manufacturing plants such as Coca-Cola in its country. How come Liberia could not create its own brand of soda and everyone buys that instead of making outside corporations rich? Our possibilities are unlimited.

The natural resources alone should bring in enough money to take care of the countries needs, but bad deals, among other things, that have offered very little of the profits and allow others to become rich has been a major problem in becoming wealthy enough to invest in one's own country. **We are the only ones that will ever invest in our country for our own benefit.** We have to look at this. We can't buy food from others, yet not produce and sell enough of our own resources to cover the cost of buying this food. This keeps a country remaining in perpetual debt. We are better than this. We must change and we will if we are willing. *We will never be a country that will thrive, as long as it needs others to survive.* Let's stop believing this lie. Let's get off the life support machines of other countries and live in faith followed by good works.

LIE #5
LIBERIANS NEED MORE MONEY

*Whoever loves money never has enough, whoever loves
wealth will never be satisfied with their income.
This too is meaningless.
Ecclesiastes 5:10 (NIV)*

Nobody I know likes being poor. Everybody loves the ability to buy or get what they need or want. Money is attractive as a result of this. Liberia citizens, like anyone else, do not desire to be poor in this life. Many reside in run-down conditions and have to fight daily to earn a meager living and get needed resources. Many Liberians think, if they just had enough money, all their troubles would be over. It may seem that way, but it's just not the case. Enough money has never been the main issue with a country like Liberia or other African nations.

The fact is, there are enough resources and money for everyone in the world to be taken care of well. We understand after looking at all the facts from the previous chapters about how much money has been poured into the country, yet many things remain the same. There have been some roads paved, new hotels, housing communities, and other things done, but most people in general are still struggling trying to function with little within this high cost of living man-made system. Many people who have received money regularly from family outside, still struggle as well. It seems that just when you think you are able to make ends meet, the cost of living increases. In our current world monetary system that includes coercive taxation, thievery, credit, debt, bondage, slavery, and exploitation of the poor, more money doesn't fix what is really wrong. These are examples showing us that the lack or amount of money is not the main problem nor is it the main answer. It comes down to our lack of understanding regarding it along with our lack of management and self-development. These are the things within our control. These are the most important issues.

Another example I will use in the point I am trying to make is there are numerous celebrities, sports stars, and lottery winners among others who came into great fortunes of millions of dollars, and yet they ended up in poverty after a few years. Even the average American who has been blessed to work, will find if they look back after working all their life, they have probably made a million dollars. Yes, it's true. Many of these people make enough in a lifetime working to become a millionaire but instead end up struggling because they didn't know how or have a plan in place to handle and maximize their earnings. How does this happen? In the words of my Liberian family, "They ate the money" that came and went through their hands.

WHAT IS MONEY?

Money is a medium of exchange. It is an accepted item of payment that transfers assets, land, and other resources. God did not create money, man did. Money is a tool created that represents value or worth. God created the valuables that gives money its value, like gold and silver. Money has to be backed by something of value and worthiness. The paper itself is not worth anything. It only has as much value as the man and banking system who created it says it has.

Money is created by man and given value according to a system so that those in that system can operate in transactions with their assets. The way man sees money is different than the way God sees it. God sees money as a tool to see what is in man's heart. It has the power to bring out the worst or the best in people. What one does with money and what one is willing to do to have it, will tell you almost everything you need to know about people. I always tell my church, if you really want to know what people value most; look at how they spend their money and time and that will tell you all you need to know. These will not lie, even if the person does. Money reveals the character of people. The Bible says where your money is, that is where your heart is. (Matthew 6:21)

MONEY AS GOD

Why is this subject important? The love of money, next to Liberia's spiritual poverty, is the most telling sign of why Liberia finds itself in such a dismal place economically. Liberia is not alone. America and many other nations are leading the way of having money and resources as it's number one pursuit causing its quality of life to suffer.

> *For the **LOVE** of **money** is the root of all evil: which while some coveted after, they have erred from the faith, and pierced themselves through with many sorrows.*
> *1 Timothy 6:10*

Money and the system this world have created for it, have become a preoccupation. It has become a god. It is no wonder why Jesus taught more about money issues than any other subject and He repeatedly warned His hearers about its power to deceive. Money has been a deceptive tool. It doesn't have to be. It can be used for good, but when it becomes a god and the desire to have it replaces what is really important, we are all in trouble.

Evil groups of people from the outside want to control and dominate all the resources. They know whoever has the resources, has the money and the power, and can control the population. With this kind of power, you can now manipulate the systems to induce what you want from the people. Wars are created. More diabolical management systems are created. You are told you must live within the system in order to survive. They don't want anybody to live independently outside the system they created. They will destroy every system other than theirs so you can come to it or be destroyed without it. In order to keep the influence, they use money. When we seek after and use their money, they can control us. The men who created a world bank money system has caused us so many problems because of its evil intent.

In fact, Liberia's bad economy doesn't begin with its citizens from within, but rather with those of other nations, who for economic reasons, have had their hands in its affairs. Neither Liberia, nor Africa's impoverished nations as a whole, can be blamed solely for its current condition. If you question this statement, just read your history and tell me what shape Africa was in before the invasion and conquest of European powers. If you research enough you will find that every effort that has been made to be politically, socially, and economically independent in Africa or with African people has been met with great resistance, killing, and destruction. It is always made to look like something other than this. America and its European cronies have lied and deceived countless millions pretending to stand for justice and bring freedom to other countries that were already free. They actually destroyed their freedoms through military force and by implementing new governmental systems for their benefit, not the country's. The truth is they wanted to keep power over money, resources, and nations. What we can be blamed for however, is giving them our cooperation in what has happened to us.

It is for the material possessions created in this system, that causes us to pursue the created money they made. The desiring of the things the Europeans brought to us was behind so many tribes selling other tribes, and helped facilitate the willing involvement in the slave trade to the Europeans in the first place. The Europeans got the tribes addicted to rum, cloth, knives and guns, copper, and glass. This was used in exchange for slaves, land, and other things. Even when the slave trade was abolished, it was very hard to stop it because African slave traders still wanted the commodities they were receiving in exchange from traders who still wanted slaves.

We were sitting on gold, yet we were selling our brothers for alcohol. We were selling our birthright and future for material possessions. Of course, we were ignorant of European schemes and being defrauded, but we were distracted with these things. In our pursuit for things, we were sacrificing our way of life. This continues to happen to this very day. God says the reason our prayers are not answered for money is because our motives are wrong. God wants to use it as a tool to meet the needs of accomplishing His purpose, not our own.

> *And when you ask, you do not receive it, because your motives are bad; you ask for things to use for your own pleasures.*
> *James 4:3 (GNT)*

Europeans will say that a main goal for invading Africa was to civilize the heathen and make them Christian. This is based on a supremist belief by itself, but if this was true: How did selling addictive alcohol, gun powder, and the other things aid them in being a Christian? They actually brought our people out of tribalism into a false religion and wicked social system that they had created. This was based on gaining possession of our land through enticement of idols, money, and possessions. This is how the nation of Israel was ruled by its enemy nations. The idols presented to them from these nations became thorns that afflicted them continually.

Money was also chosen over morals in the government structure of Liberia. Some of its key founding members made decisions to favor a small wealthy minority as opposed to building a country that could benefit everyone, especially the indigenous people.

It was economic reasons why pilgrims left England to create America, why Americans killed Native Americans and took their land, and why Africans were enslaved as cheap labor to produce wealth for the New World. Money is what men have come to worship and will sacrifice everything for; including their own conscience on its altar to obtain and retain it.

This trust in the almighty dollar has blinded the unrighteous from dealing justly with others, but worse it has crept into our church and has also blinded many of us from doing the will of God.

CHURCH AND MONEY

The purpose of this chapter is to deal with the church that has gone after the money and has ignored the teachings of Jesus. Too many of our Christian churches under the name of Almighty God and our Lord and Savior Jesus Christ have become a den of robbers.

> *Jesus went into the temple and chased out everyone who was selling or buying. He turned over the tables of the moneychangers and the benches of the ones who were selling doves. He told them, "The Scriptures say,* **'My house should be called a place of worship.' But you have turned it into a place where robbers hide."**
>
> *Matthew 21:12-13 (CEV)*

Jesus had a problem with people turning his house into a place where thieves hung out. Jesus came to worship in Jerusalem during the Passover like most of Israel did. Upon entering the house of worship, there were men who had set themselves up to prosper from those who had come from a long way empty handed and wanted to present a sacrifice to the Lord. The Lord wanted us to know that monetary and material exchange is not where the focus of the church should ever be. Once again, the preoccupation with money and having stuff took the center stage of worship. God wants communication (prayer) and fellowship. God is a spirit and they that worship Him, must worship Him in spirit and in truth for these are the worshippers He looks for. (John 4:24) He is not concerned about what we can present to Him from our hands until he has all our heart. He already owns everything else we might try to give Him.

The Holy Spirit is grieved because a multitude of pastors, prophets, apostles, church leaders, and whatever other title we like to give ourselves, have fallen captive to the god of money and have pierced themselves with many sorrows as well as exchanged an eternal kingdom for a temporary one. I would say probably half of the churches in existence, God never called them to open or start a church. **God doesn't open church buildings. He makes disciples who act like Him**. These disciples are his real church. Whenever real disciples meet, the church has gathered. These disciples are obedient to the teachings of Jesus. This is different from disobedient church members who live according to their own ways. They are not disciples of Christ. These church buildings filled with these people do not represent the Christian church but the religion of Christianity and will remain here when Christ returns because He does not recognize them as His bride. They will stay on the earth, because they belong to this world and operate according to this world's system. They have exchanged the living God for the god of this world - money.

Unfortunately, too many of our leaders in these church organizations have taken advantage of God's people and looked out for themselves; taking as much as they can to insure a resting future for them and their family.

The church bought into the deception of valuing things and property over human life. I recently received reports of an African Christian leader who stole money given to him from an American church for an orphanage. The orphanage was left with immediate needs but the Christian leader has a newly built church and home. God only knows how much money was used for his personal endeavors. My heart breaks and my prayer is for repentance and restitution to be made before he breathes his last. I don't want to see anyone separated from God for eternity, so I pray for mercy. God knows everything and nothing gets by Him. He will judge justly all who seemingly get away with abuse. God takes what you do with those who can't help themselves personally. These include the orphans and widows. He reminds us that a day of reckoning is coming.

> ***They deprive the poor of justice*** *and deny the rights of the needy among my people.* ***They prey*** *on widows* ***and take advantage of orphans***.
>
> *Isaiah 10:2 (NLT)*

At the beginning of the 21st century and still today, the prosperity gospel had taken Africa by storm. If we look with careful observation, we will see the only people who are well off and became rich were the leaders and those who were a part of their schemes. These men and woman are not led by the Spirit of God. They provide a place to *sell* their message and for people to *buy* into the belief that God is most interested in blessing them with money and things. The prosperity gospel has been successful mostly due to its popular message. Who do you know would not like God to make their life more bearable and comfortable? Money, offerings, tithings, gifts, fundraising, and pledges are emphasized. Money is brought to the altar for preachers and singers as they *perform*. Some are emotionally touched and their response is to give to the minister and singer. I'm truly concerned about the motivation behind all this.

I see new buildings, new houses, and new transportation for the man of God, but not the betterment of the poor and those who can't care for themselves. This is opposite of the way our Bible reveals the church. In Nigeria, I watched a documentary about a pastor who bought three new cars, but has no ministry to orphans, widows, or the poor. The members who gave, treat him like a god. This is called idol worship. People's hopelessness and effort to get out of poverty is exploited by false teachers who take advantage of them. These victims can't tell the truth from a lie, because they haven't sought God and righteousness, but man, money, and comfort. They seek miracles, signs, charisma, and giftings. They take advantage of people's faith and desires with manipulation tactics and force; all for the purpose of getting money. This is not God's spirit.

The church has to lead by demonstration and example when it comes to money. We must get focused on the right things. We must take the focus off of church structures, constant fundraisers to build, purchasing of new land, new signs, equipment, and uniforms. The focus of these material things leave the church looking better with absolutely no power.

How effective is our ministry work? If the church was focused on the mission of saving souls, money would not be the focus and concern. Money would be a means to the end. Churches don't save people. Pastors don't save people. God saves people and He doesn't need a church building but needs living witnesses who represent His righteousness. **The church is not a building,** but a group of people called out from the world connected to Christ through relationship. Religion is about buildings. Religion is the absence of Christ and the presence of mere men. Religion kills the power of the cross and the work of the Holy Spirit. Religion is what most of the church has become. We have seen what can be done when we have money and a building, but where is the power of God for changed lives?

What kind of life are we living right now? A life of obedience, a life of desperation, a life of fear, a life of faith, or a life of fulfilling our fleshly desires? We can't point the finger of blame at the government for corruption when it is in the church. If the church had none, people would be impacted and righteous influence would grow into the community and affect the society at large. If we sell out human lives for money and ignore the poor, what will our reward be? An infestation of corruption, waste, and theft is throughout our churches. Our churches are full of people who trust in money as their Lord and Savior.

I think some of the greediest people I know are the poorest people I know who consider themselves Christians. Don't get me wrong, there are many rich people who live to gain more, but you don't have to be rich to love and chase after money.

The Bible tells us, "The righteous with little is better than the wicked with much wealth." (Psalms 37:16) Whoever trust in his riches will fall, but the righteous will flourish." (Proverbs 11:28) Dishonest money dwindles away, but whoever gathers little by little makes it grow. (Proverbs 13:11) So, we should not take advantage of someone to get as much as we can out of them. We are not to extort money. This means obtain it in a forceful way. We should not lend money to somebody in need and charge them interest. We are not to take advantage of someone's vulnerable state for our own benefit. This is not the heart of God.

DON'T BE LIKE

Don't be like the disciple who stole money from the bag during Jesus ministry. Jesus, during his earthly ministry, picked twelve disciples and one of them was Judas. Judas walked with Jesus for three years. He heard all his sermons, especially on the dangers of trusting in money, but Judas loved money. The Bible records that he was the treasurer for Jesus ministry and he stole from the bag whenever and for whatever he wanted. Lastly, he betrayed Jesus for thirty pieces of silver coins. His life ended with him in torment from guilt, and falling from a cliff. The worse is he died without saving faith and was separated from God eternally.

Don't be like the prophet Balaam who was called on by King Balak to curse God's people. He was offered money and was insistent on trying to go get it, even though God didn't want him to. He couldn't curse God's people but he found a way to get paid by showing the king how to make them curse themselves and his love for wages cost him dearly.

It doesn't matter if we can give an accurate prophecy or not, if the motive behind it is to get paid, we will be judged by why we did it. Our works will be tried to see if they were pure. If not, all the work will be burned up. Many will say to me on that day, "Lord, did we not prophesy in your name and cast out devils in your name, and perform many miracles in your name." Then I will say, "I never knew you. Depart from me, you evildoers." (Matthew 7:22-23) This is the bending and twisting of a gift God gave you used in the wrong way.

Don't be like the rich young ruler who couldn't let go of his riches in exchange for the best life God had to offer him. Loving and serving Jesus was too high a price for him to pay when it came to all his material possessions. He wasn't willing to give them up, but God still loved him so. The Kingdom of God is like a man who found a treasure of great price (invaluable) and he sold all he had to get it. (Matthew 6:19-21) Is our faith in Christ so valuable to us that we will sell everything just to have possession of it?

Do not be like the lame man asking for money in front of the church when he actually needed much more. Money was not going to fix his problem, but just keep him comfortable in it. Are we as people of God asking for the wrong things? The man seated at the beautiful gate of the temple was at the right place but asking for the wrong thing. He was at the place where God was but seeking a worldly temporary fix in place of a permanent healing.

Do not be like the new convert who offered money to get a position and gifts in the early church because he wanted everyone's attention. He was envious and jealous of the gifts God had given to his apostles and followers. He wanted to be able to do what they did.

His heart was not right. His motive was to be the center of attention. I wonder how many church leaders are only there because of their desire for power and visibility?

Do not be like the preachers who accepted bribes in the church. Saul's sons saw their priestly position and power as a way to benefit themselves, but God was angered. They slept with the woman that came to the church and they took the offerings that belonged to God as well. They were judged by God for their actions.

The devil is the one that sets traps for all of us to fall in. Satan tempted Jesus as well and offered Him the glory of all the things in this world, all He had to do is bow down and worship him. Many people bow down and worship Satan and the idols he has set up in this world -power, money, and fame. An idol is anything that God tells you to give up for Him and you can't do it. You want and need it too bad that you are not willing to walk away and let it go. The idol of money is destroying people in and out of the church. If we walk away from it, we would find out that God has something much better for us.

DANIEL FROM LIBERIA

My friend Daniel has been tested repeatedly when it comes to money. He has passed each test and God has blessed him greatly as a result. My dear brother tells a fascinating story about how God brought him from Liberia to the United States. He is a great example of someone who valued what God valued and received an incredible promised blessing. Over and over again God tested him with opportunity after opportunity to see if he wanted his birthright blessing or would he settle for quick comfort. Working for someone else, he refused to take money he repeatedly found on their property. He found out later that they were testing him. With the chance to leave a bank with $5,000 left unattended by another customer, he instead grabbed the bag and found the customer, who had left, to return it to them. After being turned down for a visa, he fasted and prayed for God to help him. He received a call from a man he didn't know who provided a visa. When he didn't know where he would get money to travel, a lady offered to pay for his airplane ticket without expecting anything in return.

In the states, he has been favored to live in some wonderful places, work a great job, and marry a wonderful Godly woman. God has used him greatly in so many people's lives. Some would say he is a lucky man, but I say he was proven worthy by God to receive His real blessings. Many people have been tested and found wanting because they did not pass the integrity test. If God can't trust us with little, he can't trust us with much. If he can't trust us with worldly riches, how will he ever be able to trust us with the true riches from heaven. (Luke 16:11)

Many friends, family, and community members called him stupid and dumb for not taking the money that did not belong to him at the bank. The majority of these were church attending people. This is a real problem, when we see nothing wrong with getting money even when its wrong. We justify it, we think we get away, even though we know the method of how we got it was not right. We make up all kind of excuses and reasons in our mind, when the truth is, we are greedy for personal gain. We love money and like to spend it on our self and pleasures more than pleasing God.

We keep moving along and we think we are good, but don't realize like Esau we just traded away God's future promise for us for a quick dollar right now. As we continue to live this way, we delay God's true blessings and we settle for things that we call a blessing from God when it is actually something we received by following Satan's way. We take care of ourselves by unholy means and we need to understand God has nothing to do with it. Our actions and behavior showed him how much we trusted His promise. He is not pleased. "Without faith, it is impossible to please God because when you come to Him, you must believe he is who he says he is and he rewards those who diligently seek him." (Hebrews 11:6)

I wonder how many people God had desired to bless, but this is the reason why they are still struggling to provide for themselves. They valued the quick way of getting what makes them feel good, being impatient with waiting for God's best. This represents too many in the church. There is no difference between most people in the church and those that don't proclaim Christ. Why does the church continue to live by the same standards of everyone else? Like Esau despised what came from God and His way of doing things, so do many who claim to be Christians.

Money can make you feel good and be comfortable in this life but you must choose between God's way of success and this world. We will be tested on our love for money and at times you will have to forfeit it for the gospel sake. Will you be able to walk away or will you worship it? Will you choose to live for it, work for it, and worry about it?

My whole life changed as soon as I gave it all up for Jesus and started giving it away as God led me. By operating according to God's system of wealth, I not only had what I needed, but I received much more. I learned God doesn't give me what I want for my wants, but He supplies all my needs according to His riches and purpose. He is not poor and He gives me what I need every day to fulfill His purpose.

WHAT CHRISTIANS NEED TO KNOW ABOUT MONEY

There are six things I will share regarding what we must know about money. Money can only give you things. Money can't give you abundant life on earth. Money can't give you eternal life. You can't serve God and Money. Money must be invested. You can live without money.

#1 Money can only give you things.

We desire to have things in this life. Is this wrong? No. The Bible says that money answers all things. (Ecclesiastes 10:19) It is the answer to all THINGS. There is very little in life that money can't get you when it comes to having THINGS. But the Bible admonishes us:

> *You have been raised to life with Christ, so **set your hearts on the things that are in heaven**, where Christ sits on his throne at the right side of God.*
>
> *Colossians 3:1 (GNT)*

We are told to seek those things which are above and lay up for ourselves treasures in heaven. This should be our goal as believers. We are not supposed to seek after things on this earth. Things we need are supposed to come to us as a result of seeking God and His kingdom purpose first and foremost.

When money and things become the purpose for our existence, we have lost our identity as Christians. We don't know whose we are. We don't know who we have been created to be. We have forgotten that our success is not based on fame or wealth, but on our obedience to His purpose for our life. Do you know your purpose for living? Life is not about comfortability, it is about finding Him and making Him known to others. We need to find out how He wants us to do this.

Since God is not in the business of bringing our selfish desires into our life, many go get them themselves. Afterward, they have the nerve to say, "Look at how God blessed me." God never intended for us to work ourselves to death trying to get material things. These are idols because they replace seeking God and His kingdom. When we go after things in this life, we become dependent on them and on other people providing us with them or the means to buy them. We kill for things, we fight for things, and we steal and lie for things. It is the spirit of greed and commercialism. We want what we see and make all kinds of personal sacrifices to possess it. God tells us not to believe the lie. He says,

> *For **all the nations have fallen** because of the wine of her passionate immorality. The **kings of the world have committed adultery with her**. Because of her desires for extravagant luxury, the merchants of the world have grown rich." Then **I heard another voice calling from heaven, "Come away from her, my people.** Do not take part in her sins, or you will be punished with her.*
> *Revelations 18:3-4 (NLT)*

God is calling for His church to remove themselves from this wicked system called Babylon. Babylon is represented by those people and nations who are in rebellion to God. As God's chosen people, we are told not to take part in what she is doing. This is a strong message by God to His church. Will we heed his warning? If we do not, we are told we will join her when she is punished and destroyed. He that has an ear, let him hear what the spirit of God is saying. We are also commanded:

> **Do not love this world nor the <u>things</u> it offers you,** *for when you love the world, you do not have the love of the Father in you.* **For the world offers only a craving for physical pleasure, a craving for everything we see, and pride in our achievements and possessions.** *These are* **not from the Father, but are from this world***. And this world is fading away, along with everything that people crave. But* **anyone who does what pleases God will live forever.**
> 1 John 2:15-17 (NLT)

We must allow God to be our shepherd so we shall not want. (Psalm 23:1) He provides everything we need. Therefore, we don't need to chase the things of this world if we are His.

#2 Money can't give you abundant life on earth.

We were all created to live an abundant life. God wants us to be separated from this corrupt generation, while saving others. We should not live to seek after the things that will keep us from lack and make us look good. Our central purpose for getting up each morning is not to stay alive. We were not created to be afraid and be driven by the fear of not having. Our central aim can no longer be in life to just get enough to live while I do my best to get the things I like. God has much more for us than what we are settling for. Listen to how Jesus responded to a man concerned about the family estate:

> *Then one from the crowd said to Him,* **"Teacher, tell my brother to divide the inheritance with me."** *But He said to him, "Man, who made Me a judge or an arbitrator over you?"*

*And **He said to them, "Take heed and beware of covetousness, for one's life does not consist in the abundance of the things he possesses."***

Luke12:13-15

Jesus wanted the people to know that life was not about having THINGS. Life is not found in how many things you have. He said we must guard ourselves from coveting. This word means to lust after, crave, wish for, thirst after, and yearn for. We have been found longing for the wrong things as Christians. God please forgive us.

We must mention that there are things in life money can't fix or bring fulfillment in. You can have all the money in the world, but if you are sick and dying without a cure, your money will do you no good. Money can't buy you love; perhaps sex and romance, but that is not the same thing. Money can't buy you real peace of mind from terror and fear. Money can't buy you happiness. Money can't give you peace that goes beyond all understanding. Money can't give you real joy.

Things don't last nor do they give you lasting contentment. You have to keep getting things for them to externally make you feel good. It never fills the real void God put into each person to be met by Him alone. There are numerous people in life who had plenty of money and committed suicide due to loneliness, hopelessness, guilt or other reasons. Jesus said, "The thief comes to steal, kill, and destroy, but I have come that you might have life and life more abundantly." (John 10:10) **This abundant life speaks of a life that exceeds what we experience here in the earth.** We receive God's Spirit which lives inside us allowing us to operate on the earth with a supernatural joy, peace, love, and strength that can't be overcome regardless of what is going on in the world. Money and things could never give you this.

#3 Money can't give you eternal life.

Money is not everything. Money can't give anyone life after death. Your soul is much more important because it will live forever. Eternal life can't be bought. Eternal life is gained only through a personal relationship with Jesus Christ. He must become your Savior and Lord. Eternal life is found in Him. As long as we can remember the role money is supposed to play in life and we do not allow it to become our life, we will be fine. We must be careful not to get caught up in this world and forget how important this is. Jesus said,

> *For what will it profit a man if he gains the whole world and loses his own soul?*
> *Mark 8:36*

The soul of man is an eternal being. A soul never dies. When your spirit leaves your body, your soul will make its transition either to be in the presence of God or away from God in hell. We see this in the story found in Luke chapter 16.

> *Jesus said, "There was a certain rich man who was splendidly clothed in purple and fine linen and who lived each day in luxury. At his gate lay a poor man named Lazarus who was covered with sores. As Lazarus lay there longing for scraps from the rich man's table, the dogs would come and lick his open sores.* ***Finally, the poor man died and was carried by the angels*** *to sit beside Abraham at the heavenly banquet.* ***The rich man also died and was buried, and he went to the place of the dead. There, in torment,*** *he saw Abraham in the far distance with Lazarus at his side. But Abraham said to him, 'Son,* ***remember that during your lifetime you had everything you wanted, and Lazarus had nothing. So now he is here being comforted, and you are in anguish.***
> *Luke 16:25 (NLT)*

The time we spend on earth is a few years; a quick breath or vapor compared to the time we spend in eternity which is forever. The rich man in the story obviously wasn't thinking. He lived in luxury and enjoyed himself to the fullest. He could not take his money and comforts with him when he left the earth. His money would do him no good once his soul went into eternity. **Riches have the ten-**

dency to keep us so preoccupied with living that we don't prepare for eternity. A wise man makes sure his soul is taken care of. There is nothing worth exchanging your soul for. Losing your soul is the same as losing yourself forever. My suggestion is to save yourself and lose the stuff instead of collecting the stuff at the expense of your soul.

#4 You can't serve both God and money

Can't you enjoy both God and money? I believe you can. However, we are not able to serve both.

> *"No one can serve two masters. Either you will hate the one and love the other, or you will be devoted to the one and despise the other.* **You cannot serve both God and money.**
> *Matthew 6:24 (NIV)*

How can we tell which one we are serving? If your decisions are being made based on getting money alone, you are serving it. If you wake up thinking about money, go to bed thinking about money, and live throughout your day continually thinking about money, you are serving it. If you are not a giver, you are serving it. If you are always worried about how you are going to get money or make money, you are serving it. If you will lie, cheat, steal, manipulate, hide, or do anything that compromises Christ-like character in your life to get money, you are serving it.

Whatever we look to first, when we have a need, is what we trust in. When we look to God, we trust Him. When we look to man for money, we trust in money and man. On the American bills it says, "In God We Trust." Based on America's actions, I don't believe as a nation it has ever trusted the Most-High God. Only God knows where all of our hearts really are.

Basically, anything we do in the dark with money and we wouldn't want it to be seen by everybody in the light because of exposure and embarrassment, we have succumbed to the god of money. When we know what we are doing does not serve God's purpose, but our own; we have served money. It is impossible to please God when we love money because we will choose it over everything else. We must decide which one means more to us and we will have to be willing to sacrifice money for God. He will call us at times to do this so we can see if we truly belong to Him.

#5 God expects good management of your resources

EVERYTHING we have belongs to God. The earth is the Lords and everything in it. (Psalms 24:1) He put man on this earth and gave him every resource he would need to accomplish the purpose for which he was created. We are stewards and managers of what belongs to another. We will give account for every penny that God has entrusted us with. He wants to see how we handle His resources. The problem comes when we think all the money and materials we receive is ours. As Christians, we gave our life to Jesus Christ and we no longer live, Christ lives in us and the life we live now, we live by the faith of Him who died for us. (Galatians 2:20) We have been bought with a price. We are not our own. (1 Corinthians 6:20) Everything I am and everything I have is God's.

There are some people whose philosophy about money is to get all you can, then can all you get, and afterwards sit on the can. This is like the man who built a bigger barn to put all his stuff in.

> *Then he told them a story:* "**A rich man had a fertile farm that produced fine crops.** *He said to himself, 'What should I do? I don't have room for all my crops. Then he said, 'I know!* **I'll tear down my barns and build bigger ones.** *Then I'll have room enough to store all my wheat and other goods.* **And I'll sit back** *and say to myself, "My friend, you have enough stored away for years to come. Now* **take it easy! Eat, drink, and be merry!**" "*But God said to him,* '**You fool! You will die this very night. Then who will get everything you worked for?** "*Yes, a person is a fool to store up earthly wealth but not have a rich relationship with God.*"
>
> *Luke 12:16-21 (NLT)*

So many of us don't really understand how money works or how to properly use it. Most people think money is only needed for spending on things we need. Few people understand money is a tool for investing and since it is God's money, He is expecting a positive return.

> *At that time the Kingdom of heaven will be like this. Once there was a man who was about to leave home on a trip; he called his servants and put them in charge of his property.* **He gave to each one according to his ability***: to one he gave five thousand gold coins, to another he gave two thousand, and to another he gave one thousand. Then he left on his trip.* **The servant who had received five thousand coins went at once and invested his money and earned another five thousand***. In the same way the servant who had received two thousand coins earned another two thousand.* **But the servant who had received one thousand coins went off, dug a hole in the ground, and hid his master's money***.*
> Matthew 25:14-18 (GNT)

God shows us in this story a few things: He doesn't give every man equal amounts. He gives to us what He knows we can handle initially. Each man is responsible for what he does with what God gives him. As we read further, we find He returns later to see what each one has done. For those who increased what He gave them, He told them "Well done" and called them "faithful." They received more resources and greater positions. The one who did nothing but rather hid and did not increase the resources (talent or money), he was rebuked harshly, had everything taken away, and was forever removed from his Lord's presence. The same will happen to us if we continue to misuse what He has given us that belongs to Him.

Investment means you plant it, expecting to receive a greater return. We are supposed to use our money for something that outlast us. It is for a greater cause and benefit to many others. Spending is what Liberian's call, "eating the money." Once it is eaten, we have nothing else left. Good managers are investors and make more from their money while bad managers, (spenders) use it all up. Investors make their money work for them while spenders work for money. Myles Munroe says, "Money runs from people who can't manage it properly, it will never go beyond what you are capable of."

The Bible teaches that God expects you to sow seed to reap a harvest. The world teaches you that money is to spend on yourself. **The world's goal is for you to spend your livelihood making somebody else dreams come true at the expense of your own.**

> *Now **he who supplies seed to the sower and bread for food will also supply and increase** your store of **seed** and will enlarge the harvest of your righteousness.*
> 2 Corinthians 9:10 (NIV)

This scripture tells us that God brings seed to the sower and bread to the eater. What happens too often is people eat their seed and bread. When you eat your seed with your bread you have nothing in your hand to plant. How can God make grow something you never put into the ground? Don't use it all, take a portion and plant it. It must be planted in good ground. Paul says you want a harvest of righteousness. This is something that brings God glory. Pray and ask God where to sow your money. Don't let churches and pastors tell you where. God will tell you. When you plant it where God tells you, only then will you see a great harvest of return. Obedience always results in blessings.

#6 You can live without Money

I can imagine now in my head as I am writing this part, people shaking their head saying, "You are crazy, no one can live without money." Sure, I get it. We have been brainwashed to think a certain way. We think money is necessary to buy what we need to exist. Our thinking is, as long as I have money, I will be able to have what I want. This is not necessarily true.

What if you have money but the stuff you need is not available? On the other hand, what if you had resources like gas, a farm, the material and knowledge to build your own house, cotton and the ability to sew, and a person who lived with you who studied medicine, but you had no money? Which position would you rather be in? Exactly. When we see wealth only in paper money made by other nations and the materials they make, we are deceived into believing, it is the only way to survive. This is how they want us to think. We must think about what is really important like God, family, and people. We must also separate what is needed from what is wanted.

The fact is, if we have the resources we need and no money, we will have what we need with the ability to trade for other things we need, but if we have money and no resources or real estate, we don't have what we need and are dependent on getting it from someone else. If the demand is high, it may take all our money or no amount of money may even work. Most of us want money for stuff we don't even need anyway. **The more we see, the more we want. God is more interested in answering our life needs more than our money wants.**

If we really want to know how important money is to live, let's ask ourselves, "How did the indigenous people live all those years without the system of government and economy that we have become currently a part of?" Even still today, there are hidden tribes who are totally disconnected from the rat race created by man's global world system. There are societies throughout the world who live happily, enjoying life in a community with all the resources they need like shelter, clothing, food, and water. They are free and independent, without a worry. This is all without cell phones, television, jobs, cars, and paperwork. We bought the lie about needing all these things that have been created. In many ways, it's killing us without us even realizing it. You may say that's crazy, who wants to live in a primitive world. The point I am trying to make is living without money is not impossible.

I have personally lived through times in my life where it was total faith in God. I had absolutely no income coming in at all. I did not know where or when money was coming. I had a wife and four children to take care of. God had me. I didn't borrow or ask anyone for help. Everything that needed to be taken care of, I asked God.

It was a nervous time as I struggled to trust Him completely, but it showed me who He was. Now my faith is so much stronger.

When I study the Word of God and I see how Jesus lived, it reminds me how He wanted us to live. He repeatedly told us to not fear, to not worry, to trust him. He looked to God for every need He had. He lived life on a daily basis, expecting His needs to be met. God wants us to trust Him like this. This is how a child trusts their mother. Children look to us without a care. We must also keep our lives free from the love of money by being content with what we get, for God promises us that He will never leave us or forsake us. (Hebrews 13:5) Paul, the apostle, said:

> *I know what it is to be in need, and I know what it is to have plenty.* **I have learned the secret of being content in any and every situation**, *whether well fed or hungry, whether living in plenty or in want. I can do all this through Christ who gives me strength.*
>
> *Philippians 4:12-13 (NIV)*

Do we believe our faith in God, prayer, and righteous living works? If so, we must not abandon it and rely on a corrupt monetary system. Will we place our faith in God? The church must stop seeing God as only a genie to get our temporary physical desires met. God's desire is to prosper us, but to the same extent as our soul prospers. (3 John 1:2) If our soul which is first priority, is not well, it doesn't matter how much stuff we gain; in the end, we will not be well. Wealth is uncertain so we must stop putting our hope in it.

Until the church makes God its first love, loving Him with all their heart, mind, soul, and strength and putting money in its proper place, we will continue to be powerless to impact our world for Christ. What kind of person would we be today if all the time we spent chasing money, we chased God instead? How impactful and powerful would we be? We must purge our lives from the love of money. We must start looking at it from Gods perspective. We must seek first the Kingdom of God and his righteousness and all the other

THINGS will be added automatically. (Matthew 6:33) Stop loving things and using God to get them. Start loving God with everything.

> *You shall **remember the LORD** your God, for **it is he who gives you power to get wealth, that he may confirm his covenant** that he swore to your fathers, as it is this day.*
> *Deuteronomy 8:18 (ESV)*

Liberia, lack of money is not your problem and more money is not your answer. Getting God's truth, applying God's truth, and living God's truths will take you from being stuck because of money, to having an abundant life regardless of money. God gives His people the *POWER* to get wealth, so He can fulfill *HIS* purpose on the earth, not *YOURS*.

Dear God,

Forgive me for chasing the god of money. I will seek you first and foremost from this day forward. Amen.

LIE #6
ACCOUNTABILITY IS NOT NECESSARY

Why do the wicked get away with despising God? They think, "God will never call us to account."
Psalms 10:13 (NLT)

Accountability! What is that? It means we must answer to someone else besides ourselves for our actions. We must account for everything we have been given and done. We must be judged to see if we are a trustworthy manager.

Accountability only works on earth if we are first accountable to God and ourselves. People who are not accountable to God and themselves, if they are made to become accountable to others will always find a way around it. Only people who truly fear the Lord with a God consciousness will do everything possible to make and keep themselves accountable to others. Everyone is a steward of what God has given them and must be found trustworthy by Him. (1 Corinthians 4:2) The more we are entrusted with on this earth, the more God will require from us. (Luke 12:48) Righteous people do not live with guilt or cover up shameful behavior since they are required to operate according to the standards God has set.

God is a God of accountability. He is also a record keeper. He keeps records of everything. He asks for an accounting of all our words and deeds. He said, "It is not good for man to be alone. This means "to be all by himself." He needs a helper because there is safety in help. This is not just about a marriage partner, although that is one of the greatest helps a man can have. It also refers to the idea that we need people around us to help us. This is not to help us do what we want, but what God wants. Helpers can hold us accountable for our actions. Why? We have a tendency to do the wrong thing when no one is watching. We can't be trusted alone. There is always a chance for wrong. **We trust ourselves too much because we think we are smarter than the devil and know more than God.** We disregard God's warnings and advice and fall right into the pit of temptations. Pride always comes before destruction and it is the sin that precedes all the other ones. Whatever sin you fall into or struggle with, you can always trace it back to pride.

There are many scriptures that show us the importance of having wise people around us for our own protection and benefit. People who want to do what is right will listen to Godly counsel while those who don't, won't listen to no one but themselves.

> *Where there is **no guidance**, **a person fails**, but **in an abundance of counsellors, there is safety**.*
> *Proverbs 11:14 (ESV)*

There are two things we should understand about accountability: First, we will one day face the ultimate judge and give account for EVERYTHING done by us in this life on earth. (Romans 14:12; Matthew 12:36; Matthew 18:23; Matthew 25:19) Second, we will be rewarded or condemned by the Judge of all the earth for what we did. This is a guarantee. We won't be able to get out of it. We won't be able to lie about it. It will not go away by looking the other way, ignoring it, or hoping it has disappeared as time has passed.

Everything we ever said and done will be on full display and our own life recordings will testify against us. It will not be like on earth where you think you can argue your way out of it and get off with not having any consequences. There will be no place to run and no place to hide. We will be at the mercy of God. The sheer awesomeness of God's throne will render us unable to speak. The only thing erased from God's recordings is what we genuinely confessed and repented from.

I have always wondered, how people live with themselves when they know they have lied and cheated someone, stolen money or materials, plotted and killed someone, abused an innocent child, bribed someone, slept with someone else wife, or took part in many other injustices. How could they go on and not feel any remorse? This could only mean to me that evil has taken over their hearts.

This idea of accountability seems to be nonexistent throughout major places of the society, especially in churches. There seems to be very little accountability in Liberia even in day to day exchanges and small operations. The order of the day seems to be blind trust and this trust is expected and taken advantage of by many. This is a problem that is killing the country.

Accountability is just as bad inside the church community as outside. Based on studies I read, over half of the population believe their government is corrupt and almost the same believe their spiritual leaders are as well.

Much of the accountability systems in place seem to be for appearance sake. Laws and procedures are set up to look good to the public and to make them think that justice is desired and will be meted out. Many know that these things must be in place to receive money from the international community, but it's in place for that reason alone. Accountability committees are readily ignored when accusations surface. This is to keep facts and truth that will uncover ugly deeds from being revealed. When you hear someone say, "we are investigating" this usually means we are waiting to see how we can make this go away or wait for people to forget about it. Too many people get covered in doing wrong, rather than stopped in doing wrong. There's no real effort or help because either people take part in the injustice because of financial and political gain or they are afraid of the repercussions that come from testifying about the truth.

Liberia continually faces mismanagement of monetary and human resources. This is seen in every branch of service in society from governmental bodies, the health sector, and of course the church community. People question Liberians commitment to fiscal transparency and can you blame them. They hardly have any references where justice has been served for those guilty as it pertains to missing money or other discrepancies. The news reports of money theft and the like with leaders and directors of departments inside and outside of government including non-governmental organizations are regular and endless.

Liberians must be accountable to themselves personally and to each other before it attempts to be accountable to international partners. You know it's really bad when I interview two government officials and they tell me whatever project I plan to do in Liberia, know that I can't trust anybody, not even them. I was grateful for their honesty. I refuse to believe there is not someone who is really trustworthy. They may be the minority, but God always has somebody who is standing and has not bowed their knee to the idols of money and power. This is not unique to Liberia. This is a problem in every country of the world, especially my own United States of America.

When money is received by countries, it appears to be eaten up amongst those at the top. The resources seem to be shared among a select few at the top. Everybody gets their portion and is happy. The attitude is, who cares what happens to everyone else. We deserve it and they don't. The practice which is seen around the world is: if anyone tries to blow the whistle they are targeted and seen as unqualified to serve (with other thieves), publicly disgraced or set up and falsely accused, kidnapped, or dying under mysterious or accidental circumstances. When did it become a threat by wanting to serve your people with justice? Why does the culture not allow the exposure of hidden harmful secrets without these risks? Why is retaliation the standard for not playing the game that takes from the most vulnerable in the society? This is the very opposite of accountability.

If you deal with people long enough anywhere, all over the world, you will deal with people who share similar characteristics. You have great leaders and evil rulers, the greedy and generous, the wise and foolish. As we learn to deal with people no matter who they are and where they came from, we must realize they are their own worst enemy and don't know it. They want us to give them all the money to do their thing and they don't want us to question them about anything. They say to question them is to not trust them. Even in times where records are not kept well, are inconsistent, and receipts suspicious and hard to verify actual paid costs, these people are independent of wanting to listen to anybody else, but dependent on getting what they can from anyone who is simple enough to keep giving to them. Until there is real accountability with strict consequences, things will never change. We must be more careful with who we are dealing with in the meantime.

Everyone does what is right in their own eyes regardless of who the commander and chief is in a celebrated democratic setting. How can the president have any power over anyone in the government when the majority of the government officials have corrupted their way and stay in those positions of authority for excessive years? Accountability and transparency to those in this select group must be in place for a real democracy to work. As public servants, all activities, should be known to those who voted these people into office. This is necessary for our progress and without it, we will always fail as individuals and as a nation.

IN THE CHURCH

The church is supposed to be here to demonstrate to the world what justice and integrity looks like. In the church, we are supposed to hold each other accountable to the standard our Father in heaven has given us. Many Liberian Christians are only church goers; this is a big part of the social culture. The church is more of a place of belonging and acceptance. It is mostly limited to being a place of respect, position, and titles.

The church worldwide, Liberia included, has been besieged with allegations of all sorts of abuse. We have a culture of abuse and cover ups in our churches. This is backed by church hierarchy who would rather try to look good to the public than to obey God. They will do anything not to face disgrace to man. Most have no desire to change and continue to be hypocritical, lie, and cause church members so much pain. They are unwilling to take responsibility for their actions and clean up their mess.

God knows that His church is ailing due to a refusal to submit to doing things His way. There is a refusal, unwillingness, and reluctance to admit one's guilt and faults openly and privately. There is too much pride, a desire for man's respect and honor, and a refusal to be honest about the guilty and shameful behavior. It is the very thing keeping us bound from ever progressing. Those that cover their sins shall never prosper. (Proverbs 28:13) We do not like to admit our wrong. We like to ignore it, make it go away, call it the past, do anything but face it. Our refusal to righteously deal with it means the spirit of it never goes away, it only gets worse. In this place, we are now never able to move forward.

God is looking for true servants that have enough guts to say, I messed up. I blew it. I missed it. This is what people who worship God do. The worship which comes from the heart and pours out truth from the inward parts; that humbles oneself and acknowledges God is what He seeks after. He is looking for true worshippers who have His heart and are quick to say, "I am sorry, please forgive me, and I was wrong."

> ***For the kind of sorrow God wants us to experience leads us away from sin and results in salvation.*** *There's no regret for that kind of sorrow. But worldly sorrow, which lacks repentance, results in spiritual death.*
> 2 Corinthians 7:10 (NLT)

David was known as a man after God's heart because after he sinned with Bathsheba, he confessed his sin when confronted and then cried out:

> *Create in me a clean heart, O God; and renew a right spirit within me.*
> Psalms 51:10

We have been taught to hide our sins and to cover ourselves at all costs. We deny doing any wrongdoing or evil, and make excuses and give reasons for our behavior. We won't hold each other accountable because no one wants to be accountable for their evil actions. Many others who want to be righteous have been intimidated, bullied, and threatened. So many who are doing wrong are covering each other. Evil is not being exposed and done away with. It is hidden in the body like a cancer eventually growing, spreading, and affecting every part until complete death occurs. It is amazing when spiritual patients know they have a disease and won't allow God to do the surgery necessary to get the poison out of the body.

> *People who conceal their sins will not prosper, but if they confess and turn from them, they will receive mercy.*
> *Proverbs 28:13 (NLT)*

> **Confess your sins to each other and pray for each other so that you may be healed.** *The earnest prayer of a righteous person has great power and produces wonderful results.*
> *James 5:16 (NLT)*

The Bible says that Christians shine the full light of truth on everything. Why? Look at this verse:

> **We don't do shameful things that must be kept secret. And we don't try to fool anyone or twist God's message around.** *God is our witness that* **we speak only the truth, so others will be sure we can be trusted.**
> *2 Corinthians 4:2 (CEV)*

The reason why we put everything out in the open is so that WE WILL BE TRUSTED. If we were willing to be accountable to God and one another, we would overcome the stronghold called MISTRUST, that our enemy uses to keep us from uniting and receiving God's blessing as a whole church and nation. Accountability means we can't hide what we are doing anymore. We usually only hide things from others when we know what we are doing is not right. We hide our shame. The shame of the disgraceful things said and done in secret.

It is time for us to acknowledge the truth openly and plainly. **As long as we hide from our faults and encourage our children to do the same, we stay covered in our sins.** We carry a guilty conscience that will never be cleansed and create a habit that Satan can and will continually use against us while preventing any true change from happening around us. **Since we won't let change happen inside us, it won't happen outside us.** Some people don't want true change. They want external change without any sacrifice on their part. They want different without doing differently. This way seems right to them, but it ends in death since it is insincere. (Proverbs 14:12)

Most leadership positions, especially in our churches, have no accountability and it is like a dictator with absolute power. Threats and fears keep everything the way it is. People are living with known corruption and no one feels they can say anything. The continual silence is killing truth, light, and life. When we don't admit the truth, we conceal it and suffer; us and our whole land. We must stop allowing people who are hiding behind the name Christian and church positions to be allowed to continue and be supported without making them accountable.

> *A righteous man who yields to an evil man is like polluted waters or a spring that has been muddied*
> *Proverbs 25:26*

God's goal for His church is not to look good in front of others at all cost. It is not to have a culture of pride and lies. It is not to quarrel with each other. For man, *respect* is the number one need and *power* is the number one desire, but humility, love, and servanthood are the things God is looking for.

A good man is an honest man. The most dangerous man is a man that will not say he is wrong or that he made a mistake and apologize. Stay away from this type of person. You want to be around people who do their best to right the wrong as much as possible and put plans in place to make sure they don't make the same mistake again. These are the Godly leaders you can trust. This is called sorrow unto repentance. Any wrong that is justified in some way is not Godly sorrow.

One experience I had with a Liberian brother had to do with trusting him to handle monetary affairs as we determined. This person asked for money for certain people to be paid and we obliged.

When I arrived during my next visit, I found out that they had not been paid. On our following visit, I met with all parties together where face to face confrontation could not be avoided. This person stuck to his lie that he had paid everyone until it was embarrassing to all and he could not continue any longer. At this moment, he admitted he wronged others and asked for forgiveness. Following this meeting, in a private conversation with our driver, I later found out that he blamed others for my lack of trust in him, and not his deceitful behavior. He was sorry he got caught, but not really sorry for what he did. Somehow in his mind, he felt justified and saw nothing really wrong with doing what he did. He refers to himself as a Christian.

He doesn't want to yield to the Christian life as given to us in scripture which is to be like Christ. His behavior was the opposite of this. The Christian definition he has come to know is a man-made organization. He is connected to a religion. Religion uses Christ name, but it is anti-Christ in its very nature and actions. **Religion is man using God to get the things he wants from other men in this life.**

ISSUE OF TRUST

Jesus did not put His trust in men. (John 2:24) God tells us to not put our trust in man. We are to put our trust in God. So, God tells me don't look at certain people, but look at Him. I trust the God who tells me to trust Him with others. I trust the God who tells me to trust the God in someone else. We can't know who to trust, only God knows, so we ask Him. We are supposed to listen to Him as He will tell us who to work with.

I noticed when I am working with certain people and trusting God with them, as soon as I put accountability measures in place, they love to holler, "How come you don't trust me?" It reveals to me that they don't follow or understand scripture. The scripture teaches us that people must be proven.

> ***They must first prove themselves***. *Then if no one has anything against them, they can serve as officers.*
> *1 Timothy 3:10 (CEV)*

*"Whoever can be **trusted with very little** can also be **trusted with much**, and whoever is **dishonest with very little will also be dishonest with much**.*

Luke 16:10 (NIV)

<u>**Confidence in an unfaithful man in time of trouble**</u> *is like a bad tooth and a foot out of joint.*

Proverbs 25:19

We have also sent with them our brother. <u>**We have often tested him**</u> **in many circumstances and found him to be diligent** *and now even more diligent because of his great confidence in you.*

2 Corinthians 8:22 (CSB)

Here is the thing about trust. Trust is given, but you must be prepared for it. It must be tested. God tests us to see if He can trust us. In life situations we are tested to see what we can handle. With typical jobs here in America, we have reviews. These reviews are a way to grade how well we do our work. There is also a probation period. This period is usually when you first start a new job. This allows your employer to check and make sure your character, skills, and work habits will be a benefit for the company in the future.

Unfortunately, what we have now is little accountability in place. People don't know what's going on. There is no check and balance system that allows one to follow up and evaluate how faithful someone is. When this does not exist, unfaithful servants persist in positions that hurt themselves and others around them. We need to stop crying, "YOU DON'T TRUST ME." We need to realize, we can't trust ourselves, because we have an evil nature that desires to do the wrong thing. We need God consciousness and fear. We need help to do the right thing. We should be thankful when there are accountability measures in place that protect us. How many times have I checked on somebody without them knowing and found they were lying or cheating? It has been too many times to count.

We need to put external protectors around ourselves. We must discipline ourselves and make ourselves do what is needed. We must be accountable to others, submit to Godly authority, and listen to others. We will put a check system, for our lives, in place if we are serious. Without these external controls, we are more susceptible to do wrong. It doesn't matter who you are, especially if you are a pastor. The enemy will tempt God's leaders and come against them more because they are supposed to represent God and he wants to destroy all Godly influence and power in the earth.

We can't think more highly of ourselves and not be honest about our humanity and sin nature that is always wanting to do wrong. I am totally free to do as I please, but I place people around me that will keep me accountable. I allow them to tell me what I need to hear, not what I want to hear. I need protective measures in place for myself. I do not want to leave myself open to temptation to do wrong.

Joseph in the Bible ran out of the room when Pharaoh's wife tried to sleep with him. He did not trust himself to stay there. The spirit may always be willing, but the flesh is weak. There is no good thing in our flesh. When we think we are above falling, we show we really don't understand or take seriously the type of warfare God says we are in.

BE ACCOUNTABLE

The church must hold themselves accountable and hold others of the faith accountable as instructed by God. Holding our own self accountable starts with the fear of God. The other thing about accountability is, it has been given by God on earth for our protection; to keep us on the right path. We must put safety nets in our life to protect ourselves from ourselves and from hurting others and making God look bad as His representative. The Apostle Paul wanted to make sure this never happened with him:

> *I discipline my body and bring it under strict control, so that after preaching to others, I myself will not be disqualified.*
> *1 Corinthians 9:27 (CSB)*

People who want to be right will make sure there are measures put in place so that righteousness and justice prevails. The world-renown Evangelist Billy Graham never was anywhere alone with another woman except his wife to protect himself. There was a recent news story about a politician who refused to allow a female journalist to ride in the car with him. He was heavily criticized in the news, but he says these are rules he put in place to protect himself. There is a woman I know who follows the same guideline about men. These people were serious about never falling into sin as well as abstaining from the appearance of evil. These people had high moral convictions and consciousness that led them to make decisions to be right and look right before others.

People who don't care to put themselves under any restrictions or cooperate with others for their own safety, underestimate their sinful nature. The fact is that some plan to do wrong and don't want anyone watching them, checking on them, or putting controls in place to stop them. Although security cameras are not placed everywhere to track us as husbands, wives, parents, employees, community leaders, church leaders, and government leaders, God is recording everything for that last day.

HOLD OTHERS ACCOUNTABLE

When we notice a bad tree calling itself good, we need to challenge it. You as a fellow believer have a right to approach your fellow brother and sister in the faith with God's word and show them God's truth to get them to condemn wickedness, repent, and turn to do righteously. When we don't say anything to them, we are held responsible. If we keep fellowship with them, then we are a part of their behavior. We must not compromise the gospel for ANY reason. Their livelihood is at stake and our holiness is as well. Bad company corrupts good morals. (1 Corinthians 15:33) If leadership is taken into fault, you must take others and confront it. **The church is responsible for keeping each other accountable.**

> *When I tell wicked people, they will die because of their sins, you must warn them to turn from their sinful ways. But **if you refuse to warn them, you are responsible for their death.***
> *Ezekiel 33:8 (CEV)*

> *But now I am writing to **you not to associate with anyone who bears the name of brother if he is guilty of sexual immorality or greed, or is an idolater, reviler, drunkard, or swindler—not even to eat with such a one.** For what have I to do with judging outsiders? **Is it not those inside the church whom you are to judge?***
> *1 Corinthians 5:11-12 (ESV)*

> ***"If your brother sins against you, go to him and show him his fault. But do it privately,** just between yourselves. If he listens to you, you have won your brother back. But if he will not listen to you, take one or two other persons with you, so that 'every accusation may be upheld by the testimony of two or more witnesses,' as the scripture says.*
> *Matthew 18:15-16 (GNT)*

> *Do not listen to an accusation against an elder unless it is brought by two or more witnesses. **Those who continue in sin, rebuke in the presence of all, so that the rest also will be fearful of sinning.***
> *1 Timothy 5:19-20 (GNT & NASB)*

A common challenge to holding others accountable will come from those who are quick to say you are judging them. Many Christians believe that no one has a right to judge them but God. The Bible makes it clear that we as His children are not to judge sinners, but we are responsible for judging our brothers and sisters in the faith. However, our judgement must be righteous, being led by God and done in a spirit of love after we have judged our own selves to make sure we are not being hypocritical by holding people to God's standard when we are not following it ourselves.

If the average Liberian Christian says nothing to correct the wrongs they see, should we be surprised that there is no change? Preachers are sleeping with woman in the church along with other inappropriate behaviors and many won't say anything, so it continues on. We can no longer be afraid to expose corruption. We can no longer pretend it is not happening. We must obey scripture over our fear of social ridicule, isolation, threat of harm, and retaliation. We must understand, **evil triumphs because righteous people do nothing about it.**

LIE #7
SCHOOL IS THE KEY TO SUCCESS

*The fear of the Lord is the foundation of true knowledge,
but fools despise wisdom and discipline.
Proverbs 1:7 (NLT)*

I heard one person say, "the purpose of school is to learn how to learn." Someone else said, "you learn to read so you can read to learn." My own experience in school and college has led me to believe that education is advantageous because of the exposure to new knowledge and the practice of applying these new thoughts in real life. It personally helped me to understand my potential better. My critical thinking skills have been sharpened. Through constant study, observation, and insight, I am a much stronger thinker. I am not what the Bible refers to as "simple". This means easily led astray by others and their beliefs. The fact is, usually the more you know about a subject, the more you are able to do, and the more tools you have to help others.

Liberia, like most of our world, acknowledges how extremely important getting an education is. Many parents have placed it as a top priority, willing to do whatever necessary to get their children the best education they can. The opportunity to go to school and gain knowledge is treasured, even when completion of a program doesn't provide guaranteed work in a country with few available jobs. Of course, some pursue education for other reasons, such as the status they may gain from it. Either way, knowledge gained from attending school is a valuable resource in so many ways from reading to counting, to understanding how something works or where your history begins. No matter the state of society, people still want to learn, go to school, master a skill, and get a certificate of completion.

This notion that if you want to be successful in this life, you need to be educated, I am in total agreement with. The part I am not in agreement with is what that education has been made to look like. How do we determine what a good education is? Is going to school to get this education, the key that will unlock our door for success in this world?

First of all, God tells us "The fear of the Lord is the beginning of knowledge." (Proverbs 1:7) Unfortunately, most of what we call good education is void of the fear and knowledge of God. The knowledge of God is the most important element of education we need to truly be successful according to God's definition of success. Many institutions have separated God from the foundation of all knowledge and made its institutions greater than God. The structure itself has become an idol. I say this because for many, education is their god. It is where their ultimate faith lies. They believe it is the primary way of whether they can be successful or not.

Once they look to school and higher education as the cure all for success, faith in God is replaced. School studies are placed first, quality time spent with God is abandoned, and the Bible becomes an afterthought. We now will know more about this world than the God who created it. When we are not mindful and guarded, we can allow our pursuit of education to push God out. Before we realize it, we will find that we have been infected by a humanistic, secular worldview that has taught us lots of things that counter what the scripture teaches us about God's creation, life, and purpose. We can become more knowledgeable of what man can do for us than what God has already done and will continue to do.

I'm sure there are some reading this book who feel because they attended a Christian school where the Bible is taught, that this doesn't apply to them. However, that is not necessarily true. When the Bible refers to knowledge of God it is not talking about facts learned from the Bible. It is actually referring to a personal knowledge through intimate relationship. In order to help us understand better, I will share an example. I like sports. I have a favorite sports player. If you ask me his name, I could tell you. If you ask me about his family, where he played in college, what he does now for a living, how he plays, who are his friends, and what teams he played for, I could tell you all about it. You see I know all about him. Now, if you asked me, have we met? Have I been to his house or has he been to mine? Do we talk on the phone? Have we spent any time together? I would have to say no to all of those questions. I know all about him from hearing and studying about him, but I don't know him personally.

Many know about God, but don't actually know Him. We don't all have a personal relationship with Him. This is what God means and this is what He wants. This is also what God is talking about in Hosea 4:6 where He says, "My people are destroyed for lack of knowledge." This knowledge has nothing to do with Bible facts, world events, math, science, business, or anything else. He is talking about a personal knowledge of Him through time spent together. People are ruined because they don't really know God. They just have information about Him from what someone taught them. Many people don't realize He came to live in our heart. He came so that we could converse with Him intimately, like we would with a best friend.

Too many people limit education to getting information from books and going to school. The **school** is a place of assembled persons where instruction and learning take place. This is not education in and of itself. True education involves a lot more. First of all, surprisingly the word "EDUCATION" is not mentioned anywhere in the scripture. It is actually created from the Latin meaning to bring up and train. In seeking God's perspective, I would like to make mention of the words the Bible uses repeatedly when it comes to instruction, training, and learning.

Knowledge is to know intimately someone or something; to be aware and perceive, to be learned. This could refer to knowing a skill, a person, God, or a particular thing. It is to know by personal experience and function. It's only as reliable as the relationship one has to it. **Understanding** is to support or hold in the mind; comprehend, explain, to be skillful intellectually; to make sense of or figure out. We think, reflect, conceptualize, and realize. It is the activation of the mind, connected to your will, feelings, and thoughts leading to reasoning. I believe both of these definitions from God's word point us to being trained up in a particular way and with a target goal in mind.

The other word that is important here is Wisdom. Wisdom is having insight and clarity. This includes vision, inspiration, and illumination. It is the proper application to a situation or thing. This includes knowing what to say, how to say it, when to say it, and who to say it to. It is to know what to do, when to do it, how to do it, and who to do it with. Wisdom is the application of knowledge correctly. When you operate in wisdom, you are taking what you have received and hitting the target perfectly for the best results. In God's wisdom, we are maximizing a moment, mastering a subject, and giving meaning in life to a thing.

Jesus grew in wisdom and stature and in favor with God and man. (Luke 2:52) Let's look at what this verse is saying to us. Jesus wisdom from God is what preceded His high level of achievement and because of His favor with God, He had favor with men. He knew how to answer everyone, especially His critics. They were amazed many times at His answers.

We can also look at the wise king Solomon, who was the second king of God's people Israel. He was recognized all over the world for his wisdom. People would bring him gifts and come from all around the world to sit and listen to Him.

God's servant Daniel was also a very wise man who worked in the service of foreign kings and was recognized for his wisdom and excellence, even above all other advisors and wise men. His wisdom set him apart and even saved he and his friends life at one point.

The Bible talks about two kinds of wisdom: God's wisdom and man's wisdom. God's wisdom knows all and sees all but man's wisdom does not know all and can't see all. So outside of God, it appears to be wise, but next to God's, it is foolishness. It does not have the ability to take everything past, present, and future into account because it does not know all and will never have complete access to everything. God's wisdom is like having all the pieces to a puzzle to complete it, while man may have enough pieces to get a picture, but he doesn't have enough to complete the full picture. Only God has the full picture, you must come to Him to get what you need. **What sets apart one man from the rest is the one who is operating with the wisdom of God.**

School, the way we do it today, is an invention of man that does not take into account people on a personal basis. This structure is sacred for so many people because it has been in place for a very long time and this is all they know. Although it doesn't provide great results for a mass population, only a small percent benefit after completing their programs, multitudes are still convinced it is necessary. How much do we actually remember from what we learned in school? I would say not much. How much do we use in our daily life that we learned from school outside of reading and counting? Not much again. Yet, we are completely convinced this system, where our children spend several hours a day in a classroom building for most of their first eighteen years, is the only ticket available to get them to the land of promise, freedom, and a great life.

Today in the United States, as it has been for the last one hundred years, going to school is a requirement for all children. As an educator who started in the public arena almost 30 years ago, I can personally testify that our system as a whole is not good for the majority of our children. Even with all the time they spend in this system over their young life, a high percentage don't meet proficiency standards for basic Math and English or can pass a college entrance exam after graduation. The school for students has become their social world with little knowledge gained and less retained. There are always a few exceptions.

Why would this information matter to other countries like Liberia? This is important because so many follow the pattern of what they see as success from Europe and America. Their systems have become the standard of what is good, right, and successful all over the world.

What am I saying? The system is broke because it doesn't consider God's ways of how education should be done. Please stop following it and buying into its format and curriculum. We have to do things different if we want to see real success. The way we are going now is a different direction than the way God has instructed in His word. This is why our results are not much better. We can't see the connection because we refuse to think outside the box. We are stuck on the lie we have been told.

EDUCATION GOD'S WAY

Remember, learning can happen a number of ways, but the two usual ways is, it is taught and caught. Either someone is teaching and training you in something about life or you are observing, watching, and imitating what someone else is doing. One is caught and the other is taught. In both cases you are having a personal experience.

Learning can happen in a number of settings, in a classroom no doubt, but most is learned living day to day with those we are with the majority of the time. This is really important to understand because we become like who we are with most of the time. The Bible shows us the impact of this when it says,

> *Keep company with the wise and you will become wise. If you make friends with [foolish] people, you will be ruined.*
> *Proverbs 13:20 (GNT)*

We will highlight the three main KEYS from God's Word that must be followed for education to be successful.

#1 Parents

The scriptures tell us the responsibility of teaching children have been given to parents first and foremost.

> *You shall teach them diligently to your children, and shall talk of them when you sit in your house, and when you walk by the way, and when you lie down, and when you rise.*
> *Deuteronomy 6:7 (ESV)*

Train up a child in the way he should go; even when he is old, he will not depart from it.

Proverbs 22:6 (ESV)

The word of God instructs parents to teach and train their children. This scripture means each child has been given a specific purpose by God and we are supposed to train them up according to that purpose. All other teachers play a supporting role of training. When we don't follow this command, we are not following the order of the Lord and shouldn't be surprised at the unnecessary challenges we will face in and with our children. If you think hard enough, you will discover many problems we have is a direct result of our decisions that do not follow God's decree. We have a tendency to want to blame all problems on evil, the devil, and other people, but it is not the case most of the time. The person we see when we look in the mirror is responsible for most of our problems whether by ignorance (not knowing better) or by disregard.

I have learned that success of the students is much more connected to their parents and home life than what the school is doing. How much of what we do today is learned from our parents or guardians who raised us? Almost everything. Most of our meaningful learning took place at home. We have a need to connect what we are learning from the outside to our daily life at home.

God gave specific instructions to these parents for training their children in scripture: Mary and Joseph about Jesus, Elizabeth and Zachariah about John the Baptist, and Manoah and his wife about Samson. These stories and other verses in the Bible illustrate that God had a plan for each and every one of our lives before we were ever born. He knew about us. He gives us to our parents and they are to receive instructions from Him regarding our purpose and how to train us up.

When parents allowed other people to be in their children's life, it was people that were going to help bring them into the purpose God gave them. Hannah did this after she dedicated her son Samuel and he lived at the temple with Eli, the priest. Timothy's mother allowed Paul to mentor her son and become his spiritual father; after she had already taught him.

You are the key to your child's destiny. It will be hard pressed to find someone who cares about your children more than you do. There are unfortunately too many parents who are dis-attached from their own children, but I believe most parents love their children very much and want the best for them. Some children have guardians who act as parents, like in orphanage homes. Either way, our children need guidance from a loving supportive parent figure who will always be there and support them through each stage of their life.

I believe every child born deserves the opportunity to learn and grow. He must have his basic needs met of security, food, shelter, clothing, and belonging (love). It is on this foundation that they can then focus on learning and growing and becoming who they were created to be. Only after having the necessities, can they give attention to working and acquiring the skills they need to be their best them. Many students fail in education because they are missing this foundational piece from home.

Remember, anything anyone else does with and for our children should be reinforcement of what we are already teaching and doing with them at home. Never put the sole responsibility of your child in someone else hands, this includes their school. It is our responsibility to take care and teach them. People and family can help, but they should never replace you. Don't ever give them up because you can't feed them, rather cry out to God and He will provide. Don't ever give up on them because they need you. God loves them just as much as you do. He will help you care for the children He blessed you with.

#2 Purpose

Mary and Joseph were told by an angel, they were going to have a son. They were told to name Him Jesus. They were also told what His purpose was.

> *And she shall bring forth a son, and thou shalt call his name JESUS: for **he shall save his people from their sins**.*
> *Matthew 1:21*

Manoah and his wife were also told by an angel that they were going to have a son. They were told he would be set apart by God from birth, he would be a deliverer for Israel, and he should never have his haircut. His wife was told she must follow the command to not eat anything unclean or take strong drink. Elizabeth and Zacharias received similar instructions in a similar way about their son John the Baptist. He was given his name by the angel, who also told his parents the boy's purpose.

The reason why this is important to us is, we are no different than them, from the standpoint we were all seen by God before we were created and He already had a plan and purpose for our lives. He told Jeremiah, "I chose you before I gave you life, and before you were born, I selected you to be a prophet to the nations." (Jeremiah 1:5 GNT) Look at what some other verses of scripture tell us:

> *Your eyes saw my unformed body;* ***all my days were written in Your book and ordained for me before one of them came to be.***
> *Psalms 139:16 (NIV)*

> *Listen to me, O islands, and pay attention, O distant peoples:* ***The LORD called me from the womb; from the body of my mother He named me.***
> *Isaiah 49:1 (BSB)*

> *But when **God, who set me apart from my mother's womb** and called me by His grace, was pleased*
> *Galatians 1:15 (NIV)*

One of the saddest things I come across in my travels while preaching the gospel, is when I ask people, do they know their purpose for living? Do they know what God created them to do? The majority readily admit that they don't have a clue. If we as adults don't know the reason for our existence, how will we be able to help our children know their God given purpose?

Too many of our children sit in school with their mind on other things. The old saying goes: You can bring a horse to the water, but you can't make him drink. This explains what happens most of the time in the classroom. When children are not interested in what is being taught, little to no learning will take place; no matter how good of a teacher you are. Where a person's interest is, they will soak up the most information. This is when we want to know. Our will to learn is most important in gathering knowledge, understanding, and wisdom.

A person's will to learn is high when what they are studying is connected to their life purpose. I love to help people find their purpose. There are several things that help us determine our purpose. God's call, our gifts, and our dreams. We will find our purpose in the things we have passion about. I believe we should let students pursue their individual passions as early as possible. Children who want to learn should be able to have access to the tools and resources that will help them learn as much as they can about the subject that interest them most. Experiential learning will always surpass classroom learning. Practical hands on training is always the best training. We must provide our children and young adults the opportunity to explore. They must have access to study from life books.

We should never underestimate what a person can do. Everyone has the potential to touch the world with their gift. They could be the next great physician, scientist, or communicator that changes this world. We could be missing out on the benefit of their gift because we refuse to invest in them. We, as a total society, are the ones that will get hurt the most. We must recognize the special gifts in our students and their aptitude to learn and invest in their success. This is our future.

Education must be more targeted for it to work for our youth. We don't want them to be a copy, but an original. Everyone is trying to copy and mimic what they are being told. They are doing exactly what someone else does. Society plans it this way, but God wants us to be the unique original He has made us. Let us stop trying to be like someone else.

We were given a purpose to benefit others. Let's ask ourselves: **Am I doing with my life, the purpose God has for me?** God never created us to do whatever we wanted outside His purpose. If you are a Christian, your life is not about you and how much knowledge you have. It is only about finding out what God had in mind, when he put you on this earth. He has a perfect will for your life and He leaves it up to you to accept or reject it.

#3 Teacher

It is necessary for everyone to find the people that God will use in their life to perfect the gift that He has given them. When God has given us an assignment in life, He prepares us for it. Many times, He uses others who are already doing what we are supposed to do and have mastered the skills for that particular work. We must complete our training in order to be ready for our time. This can be called a master and servant relationship. Sometimes it was referred to as a father and son relationship. Today, we may use words such as teacher and student, mentor and mentee, instructor and apprentice.

> *Students are not greater than their teacher. But the student who is fully trained will become like the teacher.*
> *Luke 6:40 (NLT)*

In scripture we find many examples of those who learned and worked closely under other men in order to fulfill their God given purpose. We have Samuel with Eli, Solomon with David, Joshua with Moses, Elisha with Elijah, Timothy with Paul, and the disciples with Jesus.

If you are ever going to come into your success, you will have to be trained by the right people who are doing the right thing. This training doesn't need to happen in a classroom. The learning happens through regular interaction. I recently found out that when Jewish boys are being prepared to be a Rabbi, a name for a spiritual leader in the Jewish community, they are not only taught the material they read and speak, but they wear the appropriate dress and follow the

Rabbi leader wherever he goes, so they will know how to walk, talk, interact, and live out the role daily. This is real instruction and learning. **Whatever is taught may not be caught, but whatever is caught doesn't need to be taught.**

If I was a parent needing to put my child in a school or program that works best for them, what would be the most important things I would look for? Based off what I understand about God's word, a few things would be necessary. First of all, my children would need to be in a school program that is connected to their gift, passion, and purpose. This is their destiny. Next, those that will be leading and teaching them would have to be righteous people. Their lives would need to reflect the character, behavior, ways, and mannerisms that God wants from people. Lastly, they would need to possess the skills, knowledge, and wisdom to impart to my child the things they would need to have in order to fulfill their purpose.

Remember, depending on our children's calling, we may not need a school. We may need a person instead who can teach them what they should know. However, we should never put our child with someone just because they have a bunch of knowledge or because it is convenient or free. The teacher must have a fear and personal relationship with God exhibited by Christ-like behavior. Remember, the Bible says the student will become like the teacher at the end, this is not only in skill but also in character.

FAITH & ACTION

We need to see God's people who believe in what God can do, not what the education system can do for them. We need those who believe in the gift and purpose God has given them and their success is not dependent on what man's system does or the need for it. God is not dependent on a college degree to get His children where He wants them. We have to take our limits off of what God can do versus what man says we need to do. God gives us the power to get wealth. (Deuteronomy 8:18) The gift God gave us is able to bring us before great men. (Proverbs 18:16) Our potential is unlimited with God.

One of my recent favorite faith stories is about a man with the last name of Mulli. He was abandoned by his family as a six-year old child and grew up begging on the streets in the country of Kenya, doing whatever he needed to do to survive. He had no family, no place to stay, and no food. It was as a sixteen-year old teen that he had reached his lowest point, was about to give up all hope, and considered suicide. During this period, someone reached out to him and invited him to a Christian meeting. It was that night that he heard the good news and surrendered his life to Christ. His life was transformed and his thinking was changed. He soon afterward got a job, saved up money, and started a transportation business while doing other ventures. God blessed him and he became a wealthy business man. Then he received a burden from the Lord to save the children on the streets who were just like he was. Soon, he left everything to care for abandoned children on the streets and to date, over 23,000 children have been helped and thousands of children have found hope through God using the life of Charles Mulli. God is amazing with what He will do with a person whose life is submitted to Him.

My other favorite story is about the boy who created electricity. From a small unknown town, a young boy in Malawi was discovered. He was unable to go to school because it was a famine where he lived and his family could not afford to pay the fees, but his desire to learn caused him to take advantage of whatever he could read and experiment with. He fought through many personal and family challenges and learned what he could until he had built his own windmill to produce energy and make light for his family and community. His breakthrough got him recognition and opened the door for an opportunity, as he was sponsored to go to school in the states to maximize his potential.

Do you see how his refusal to give up and do his best with whatever he had regardless of the obstacles in his way allowed God to do the rest? **Faith in God is seen by how you respond to adversity.** Do you still believe God? or Do you believe more in what is happening against you? No matter your background, you are not limited until you lose your faith in God and place it in man's limited system.

There are people struggling who have several college degrees. There are others who are worth millions who barely finished high school. They just tapped into their purpose. They were not afraid to take risk. They refused to give up. They were not afraid to be different.

The worst thing you can do in this life is to try to be like somebody else. God created you different to be different. There are ordinary people all over the world doing extraordinary things and making an impact. Stop trying to fit in with everyone else and dare to be an original. Stop trying to do things to impress others and instead do something original to make a name for yourself being what God created you to be. Maximize your gift and do something nobody believes is even possible. **Think higher than what you are being told to think**. Shame on us if we settle for being an average, normal human when we were created to standout.

I was recently reading an article on hundreds of young millionaires. Many of these people were the average age of fifteen years old when they implemented a good idea that made them millions. Everything from making grandma's jam recipe to building social websites, teaching others, designing, singing, and selling original creations. In my personal study of wealthy people, although the majority of them went to college, it wasn't the subject matter they learned or their degree that made them wealthy. It was their ability to dream, have vision, think, plan, act, and never give up. They dared to do things nobody else had done and some even dropped out of school to pursue their own ideas.

A black man named George Washington Carver came up with 300 inventions using peanuts. This was a man who was a thinker and innovator. He did not have the support, access, or human resources other men had. He just had a creator, his mind, and a work ethic. He maximized his potential; using all his abilities and giving his very best.

The truth is you are one idea with hard work away from changing your whole life and impacting the world. We are the biggest wasters of human and financial resources. We are the biggest wasters of time. We have little faith in God and have no faith in ourselves. We don't act. When we do, we give up easily or procrastinate and waste time on activities that don't help us get where we want to go. We finance other people's ideas by buying the stuff they create, without pursuing our own. When we do work hard, it's at the futile things. Some are professional scammers or thieves instead of using that intellect to help our world. They only see success as having things in life, even at other people's expense.

We can no longer just do what other people are doing or what we already know. We must get a vision for the uniqueness inside of us. We are not here to make celebrities out of others who are living their dream and not make time to participate in making our own dreams come true with God's help. **All of this teaches me that we can have a great education, but if we have a bad belief system, it doesn't matter.** If we have a great belief system, combined with work ethic, we can thrive even without schooling.

BEING A SELF-LEARNER

We can't only depend on others to teach us always. At some point we have to be hungry and thirsty enough for the knowledge, understanding, and wisdom we need. We must seek God first followed by the places and things from Him that will fill our appetite and quench our thirst. We will have to be a self-learner if we plan to be successful in what we do. Let us develop a love for learning and take advantage of everything we can. We must discipline ourselves, manage our time and resources properly, and maximize our opportunities in order to grow in our mind which will result in the effectiveness of the actions we take. The more we commit to learn and practice what we learn, we will grow spiritually, mentally, emotionally, and physically.

THE ABILITY TO THINK

When it comes to presenting themselves through writing and speaking, many Liberians are great at memorizing, copying, and borrowing what they've seen, heard, and learned. From the initial appearance, this may look good. I will never forget watching a movie called Curly Sue, where a little girl who couldn't read had memorized spelling one very big word to give all the impression that she was very smart when in reality it was a cover for her illiteracy.

The first step in growing in knowledge is to acknowledge what we don't know and stop pretending. There is no shame in saying we don't know something or we don't know how to do something. I love the fact that many people want to try to figure out things on their own, but the wise man listens and gets understanding. Learning by experience is great, but ignoring help causes things to be ruined and people to get hurt unnecessarily. If you are too prideful and you don't like to be told anything, you will never be able to become what God wants. Once we get passed this initial stage of pretention, we can deal with the deficiencies that we have covered up so long.

In my own testing of students I worked with in Liberia, I found that for many there was a major struggle with problem solving. It was very hard for many to transfer basic math concepts and be able to apply math rules to figure out answers. I believe one reason is thinking is focused on day to day living. The majority are inclined to work with their hands and feet. I have learned when it comes to problem solving and critical thinking it takes lots of work and practice. When you don't fully understand something at first, you will eventually, if you keep going. Our understanding becomes better and things get easier as we put time in. In the long run, our patience will be rewarded and our learned skills will place us above others.

Many are too impatient for this, so as you teach them, as long as you are there they will do it, but when you leave they will go back to doing things the way they have always done them. This means absolutely no progress in mental skills. This will become evident in the overall work. The reason why developing your thinking skills is so important is this is how you are able to be a good problem solver. Those who make up this group are your directors, executives, and supervisors all over the world. People are willing to pay big for people who know how to solve problems.

Learning with other students is good when we are able to glean from others and consider others views while we study and learn. We were meant to take in information and process it to make it our own. Schools were not created to help us think independently but to follow what everyone else is doing in the class all the way to the job market. Schools prepare us to work for someone else. It was God's desire that men have dominion over the earth. The more leaders we have leading, the better quality of life we can produce for our nation. If we want to see growth in our life, we must be able to FOCUS with our thinking.

THE IMPORTANCE OF READING

A good portion of our society doesn't read books and this is a big problem when it comes to advancement in a country. Reading is the way you gain information and grow your mind. One European leader I heard about, a savvy business man said, "Africa doesn't need more money, they need books." I am in total agreement, but while this remark, as statistics show, may be a true fact for the majority of Africa, it should be explained why this is the case. Making blanket statements without looking at the cause is deceitful, because it suggests that the problem lies solely with those who don't read. When we are able to look at the cause and effect and how we got here, then we can put the right plan into action to fix it.

There are challenges in Africa like any other place in the world, but at the same time there are also unique problems. Here are six challenges that affect the advancement of literacy in Liberia and other countries: illiteracy, access, tradition, lifestyle, education cost, and leadership.

Anywhere we go in the world, we will find the literate, illiterate, and those in between. The difference is there are much higher numbers in Africa and in Liberia. This is partly due to the war which disrupted schooling for more than a decade. Even for many who can read, they can't always comprehend what they are reading. The most unfortunate thing is that ordinary people who have limited reading skills are left way behind those in the society who have had great academic training.

We also do not have access to a lot of good books. There are very few choices around for many people in many places. I don't believe Liberia has an actual public library and you won't find major book stores. It appears people have the Bible but not many read it or are able to. The younger generation has technology which gives access to reading material, but I would not consider the social media they are constantly on, good and educational reading material for life growth. Greater accessibility to internet service and a disciplined practice of looking at the right things would be helpful.

We must also take into consideration the history of living in an oral tradition culture where things are passed along through hearing stories. When this is the custom, it could be tough to get people to read the Bible or any other material individually instead of listening to someone else tell them what it's about. It is no different than Americans who would rather watch the movie than read the book about the same story. Those who are able to read, read written texts out loud to others. In many places, people learned by repeating what they heard. Many people have grown up on what is called "rote learning" which is memorization based on repetition. For many with this tradition, listening together is good because it creates community. In most oral cultures everything is done together in a community. This is opposite to the individualistic focus of other countries.

We also can't forget how the people of more undeveloped nations use the majority of their time trying to make a living to survive. This many times includes needing the help of elder children who can't attend classes. Those who can and would like to read after the work day don't always have the ability to read at home at night due to lack of electricity.

Another issue is the education cost in Liberia, even in so called government schools there are costs. Problems with teachers being paid hinder consistent learning among other things. Therefore, the country is mostly made up of private schools instructing the children. Cost may include tuition, registration, graduation fees, uniforms, and materials. Many can't afford to send their children. Many miss out on the opportunity to learn to read because of poverty. Even when their children can read, they struggle to pay for any books for purchase that will support regular reading and growth.

Leadership, especially in the church, has played a huge part in society with non-readers probably more than any other place. The speaker who shares God's Word represents authority. The hearers have become accustomed of placing their trust with their preachers and have become totally dependent on this person for correct information. They don't read for themselves or question what is read and interpreted. Those leaders who have not been trained may interpret texts incorrectly and use their position to dominate listeners on what to think and believe.

Lastly, there are those who are highly motivated and have taught themselves to read well. I encourage everyone to make reading a habit. This is the only way you get better. **Reading is a necessity if you want to grow**; especially the Bible. I am concerned that the Bible is not reaching the heart and minds of hearers in many churches in Africa. It is the greatest book you could ever read. If you just read the Bible consistently daily for one hour, your mind would be transformed. I would suggest for Biblical understanding and correct application, start by seeking the truth through prayer. With the help of the Holy Spirit, He will illuminate God's Word. I have heard of many people who have learned to read by reading the Bible. I'm not surprised since the Bible is a supernatural book and God wants to reveal Himself to us through the words on its pages.

THE CORRECT USE OF KNOWLEDGE

Knowledge is not power in and of itself. Knowledge is just knowledge unless I do something with it that helps me and others. In fact, if applied wrong it could be deadly. That's why the scriptures say,

> *Wisdom is supreme; therefore, acquire wisdom. And whatever else you obtain; gain understanding*
> *Proverbs 4:7 (BSB)*

I fear we have left God's knowledge for man's and pursued their type of life, their goals, their dreams, their hypocrisy, and their superior attitudes. So, we could look like them, talk like them, and attempt to have the things they have. We have been seduced by an ungodly culture that is anti-Christ.

Are our dreams, visions, and goals being considered in this process? Are we being told what is best and we believe it? We must find out from God as His child what He has designed as best for us and the children He has given to us.

The knowledge of man is not the key, nor has it ever been the key to success. It is a key to unlock opportunities in this world we live in, but success is not making a lot of money. Success is not having a lot of friends. One of my favorite authors, the late great Dr. Myles Munroe defines success this way:

SUCCESS IS YOU DISCOVER YOUR PURPOSE AND COMPLETE IT BEFORE YOU DIE. SUCCESS IS MEASURED BY WHAT YOU HAVE DONE COMPARED TO WHAT YOU SHOULD AND COULD HAVE DONE, THE ONLY PERSON WHO KNOWS HOW SUCCESSFUL YOU ARE IS YOU AND GOD. IT IS POSSIBLE TO BE SUCCESSFUL IN THE WRONG ASSIGNMENT, SO THE KEY OF THE SUCCESS IS ASSIGNMENT, AND THE PURPOSE MUST COME FROM GOD.

My own definition of success based off what God has taught me is: Success is hearing your Maker say "Well done, good and faithful servant." Success is finding out what God created you to do and doing it to the best of your ability. **Success is connected more to what God wants from you, than what you want from Him.** This means you can have everything that life has to offer you and still not be successful. A house, money, good position, or ability to travel and it doesn't matter because none of these things mean success to God. It only means success to man. It is a wasted life if you live by the world's success and never fulfill your God given purpose. God put us here for Him, not for us. We should not be looking for the meaning of life without Him.

We may find we have been living the life others have made us believe is worthwhile. We may find we have been trying to fulfill our passion without submitting it to the one who gave it to us along with our life. He is waiting. His ways are easy, but the way of someone who does not yield to Him is hard. There is a way that seems right to a man but it's not and it ends in unfulfillment. We must trust in him with all our heart and lean not to our own understanding, in all our ways submit to Him and he will direct our path. (Proverbs 3:5-6) We should be tired of the roller coaster ride of life and doing things the hard way. He says, "Come unto me all you who are weary and carry heavy burdens and I will give you rest, take my yoke upon you and let me teach you because I am humble and gentle at heart and you will find rest for your souls; for my yoke is easy and my burden is light. (Matthew 11:28-30)

Don't believe the lie knowledge is everything and the more knowledge you have the better off you will be. The knowledge of God is most important. The greatest education does not come from world books, it comes from the Book of Life. More than this, true success is gained from the wisdom of God. In other words, you can have a doctor's degree and know many things about Science, Math, English, and History and miss life's meaning. It is not the knowledge of Bible facts or of this world, but the knowledge that comes from a relationship with Him that brings success. All other knowledge is worthless unless we allow the Spirit of God to use it in proper application to our life resulting in success.

> *Not only those things;* ***I reckon everything as complete loss for the sake of what is so much more valuable, the knowledge of Christ Jesus my Lord.*** *For his sake* ***I have thrown everything away; I consider it all as mere garbage, so that I may gain Christ***
>
> *Philippians 3:8 (GNT)*

Many of our solutions compete or go against God. Our answers to world problems concerning family, church, school, business, health, government, resources, and human relationships are different than God's. This knowledge derived from our world attempts to decide good and evil apart from God. Our knowledge says, what do we think? God's knowledge says, what does God think? Don't let the world tell you how to live, but let God tell you how to live. This is what truly matters.

The world will try to convince us that God is not enough and there is more to life than Him. They will tell us that we will be left out and missing out if we make God the priority. This is a lie. Making God your number one priority is the best thing you can ever do. I will always seek God's knowledge and wisdom beyond what the world is saying. I train myself to ignore and refuse knowledge that goes against God. I will not be infected by it nor participate with it.

We have more knowledge today, but less fulfillment. Man has made it his purpose to acquire more and more knowledge without God. **Man's increasing knowledge of everything without God's input is not his power, but rather his downfall.** It is only when a man gets more knowledge from His Source, that he is empowered in his thinking. This knowledge alone will serve a useful purpose. Knowledge itself is fleeting without God's purpose and meaning. The wise king Solomon, who did everything he wanted to on the earth, said it best:

> *But, my child, let me give you some further advice: Be careful, for writing books is endless, and much study wears you out. That's the whole story.* ***Here now is my final conclusion: Fear God and obey his commands, for this is everyone's duty.***
> *Ecclesiastes 12:12-13 (NLT)*

LIE #8
LOOK OUT ONLY FOR YOURSELF

Afterwards the lord asked Cain, "Where is Abel?"
"How should I know?" he answered.
"Am I supposed to look after my brother?"
Genesis 4:9 (CEV)

What is selfishness? It is lacking consideration for others. It is being concerned chiefly with one's own profit and pleasure. It is the excessive or exclusive concern with one self and the seeking and concentrating on for one's advantage. It is to focus on one's own wellbeing and disregard others. A selfish person is the one who puts their own needs first. They are primarily concerned with themselves and seek only those activities that fulfil their own desires and wants. A selfish person only tries to satisfy their own pleasures, they have little consideration for other people's needs and they worry only about their own comfort. When you make life difficult for others just to meet your own ends, that is being truly selfish. When you have a huge amount of interest invested in yourself and don't think about the wants and needs of others, you are living your life in direct opposition to the heart of God.

This is called me, myself, and I, living for my happiness versus living for God. We human beings are selfish by our own sinful nature. **All selfishness is sin and all sin is selfish.** We don't deny ourselves what we want easily. In fact, the more we give ourselves what we want, the more self-centered and selfish we become. Feeding our insatiable desire only makes it grow and want more. God is waiting for us to give up our life for His. We are unhappy when we can't have what we want. We do not realize our true unhappiness comes from us living our own life without God. Real happiness and contentment come from denying ourselves and losing our lives. It is a hard process to get to this joyful stage though. We have to work through so much pride and selfishness.

Everything Christians are commanded to do is for Jesus sake. Our purpose on the earth is not about us. It's about serving others. Our goal can't be to personally benefit. We do what God wants for Him alone, otherwise we are acting in selfishness. Many people who attend our churches think their whole life is about them, how they can be happy, feel good, obtain materials, and get positions. They don't realize this mindset is rooted in selfishness.

Most selfish people are skilled manipulators by instinct who believe that they are more important than everyone else. They can hurt you very easily. They may make you feel confused and lost or guilty when they think you aren't giving enough back to them. Here are a few very obvious signs of a selfish person that you should pay attention to: They always need something from you. They are constantly looking for a favor. They are not willing to give to you in return or complain they have nothing. They remind you that you have more than they do and you should share. They expect special treatment by you. They are initially friendly in wanting to connect with you. **They see nothing wrong with using you to get what they want and desire.** They are not grateful for what you have done for them already. They will react with agitation if you refuse them. They will try to make you feel bad if you don't do for them.

Where selfish desires and envy is, there is evil practice. When you serve only yourself, you are making the ruler of darkness happy. This is part of His mode of operation. His aim is to get people who serve themselves.

> *Don't be selfish; don't try to impress others. Be humble, thinking of others as better than yourselves. Don't look out only for your own interests, but take an interest in others, too.*
>
> *Philippians 2:3-4 (NLT)*

I have never seen a bride so in love with herself that she forgot about the man she was getting married to. I have never been to a wedding where the bride didn't show up, but rather left to go enjoy herself and see how much she could get for herself. The brides I saw were more interested in how they would look to their new husbands. They wanted to look their best for Him. They wanted to please Him. Can you imagine a bride so stuck on herself that she completely ignored her husband? That would seem unimaginable. Yet, Christians are called the bride of Christ and we are so in love with ourselves, our positions, titles, wealth, and lifestyles that we have forsaken our husband. We are no longer interested in His purpose and will being done. We are no longer making sure His sheep get fed. We have abandoned the people we have been called to look after, so we can look after our own selves.

In your relationships with one another, have the same mindset as Christ Jesus.
Philippians 2:5 (NIV)

What of kind of mind does Christ have? The verses that follow tell us that Christ, although being equal to God and residing in the perfect place we call heaven, came down and took on the lowly human form and suffered a death in obedience to God to save the creation. This is love. Love does what is best for everyone else at one's own expense. Love lays down his own life for others. This is the love God tells us as His children to emulate. This is the love that is missing in action in most of our churches. He became a servant. He made himself of no reputation. This was his intent and motivation. He had already decided he would serve and would not in any way desire any prominence. Church leaders, we still have a lot to learn. God is still looking for His leaders who say, "God it doesn't matter if no one ever knows my name, as long as you are glorified I will be satisfied."

1 Corinthians chapter 13 is known as the love chapter. It defines love for the believer. It explains the priority of love which is above spiritual gifts, knowledge, and anything else. It basically reminds us that without love, absolutely nothing else matters in life. It reminds

us that for it to be real love, it will not seek anything for one's own self. 1 Corinthians 10:14 tells us not to seek our own good, but the good of our neighbor. What have you done for others? What attitude do you have in regard to others? How do you treat others?

Jesus washed His disciple's feet. He served them and demonstrated what He was all about in that one act. He was not looking for them to give him anything or get anything from them. He was always looking to give and serve. God's kind of love is seen in sacrifice. True sacrificial love cost us something and we get nothing physical back out of it. This is the opposite of what we see from the leaders in our churches today. Everyone else doing for them. They are being served. Their greatness is being talked about. Why are we talking about men's greatness when they are not willing by example to give up anything for God and anyone else?

God's salvation is seen by what we give, not by what we take and hoard for ourselves. Jesus told the rich young ruler, "If you want to be perfect, give all your money to the poor and follow my lifestyle." After Zacchaeus, the tax collector hosted Jesus at his house, he decided to give half of his money to the poor and repay double anyone he had stolen from. Jesus responded that salvation has come to this house. The kingdom of God is seen when its citizens are taking care of the poor, not taking for one's own self.

The mother of two of Jesus disciples asked Him to let her sons sit on the right and left side of his throne. (Matthew 20:21) They were trying to position themselves. Jesus didn't laugh, He didn't scold them, He didn't seem to be upset. He knew human nature. He just taught them. He knew the motives of people's hearts. He trusted that God was going to reveal His purposes to them and His spirit would prevail eventually over their fleshly desires. They were no different than we are today. The desire to be great and have prestige mattered to them just like it matters to us. God knows how to help us care about what really matters to Him if we let Him.

We have a vision of how we think our life should be and God has a vision. We must be careful not to try to make God's vision into ours. People want what they want so bad. If God has given us a vision, He will require from us to lay it down and trust Him with it.

So many hold on and refuse to give it to God, not understanding if we die to the dream and release it to God, it would resurrect in righteousness. As long as we insist on trying to make it happen our way, we struggle and lose it. I have experienced this first hand with myself and watched others labor in vain as God remains silent until they are willing to die and accept doing His thing, His way.

Abraham gave up Isaac. God allowed Jesus to die. Unless a kernel of wheat falls to the ground and dies, it remains only a seed (all by itself); but if it dies, it bears much fruit. (John 12:24) This principle of dying and being resurrected is the only way new life is produced. All that is from our old nature must die. This is the process that God uses to bring us to a place of total unselfishness. This is the process so many fight against. Man does not want to die to gain his divine nature. He wants to live according to his sinful nature. He doesn't want to give it up. He likes it too much. He wants to put a divine nature cover over his sin nature. This is what religion does. This is why religious people never change. This is why they continue to do evil things. God said we must lose our lives so we can gain it new in Him.

I've never seen so much selfishness and pride among so called Christians. Pride is killing the church. Selfishness is killing the church. People are not willing to work together; instead they live by worldly principles: If you honor me, I will honor you. If you love me, I will love you. This is the same type of love the unbelievers have for one another. So, how are we any better? Churches all serve the same God and all believe they are saved by the same Savior, yet behave in a manner that tells our world we are not together.

The Bible says they will know we belong to Him by the way we love one another. **The way we love our fellow man is the main determinant of how people can identify who we belong to.** How do we take care of one another? The world takes care of their own sometimes better than churches. Families take care of one another, while some churches and pastors take care of themselves and let others starve. We need to see our churches take care of one another.

Nepotism is a real issue in our churches in many ways. This is where one's concern of themselves, personal family, and close friends interferes with doing what is just and right in God's eyes. This is where leaders look out for self. What is right and fair goes out the window. The goal is not justice, it is a survival operation according to man's ways; trusting in what one can see instead of what God is saying. We may say God understands and God is not going to make a big deal about it. The fact is everyone else is not treated equally.

There are too many churches that sacrifice God's will being done because of family preference. People are placed in positions they don't belong. People are not corrected or disciplined when they do wrong. They are given special privileges and advantages over others. I remember hearing a messenger of God share her testimony of how God used her greatly preaching around the world, but at home she was dealing with a drug addicted daughter. At her most painful moment in prayer, she told God she would not preach to others until her daughter was set free. His response to her was that He couldn't use her if her daughter's soul was more important than anybody else.

Jesus said, "My mother, brothers, and sisters are the ones that do the will of God." (Mark 3:35) He said this as he pointed to those who were around Him, when they told Him His natural family was calling for Him. The blood of Christ that makes us a family must not give way to family blood in opposition to God's purpose. God cut off a priestly family forever, because after many warnings, the head priest refused to restrain his disobedient sons who were functioning under him. (1 Samuel 3:13) God takes this stuff seriously.

HOW CAN WE SAY WE LOVE GOD?

I visited Liberia in late spring of 2014. At the hotel I stayed at, I ended up speaking to lady who was working as a security guard. She had not been paid for six months. Yet I paid the owner of the hotel a good sum and there were others who also stayed at the hotel. I couldn't understand why a Liberian Christian business owner would allow a woman to work every day for them, promise to pay them, and when he received money never made sure they received something in pay. I found this type of behavior over and over again. I actually started paying my drivers myself before I would leave because I knew there was a good chance that the owner of the vehicles we were renting, would pay the driver little or nothing of what I gave him after we left. I can't figure out why some people would do this to their own fellow brethren. Anytime someone would allow someone else to go without, when you have it in your ability to give them what you owe them is beyond evil to me.

> *If we have all we need and we see one of our own people in need, we must meet their need, or else we cannot say we love God.*
> *1 John 3:17 (CEV)*

The great love of God has been demonstrated to us by what He has done for us. While we were yet sinners, Christ died for us. (Romans 5:8) He paid the biggest debt we would ever owe. He met the greatest need anyone of us will ever have. We owe Him our life. He wants us to give our lives in loving others with the same love He has loved us with.

JEALOUSY

Jealousy and envy run rampant everywhere, but I personally have never quite seen it like I had until I went to Africa. It was so bad at times I thought I was dealing with ten years old instead of forty-year old men. The competition, fight, revenge over the littlest things really surprised me. I can remember upon my first few visits, my first Godson asked me one day to please do not let anyone else know anytime I do anything for him because it would be very bad for him.

I was told if people know you receive support or have someone connected to you outside, the word gets around in that community to not help you because you already have help. Any outside connection means people expect you to help them because they assume it is in your means to help them because of your contact. If you don't help them, people are mad at you. It is hard enough to deal with the difficulties of life but adding the daily pressures of unrealistic expectations and jealousy from community and family members can be too much.

When you start helping one, everyone wants you to help them as well. It never occurs to anyone that you are a limited human with limited resources or they figure it doesn't hurt to ask for a million, the worst you can do is say no. Being able to do for one student while another one is missing out on an opportunity does cause jealousy with some family and members of society; maybe even to the point of robbery and physical harm. Some people would rather not see you have or move forward if they can't have the same thing. Like kids fighting on a playground, everyone wants to make sure they are heard, they receive attention, and they are satisfied.

God does not deal with His children all the same. He loves them all the same. Some receive things from Him at different times. Some don't receive the same things. God issued talents to three different men and they all received a different amount. God paid workers who worked one hour for Him the same amount of those that worked the whole day based on His agreement with them. Of course, the ones who worked longer were mad at His generosity. From a juvenile perspective, you may think this is unfair. We all think fair means the same. God loves us the same but gives us what He knows we can handle and what He deems necessary for His plan to be fulfilled in each of our lives.

He wants to see how faithful we are in what He gives us to do. What will we do with the little we have been given? He will take the little and give it to someone with a lot if we prove unfaithful to manage it correctly. I believe everyone in their life gets a time to manage something. What do we do with it when we get the chance? We can't be mad at someone else if we blew our chance. We can acknowledge we messed up, ask God for another chance, and do better on the next round.

Our major problem with others is we compare ourselves to them. This is the worst thing you can do. God never created all the people on the earth to look at each other to determine their worth or value. We covet what someone else has. We are envious of how blessed someone else may be. This is because we know church, but we do not have God. Our eyes are on the wrong thing and when that happens it will mess up our perception and we will find ourselves thinking and acting wrong.

We are a community that is supposed to look out for one another. We must do what is righteous and encourage righteousness. Love your neighbor, celebrate with them when good happens to them. Your response and actions determine whether God should give to you as well. We reap what we sow. If we sow unhappiness, discontentment, complaining, and jealousy, then this is what we will receive in return. Bless your neighbor.

The first sibling rivalry, from the first brother relationship, was between Cain and Abel. These are the first two children from the first father and mother. We are all related by the way. We can relate to them because we have the same sin nature and natural tendencies.

As we can see from their story, Cain and Abel was responsible to God for what they both did. Both were accountable for their own actions to God. They both presented themselves to God. It was during this process one was favored and the other one wasn't. The reason given was not that of preferential treatment, but of God's requirements and standards. It is amazing to me how many people do not want to do what God requires yet they get mad at others who receive the benefits of their obedience. Cain was angry because God did not bless him. He could not direct his anger at God so he directed it at his brother as though it was his fault. Instead of him desiring what God required for his own blessing, he chose to kill his brother instead. **Jealousy exist because we want what others have, but we are not willing to do what we need to do to get what God has for us.**

When we do not address the real reason for our dis-satisfaction, we will take it out on others. Others are not responsible for whether God blesses us or not. Stop believing this lie. God blesses whoever regardless what people think about them. When God gets ready to bless you, he doesn't need another man's permission to do this. When you believe it only comes through man, you miss how big God really is. It was Cain's anger that Satan used to cause him to harm his brother. His thoughts led him to this. Wrong thoughts lead to wrong actions. Afterward, he did not even want to take responsibility for how he responded to his brother and what he did to him. However, God sees it all. He hears the testimony of the poor, the exploited, the orphan, the abused, the misused, and even the murdered.

CHURCH HINDERANCES

Spiritual leaders must give account for how they treat their members. (Hebrews 13:17) Spiritual leaders must give account to God for what happens to you under their care. What a responsibility! They want to say, "You must listen to me as your overseer." Do we understand we must take responsibility for our advice and example? We should not presume to be teachers, because we will have a greater responsibility. (James 3:1)

We have been guilty of doing many things that were not done to benefit the whole congregation. Decisions have not been made to benefit the majority, but rather to benefit the leaders. **If you succeed, while everyone else around you struggle, and you refuse to help remove this disparity, you are a part of the problem.**

Many in our churches will keep somebody else's money when given to them to give to another. Many will eat and steal the money. Many will borrow with no intention to pay back. Many will make promises they do not plan to keep. These things are common and correction has been disregarded by those whose goal is to have at all cost. My heart breaks and Gods judgement is reserved for such. These may be deacons, pastors, worship leaders, and so-called church members but they are not followers of Jesus Christ if they refuse to follow in His footsteps. Christ doesn't allow us to treat people any kind of way and keep going without regard to what we have done. This is not allowed in His kingdom.

> *So, if you are offering your gift at the altar and there remember that your brother has something against you, leave your gift there before the altar and go. First be reconciled to your brother, and then come and offer your gift.*
> *Matthew 5:23-24 (ESV)*

This can explain why we are missing the presence of God in Christian churches. The sacrifice of praise and worship we offer to God is not received by Him, until we make things right between ourselves. Like Cain, God doesn't receive the gifts we bring that do not meet His requirements and standards. Gifts to God that have unforgiveness, jealousy, deception, lustful behavior, greed, and the rest attached to it are never received by Him. God is looking for His people to repent. This is to change our mindset, turn around, and start going in the other direction; which is the right direction and do what is right.

Another Biblical example of how important this principle is, is found in 1 Peter 3:7. Our prayers are hindered if we do not honor our spouse, particularly husbands with wives. God says that we are heirs together. He does not prefer a man over his wife. We are all impacted by what we do to each other. God holds us responsible for how we treat one another.

A religious church leader wanted to justify himself regarding the commandment to love your neighbor the same way you love yourself. (Luke 10:28-32) As an expert in teaching the law, he held preferential treatment to Israel as opposed to those outside referred to as Gentiles. Jesus understood this, as this man wanted to know who exactly Jesus was referring to when He used the word *neighbor*. Jesus then begins to tell a story about a man who was mugged on the way to Jerusalem by thieves. They stole his stuff, beat him, and left him half dead in the road. A preacher walked by him, a church worker walked by him as well, but a despised Samaritan sinner outside of the church had compassion on him and took action to care for him at his own cost. Jesus wants us to tell Him, which one was the neighbor? Which one obeyed the commandment? Of course, it was the one who had mercy.

Jesus made sure when He told the story to let the Jewish people know it was a Samaritan who received Gods approval. This was important because the Jews despised the Samaritans. God wanted them to see that when it comes to doing right versus doing wrong, this is what matters to Him most; not where you came from, who you know, what church you go to, or what position you have. God doesn't care about that stuff. He cares about how you treat people. He said, "Go and do the same thing the Samaritan did." What is wrong with us? Christians see people in need of care and could care less. Where is the mercy and concern from the God we say we serve?

The King of Heaven will judge all nations, He will separate those that belong to Him from those who don't. (Matthew 25:31-46) He will say to those that belong to Him, you fed me when I was hungry, gave me drink when I was thirsty, clothed me when I was naked, looked after me when I was sick, and visited me when I was in prison. He says, "When you did it to the very least of these brothers who belonged to me, you did it for me." Those on the left considered goats will be told to depart into an eternal fiery punishment because they did not do these things unto the brethren. God says they did not minister for Him and to Him. We need to listen to this message. This is not just a story. It is God telling us something we need to understand. We are each other's keeper in God's eyes.

Heavenly Father,

Forgive me for being selfish and only looking out for my own best interest. I now understand this is not your heart. I have bought into the lies of this culture. Forgive me and cleanse me from this mindset and the habits I have formed. Fill me with your love and let it flow out of me to others from now on. In Jesus Name. Amen.

LIE #9
LYING IS NOT A BIG DEAL

The Lord hates lying lips,
but he delights in people who are trustworthy.
Proverbs 12:22

Every human being, I imagine, has been guilty of telling a lie at some point in their lives. From many people's perspective, lying is necessary sometimes to accomplish an end, such as a way of surviving, or it is needed to prevent shame and to keep a good image intact. Because of its common use all around us, I believe most have accepted it as the norm. We don't see it being a big deal and don't believe it has a detrimental effect on our lives.

In fact, we have even divided lies into colors to determine what we can accept or not. We have white lies as opposed to a regular lie. We have placed them in categories by size. Some are seen as a little lie while others are referred to as big fat lies.

Here is some of the human reasoning we use so we feel comfortable with telling a lie:

- Everyone has lied before and lying is done by everybody in some way so to expect someone not to lie at all is unrealistic.
- It is natural to tell a lie. Nothing is wrong with telling a lie.
- Lying is justified to get what you need or want.
- Some lies are necessary as it prevents shame or further damage.
- Some lies protect me and others and are needed for safety reasons.

- We should accept people lying as long as it doesn't cross a certain line.
- There are much worser things than lying like murder, abuse, stealing, etc.
- You must survive at all costs, even if that means you need to lie.

As those of us who attend church and see ourselves as Bible believing children of God who serve His purposes, we must look at God's perspective on this topic to gain the truth. How important is this subject to God? How important should it be to us? We must find out what God thinks about this behavior called lying.

We find in scripture that God's nature and character is Holy. He is light and there is no darkness in Him at all. Most of all, He is truth. He is absolute truth making Him trustworthy, dependable, and without falsehood. He would NEVER deceive or go against truth. For Him to do so would mean He could not be God. His very essence doesn't allow for anything but truth. God is truth and determines all truth.

The Roman governor Pilate asked Jesus to define truth to him, when He was brought before him by the nation of Israel who condemned Him to death. Jesus said, "He was the truth and all that heard His words heard truth, but not all responded to this truth." (John 18:37)

God's very being, nature, and character is truth. It is who He is. It is what He represents because it is of Him. Once God has established how He will work, He must abide within the limits of His own word in order to prove He is the only trustworthy and dependable God there is. He knows all things and is perfect in all His ways. He is also the creator, originator, and beginner of all things as well as the ending.

Since God is truth, He is unable to lie. The Bible says,

> *…So that by two **unchangeable** things, in which **it is <u>impossible</u> for God to lie**…*
>
> *Hebrews 6:18 (ESV)*

*In hope of eternal life, which **God, who <u>never</u> lies**...*
Titus 1:2 (ESV)

***God is not man, that he should lie**, or a son of man, that he should change his mind.*
Numbers 23:19 (ESV)

*I write to you, not because you do not know the truth, but because **you know it**, and because **<u>no lie is of the truth</u>**.*
1 John 2:21 (ESV)

God **CAN'T** tell a lie. God **WON'T** tell a lie. He can't change His mind in regards to who He is and how He acts. A lie is the very opposite of truth. There is no deception found in the truth, none whatsoever; not even a little bit. God is the only one who determines what a lie is and how bad it is.

What do we call a lie?

Let's define and understand what a lie is. ***A lie is a falsehood spoken for the purpose of deception.*** Its intention is to represent falsely and it is a violation of the truth. IT IS FALSE. It is deception spoken with the goal of making someone believe something that is not true.

Where did lies come from?

Lies come from Satan, the devil, adversary of men, rebel against God, the deceiver, and opponent of truth. He is called the Father of lies. He has no truth. He is the inventor of lies and therefore lies are his original language. He is evil. Any deception known, its root always comes from the influential work of Satan, our enemy. A lie includes anything that is not fully the truth, including keeping back part of the truth, a partial truth; not being totally honest or forthcoming; hiding information, not being clear, and pretending about a particular thing.

However, another definition is: a twisting or bending of the truth. This is what the enemy of God does best. This was seen in the very first lie. What makes a lie so deceptive is that there is usually some truth attached to it. The devil mentioned some truth but spoke what was opposed to God's word. He was changing the meaning of what God had said to make it into something He never said and meant. In the original garden, the serpent, possessed of the devil, said "Did God really say that you would die? You will not die. He knows what you will gain instead." We must understand that **you can't have a lie unless there is a truth first.** We know that all truth comes from God above. Anything that is not the absolute truth has been introduced by an enemy of God. In order for us to operate in a lie, we must choose to ignore the truth and change it like Satan did.

In the temptation of Jesus, the devil asked Jesus to do something that would satisfy His natural desires, three different times. The second time, he even quoted the scriptures to try to confuse Jesus. He wanted Him to do something God never intended. It was his effort to take the perfect word of God and change its original purpose so it could be used in a way that seemingly benefitted man on the earth while rejecting God's truth at the same time. Satan turns everything around that God made perfect. Let's see what the scriptures tell us about him:

> *…who is called the devil and Satan, the deceiver of the whole world.*
>
> *Revelations 12:9 (ESV)*

> *You are of your father the devil, and your will is to do your father's desires. He was a murderer from the beginning, and* **has nothing to do with the truth, because there is no truth in him. When he lies, he speaks out of his own character, for he is a liar and the father of lies.**
>
> *John 8:44 (ESV)*

> *Put on all the armor that God gives,* **so you can defend yourself against the devil's tricks.**
>
> *Ephesians 6:11 (CEV)*

The devil is a liar. The devil is the father of lies. The devil does not know how to operate in truth because he has left the truth. He has nothing to do with truth. His characteristics are not the same as God's. His characteristics are only consistent with who he is. He is a deceiver, a trickster, and someone who is looking to fool humanity.

How did we come to believe these lies?

We understand thus far that our enemy, that opposes God and everything that is in the light and is righteous, is a liar and deceiver. As the father of lies, he is a master deceiver. This is something, as we can see, that the evil one has been doing a very long time. What makes his lies work is his ability to mix it with the truth. He is great at putting attractive bait on a hook and catching men on the earth. The goal is to keep us locked up, so we won't be truly free. Man was created in the image of God but fell under the trap of the devil. From the beginning when the first man and woman existed on the earth, his plan has been at work. It was always his desire to influence us so that he could control us.

Today, he has twisted the knowledge given to man to be used in a way that God never intended. Man uses his knowledge against God instead of operating with God's understanding and wisdom. Man has forgotten that the fear of the Lord is the beginning of knowledge. (Proverbs 1:7)

The goal of the enemy is by getting mankind to believe and tell lies, they will lose the place of authority in the earth God gave them. When we succumb to these devices and do the opposite of what we were created for, we are now limited to this earth without the power or spiritual fortitude to fight the evil spirits we have allowed to gain control.

Satan's lies appeal to us because he finds something in us we really want, even if it cost us our soul. He finds something we are willing to sacrifice to get; something that we can't seem to resist and live without. When our natural appetite rules, we can be fooled and bought. We find ourselves functioning at a level God never intended, being swayed by earthly influences. The main battle is the stronghold of the mind. The only way the enemy wins is to make you believe the opposite of God's truth.

Since humans have become so removed from their first state in which God made them as perfect and are unfamiliar with God's original intention, they have become numb to lying. It is part of one's evil sinful nature to not tell the truth. It is part of the fallen human condition we have as a result of sin.

How does God feel about lies?

We know what man thinks, but how does God see it when mankind tells a lie. The following verses give us an idea:

> *There are six things that* **the LORD hates**, *seven that are an abomination to him: haughty eyes,* **a lying tongue**....
> *Proverbs 6:16 (ESV)*

> **Do not lie to each other**, *since* **you have taken off your old self** *with* **its practices**.
> *Colossians 3:9 (BSB)*

> **You shall not** *steal, nor* **deal falsely**, *nor* **lie to one another**.
> *Leviticus 19:11 (NASB)*

> *A* **false witness** *will not go unpunished, and* **he who speaks lies shall perish.**
> *Proverbs 19:9*

> **Lying lips are abomination** *to the* LORD: *but* **they that deal truly** *are his delight.*
> *Proverbs 12:22 (NASB)*

We are told throughout scripture that lying is not acceptable to God. Yes, lying is a bad thing from God's perspective. Lying is wrong – any shape or form. A lie is not the truth. Lying is a disgrace in the sight of God because it goes directly against Him. He is Truth. A lie can never become a good thing because it itself is a breaking of God's law. Wrong never becomes right. We can't guard truth with lies. We can't guard truth with silence. There is never a situation where lying is fine. There is no lie that can be excused or justified in God's eyes. God has a set, perfect standard where He does not allow anything to slide and be justified according to our opinions.

Lying is an evil practice. The Bible is very clear on God's stance when it comes to lying. Do not do it. God says it is an ABOMINATION. These are strong words. He says the same thing about homosexuality. Wow! So many have been deceived by the devil to think it is harmless. You will not find a scripture where God approves of lying. When God gave His servant Moses the Ten Commandments that He wanted His people to obey, one of them was "Do not speak falsely about your neighbor." God's people understood they were not to tell lies about, for, or to their neighbors. Liars are put in the category of those who practice ungodly and sinful behavior. (1 Timothy 1:10) Liars shall never enter into kingdom of God, but shall be condemned to everlasting punishment according to Revelations 21:8, Revelations 22:15, and Revelations 21:27.

In John 8:44, Jesus is speaking claiming that those who practice telling any kind of lies has a father, but it is not God. They are the children of the devil. He says sons and daughters are like their father. You will take on the character of your parents. So, when you deceive others, who are you acting like? Those who practice lying are following in Satan's footsteps and he has become their father. Spiritually, if we want God to be our Father then we must decide to put lying away. The only way we can become a child of God is to repent and leave our sinful ways that does not bring glory to God, nor please Him, or represent Him accurately.

In Acts chapter 5, Ananias and Sapphira lied in the presence of God and fell dead because of it. The Apostle Peter said to him, "Ananias, why has Satan filled thine heart to lie to the Holy Ghost." Do you see who is responsible for causing a person to tell a lie? He adds, "Why have you planned to do this in your heart? You have not lied unto men, but unto God." If the presence of God was truly to show up in our meetings, I wonder how many people would fall dead from telling a lie in the church. How many would fall out from pretending to be something they are not, or for making others think something that is not true? Lying is a light thing to man, but it is a serious thing to God. It is only His mercy and many people's ignorance that allows Him to let them live and continue in their deception of believing it is not a big deal.

The excuses of: "everybody does it," "God does not expect you to be perfect," and "it's hard not to," won't work forever. We all understand this, but this doesn't change the fact that God doesn't want us to practice wrong behavior. We must get in our minds that this is wrong. This is not good. This is unholy. God is Holy and He wants me to be Holy. I can't accept this because God does not accept this no matter how I may feel.

When a person has a true encounter with God and he is put in right standing with Him, he no longer wants to lie. God cleans him up and he loves what God loves and hates what God hates. This is how we can tell who is righteous and who is not.

> ***A righteous man hates lying***, *but a wicked man is loathsome and comes to shame.*
> *Proverbs 13:5*

Real Christians don't practice lying. Lying is a sin and Christians don't practice sinning.

> ***Whoever makes a practice of sinning is of the devil,*** *for the devil has been sinning from the beginning. The reason the Son of God appeared was to destroy the works of the devil.*
> *1 John 3:8 (ESV)*

It's impossible for Christians to continue to have lying lips according to scripture. They don't live a lifestyle where telling a lie is fine. All who belong to God are convicted by the Holy Spirit if they tell a lie. Those who really love God and cherish their relationship with God will repent, confess, and make right the wrong they did. They can't just keep going pretending it never happened. **If**

you believe you are a man or woman of God and you see nothing wrong with telling lies and you are not grieved about it, you do not belong to Christ yet. God requires that you fix the lies with confession. If you confess your sins, he is faithful and just to forgive you and cleanse you from all unrighteousness, but if you say you have no sin, you call him a liar and you are the one deceived and do not have the truth. (1 John 1:9-10) You must agree with God and see it the way He sees it. **The only way to fix a lie is to tell the truth.**

What we lie about?

We lie about how much something cost; how much is needed; our needs; how many of something we had; where we are going; what we did; what we saw; why we did something; What we don't have; What we said; our weight and our age, and more.

The main need for men is RESPECT. This is so important to men and I don't think we can live without it. **We will do anything to protect our image, especially LIE.** God can't trust us until we care more about Him and His image than our own.

Why do we lie?

We lie for many reasons: I believe the main reason is because we are afraid. Fear is why most people lie. We lie when we fear what man thinks and what they may do to us. We see this in scripture with Rahab, Abraham, Isaac, Jacob, Joseph brothers, and the midwives in Egypt among others. We lie because we fear losing out, not having what we want, and not looking our best. We don't trust that God will do what He says He will do, so we take matters into our own hands by using methods that don't represent Him. We abandon God's truth and decide to accomplish our purpose according to our will and our way instead of His. We know it is wrong but we feel we must do what we must do right now. We don't believe the truth works better than a lie. We don't believe the truth will save us, but a lie will.

This is not God's thinking, it is man's and it is inspired by Satan, the father of all lies. The goal of lying is to not take full responsibility. You are not submitting and making yourself accountable to God.

Lying is many people's method of getting what they want. It is then used to cover one self, cover someone else, and protect someone else. We say, "God understands." He understands we just agreed to the devil's method. We trust His word greater than God's word. We have saved our body, but compromised our spirit man in the process. We are in trouble and we don't know it because we have placed our confidence in man and in our enemy's way of doing things. Though years go by, we have been fooled from seeing that there is a way that seems right unto a man but it ends in death. (Proverbs 14:12) Death starts inside not outside. Death is to be separated from something. For example: physical death is the removal of our spirit from our body. We leave this world for another. In the same way, lying separates us from God, who is the truth.

God will never condone our lying. I believe He knows one's heart and the motive and is still never accepting of a lie, no matter how much we justify it. Would God lie to get what he needed? God would never give us more temptation than we can handle or put more on us than we can bear. (1 Corinthians 10:13) He wants us to trust Him and be steered from this serious error. He doesn't need our help in lying to save or help us. This is the opposite of His nature. We must never neglect the truth even if it cost us our life. (Revelations 12:11)

Lying is what the unredeemed and ungodly practice. When we just can't seem to help ourselves, do we realize what really happens to us every time we tell a lie? What did we just exchange for that lie? We gave up Godly character, our integrity, compromised moral consciousness, the respect of unbelievers and believers, and we abandoned the God part of us. We brought ourselves low, down to a lower level. We became untrustworthy and unfaithful. We profaned our name as well as God's. Did you know that a good name is better than riches? (Proverbs 22:1) Good from God's perspective, not from ours or another man's opinion. We experience spiritual death, meaning there is a separation between us and God, because God does not fellowship in darkness. Every time we lie, we are further separating ourselves from Him and His presence. When we lie, we lie to God, not just man. We must renounce lying.

The person who has God living in his heart and life is immediately convicted, they repent and are made conscious when they are not speaking the truth. If they don't, they are living a lifestyle of deceitfulness. Some people who are intent on justifying themselves, just refuse to call a lie, a lie. Lies and deceptions are seen by all of these activities:

- Telling somebody something that is not the truth.
- Making someone think something that is not truthful.
- Allowing someone to believe something you know is not true.
- Sharing something and knowingly keeping back part of the truth.
- Sharing something and adding things to the story that did not really happen.
- Making something look differently than what it actually is.
- Getting someone to focus on something else to hide the real problem.
- Using a reason to do or not do something when you know it is not the real reason.
- Pretending to know something you don't know.
- Pretending not to know something you know.
- Keeping the truth from somebody due to fear of how they may think or feel about you or react.
- Sharing something about someone or yourself in a way to make them see things in a way that is not completely the truth.
- Sharing or doing things in order to accomplish a purpose that you hide from that person.
- Doing or saying things for the sole purpose of getting a reaction or manipulate another person.
- Blame someone for something when you know you are partly or totally to blame.

- Blame something on something else that is not the actual problem.
- Make a promise and don't keep it.
- Tell yourself something that is not truth.
- Telling somebody you will do one thing when you plan to do something else.

All of these things fall into the area called a lie. For many, lying has been made a lifestyle, habit, and routine. Lying has become a normal part of our church community as well. I can hear some people saying, "Why are you calling everybody a liar?" Everybody is not, however, if you regularly practice doing any of the activities mentioned above, then God has called you one and the Bible says, "Let God be true and every man a liar." (Romans 3:4)

This is one of the many hidden sins that the church does not deal with. Who wants to hear a message on lying? Immediately, we know it will be convicting and we must humble ourselves and repent. We know sermons like this does not make people feel good about themselves. We don't want to offend people. We are afraid people will get mad and not return. We want them and we want their monetary support. We also don't want to preach on something we are participating in ourselves. This would be too uncomfortable. When we preach God's standards for operating in this world, we know we are the leader and example in actually obeying it. The people hold us accountable and when they see us failing, they will remind us of our hypocrisy.

Some Truths about lying

If we practice lying, the enemy is able to use it against us. God is unable to bless us because we have aligned ourselves with the powers of darkness. Sometimes people actually believe because they benefitted from a lie, that God blessed them. This couldn't be any further from the truth. The enemy rewards those who use his methods, but in the end, they are destroyed. When we sow lies, we reap lies and we always get back more than we plant. The enemy will let people believe their lies work until they become so deceived, they don't realize they are getting lied back to by the father of lies. When you deal falsely with people, he will make sure someone deals falsely with you.

The patriarch Jacob was a deceiver until God changed him. After deceiving his brother twice, Jacob met his match with his uncle Laban who deceived him at least ten times. You don't realize the fire you are playing with when you practice falsehood. The greater deceiver always wins. We need to make a choice right now to allow God to intervene before we drown in our lies and lose our lives.

When we live a life of lying, we are revealing to the world that we are not Godly people. We are functioning as an immature human and have not become a real man or woman yet. Only grown up boys still lie and deceive because they haven't been prepared and made ready for the transition into real adulthood. In 1 Corinthians chapter 13 we find this:

> ***When I was a child, I thought like one and I played games like one – I pretended, but when I became a man, I put away childish things.***
>
> 1 Corinthians 13:11

Perhaps, you are a man now in a grown body but still playing childish games. For example: usually boys can't accept losing while men learn from it. Boys may cry from falling, men have learned to get up and do it better so they won't fall again. Boys may cheat to succeed while men of Godly stature refuse to take a shortcut and cheat because they value themselves too much. This verse is speaking about one becoming mature, complete, finished, and having experienced the growth to function at the next level. Are you ready to grow up and function at God's level?

The reason for lying never justifies the lie. As soon as you make an excuse why, it will allow you to lie more easier if you feel you have a good enough excuse.

Don't be a fool. When people lie, they lie for them, not for you. **Lying is always the companion of selfishness.** It's about their own self-worth. They are dealing with their own fears.

Liars will attract liars. Look around you, liars don't hang out with truth seekers. Those connected close to you are liars as well if you practice lying. When you practice something, you are involved in it regularly. You might take a day off here and there or might be on vacation, but when you are back in the regular routine of life, you are dealing with others in your practice. People who lie become good at it. Good liars are prepared in advance with back-up lies. They learn to cover their tracks with more lies.

Do not withhold the truth from any child or person for any length of time. It's like believing a lie and when the real truth comes later it usually crushes them. The later it takes to get the truth, the worse it seems when it comes, because people feel like they have been living a lie until that time. It's one of those things where everyone wants honesty but doesn't always want to be honest. What happened to honesty? When is it good to tell a lie? Never! There is absolutely nothing we should lie about.

We can't lie to obtain something and then say God blessed me. Please do not use the devil's behavior and lifestyle to gain something and then attribute it to God's blessing or God helped you or God led you. No, you relied on your fear which did not come from God. Your fleshly behavior has nothing to do with the Spirit of God. There is no way we can associate the two, nor justify the action to a Holy God.

Fooling people is a form of lying. God is not in the picture. 2 Corinthians 11:14 states the enemy will disguise himself. He disguises himself to be something good when he is not. He makes himself to appear to everyone as someone he is really not. So, when we pretend to be something to others we are not, whose footsteps are we following? Who is our daddy?

How do we get rid of these lies?

We have to ask God to show us if there is anything in us that we need Him to shine His light on. Ask God to search you. The issues of a man's soul are very deep.

If I can tell on myself, I didn't realize it but I had lied to myself for years. I was deceiving myself in a certain area about a certain thing. I just couldn't see it. My wife had brought it up for years, but I refused to believe it. God brought me to a place in my life where I could not deny it anymore. **Your lie will always show you who you are and where you are.** You will never be able to receive your full benefits as a child of God until you face your fears to remove lies. God's truth is the foundation needed in order to get us to the place He wants to take us.

The only way to defeat and remove lies is to TELL THE TRUTH. The only way to fix this is to acknowledge your lying ways and change them. Confess and repent. You must decide if you want Him or your lies because you can't have both. How can two walk together unless they be agreed? How can God and Satan fellowship together when they have nothing in common? Lying is the lifestyle of Satan while speaking truth is the lifestyle of God.

> *When the Spirit of truth comes, he will guide you into all the truth, for he will not speak on his own authority, but whatever he hears he will speak, and he will declare to you the things that are to come.*
>
> *John 16:13 (ESV)*

God promises all believers He would send them the Holy Spirit. This spirit is also called the Spirit of Truth. This Spirit of Truth will lead, guide, and will only speak that which is in agreement with God who can't tell a lie and His son Jesus who is the Truth.

We don't expect those that live around us who do not know Christ, to embrace this truth and obey God's word. The healing of our nation is not up to them. **If we can get all the church attending Christians, who claim they have a relationship with Jesus to stop lying, you will see an immediate impact on the culture.** If we could get all the preachers in the churches who are lying to stop, we would see an immediate change in the nation. I'm not accusing any persons, but rather I am challenging the Body of Christ to take this subject as serious as God our Father and our Lord Jesus Christ does. Let's begin today to clean up this area in our lives. We can no longer let the enemy downplay this as not a big deal, thereby giving him an open door to do his work in our homes, churches, and nation.

I have been in ministry over 30 years and I am still always shocked when I encounter or hear a story about people who act spiritual but lie through their teeth. I'm talking about the church in America. I say this not in judgement, because I have been guilty of lying on occasions over the years. I've practiced for many years not to, because the way that the Lord deals with me is: He makes me go to people and confess. As humbling as that is, I make a practice of not being put in that position. I do not stand in judgment of no one, I just want all of us to strive for what God has said. It all starts with an acknowledgement, repentance, and a decision not to practice this moving forward.

In my personal experience with Christians in Liberia, revelations from other missionaries there, social media and chat room discussions, and many Liberians themselves I must say this is a BIG problem. The problem is too prevalent to ignore. One missionary to Liberia, during her mission trips there, dealt with lying so much that she referred to Liberia as LIE - BERIA.

You may feel insulted and I'm sorry if you do for that is not my goal. I only want to make a strong point. Of course, we know this does not refer to all, but for many it does. I am not referring to the outside world as much as I am referring to those in the church community. This is not an easy subject, but I know God asked me to deal with it. I pray that we know the difference between conviction and condemnation. Jesus did not come to condemn us but to save us. He saves us by convicting us of sin, so we can confess it and be clean. He said to those who believed on Him, "If you continue in my word, then you really are my disciples; and you shall know the truth and the truth shall make you free." (John 8:31-32) Let's be free. Join me in a prayer from your heart, if you need to make things right with God in this area.

Dear God,

We come before you asking your forgiveness. We needed to be reminded of who you are and what you stand for. You stand for truth. We confess our sin of lying. We repent of the lies we have told. We surrender our lying habits and the excuses we give to justify them. Clean us and make us whole. We know this is your perfect will for our lives. It's not our families, churches, government officials and friends we need to pray for about this; it's us Lord standing in the need of prayer and in need of your grace. You said if we confess our sins, you are faithful and just to forgive us. You also said if your people humble themselves and turn from their wicked ways, only then can you hear our prayers, forgive us, and heal our land. I receive your forgiveness. Thank you, Lord. Now help me by the power of your Holy Spirit as it is my desire to walk in truth from this day forward and I am committed to it. In Jesus Name. Amen.

LIE #10
SEXUAL IMMORALITY IS NORMAL

Since you are God's people, it is not right that any matters of sexual immorality or indecency or greed should even be mentioned among you.
Ephesians 5:3 (GNT)

Me and Dan spent some time together. I was looking forward to this conversation. Here I was an American that was being led to write a book to the Liberian church community, dealing with the taboo subjects that most people are silent about. I wanted to know from another Liberian who grew up there what was the mindset or thinking in regards to sexual relations in the society.

Dan himself grew up believing he was a Christian even though he had relations and fathered children with a woman he had never formally married. I asked him if he saw anything wrong with being unmarried and having sexual relations as a church going Christian. He said it was what everyone he knew did around him. It is the culture. It is accepted.

When I asked him, if he knew what he was doing was considered sin in the Bible, he stated yes. He said he just didn't give it much thought. The limited times he would read the Bible, if he read something on any sin that confronted him as ungodly behavior, he would just close his Bible and open it up to another passage that wasn't so convicting. Like many in the church community think, if we somehow ignore it, we don't have to think about it and it will go away. I guess this is a way to reject guilt. He was never challenged by the Christian pastors because they did not preach against it. Many of them practiced the same behavior. In fact, some Christian leaders in high positions even suggested there was nothing wrong with being with girls as young as fourteen years of age. I went out of my way to try to understand those who grew up in the Liberian culture and the thought process that went into how people lived when it came to their sex lives. I was very grateful for the input from so many. These things were truly hidden from me.

Liberia's community has a majority made up of indigenous and native tribal people and with it they carry their traditional African religious customs. These customs included having more than one wife or having multiple relationships and children without ceremonies. It is what we may call, common law marriage today in America. I enjoy learning about people, culture, and customs as these have been the way tribes lived in their small villages many years before the Americo-Liberians appeared. The Americo-Liberians came creating their own system of orderly living, religion, and governmental structure.

We do not put down or criticize the native social views. We should expect and accept others beliefs on how they choose to govern their own lives. What is not acceptable is to mix these beliefs with Bible truths because they are in conflict with each other. For example: Polygamy has been around since the beginning of time, even practiced by Biblical patriarchs. It was man's idea, allowed by God then, and caused many problems. However, we can never find anything showing God commanded or supported it. We can only find abundant scripture commanding marriage to be between a male and female becoming one. (Genesis 2:18, 1 Corinthians 7:2-5, Matthew 19:4-6, Colossians 3:18-19, Ephesians 5:22-33, Genesis 2:22-24, 1 Peter 3:7, Matthew 5:27-28).

The scripture makes it clear that fornication (sex outside marriage) and adultery (sex with someone other than your spouse) are both sins that if practiced will keep you from entering the kingdom of God.

> *"You have heard that it was said, 'You shall not commit adultery.' But I say to you that everyone who **looks at a woman with lustful intent** has already committed adultery with her in his heart.*
>
> *Matthew 5:27-28*

> *Do you not know that **the unrighteous will not inherit the kingdom of God? Do not be deceived**. **<u>Neither fornicators</u>**, nor idolaters, **<u>nor adulterers</u>**, nor homosexuals, nor sodomites,*
>
> 1 Corinthians 6:9

It is **IMPOSSIBLE** to be a real, authentic Christian and practice this lifestyle of ancient African customs. **A choice must be made.** To intermingle the ways of both is to renounce your life as a Christian. It is to live in a false reality that you are in right relationship with the God of heaven who created everything. It is to deny Jesus Christ, the only way to God and His message. Lastly, it is to grieve and be in direct noncompliance with Holy Spirit, who is holy and would never be in the presence of immoral and sinful living as He has determined such behavior to be.

In African customs, marriage is a process rather than the event westerners have made it. In God's sight, marriage is a covenant between two people that includes God in the middle of it. Despite Christian insistence on monogamy, history shows that the African custom solidified marriages by children and men of success. Many men were known to have a ring wife and a country wife. Research shows that even up to today 25% of marriages in West Africa may be polygamous.

I was thinking about polygamy specifically in Liberia. I understand that the Muslim religion which is predominant in some of Africa, Middle East, and Asia legalizes this custom as a way of life. In some other countries it is illegal, but not criminalized, while in others it is illegal and criminalized. Despite these legal set ups, the longstanding customs and traditions of many of those native from the hinterland prevail in many ways. It appears to be saturated in the blood line and irresistible to function any other way. Even those who do not practice polygamy, the marrying by one man to many wives, will be found to have mistresses and girlfriends with no legal responsibilities to these women or the children they may produce by them.

Between 1910 and 1930 there was a converted Christian African preacher from the Liberian country who was responsible for converting thousands to the religion of Christianity. Though other evangelical missionaries had visited by then, none had the success of William Davis Harris. He was known as Prophet Davis. His conversion and ministry seemed real. He gained the recognition of African traditionalist by challenging them to not remove but replace their fetish practices with a different power; the power of the Holy Spirit. His ministry was demonstrative and won many over. The only concern Christian imperialist of the time had with him was the fact that he had several wives and didn't see anything wrong with polygamy.

Today, there is a great mixture of ancient beliefs with Christian beliefs forming something other than what was intended. We will follow the culture of our world if we don't hear the Word of God. The Word of God is counter to the way our world and man does things. God has a way for us to live. Many Liberians haven't addressed this issue because they haven't committed themselves to knowing and obeying God's word as well as teaching others to observe God's command like He told us to do. In Matthew 28:20, Jesus told His disciples, "and teaching them to obey everything I have commanded you."

Without teaching the truth, we are in danger of a new generation following who will not know the truth and will copy everything they see. They will also become what they follow after. The sins of the fathers are followed by the children to the next four generations. This wrongdoing becomes accepted and nothing changes year after year, decade after decade. Those who choose to live a righteous, pure life in this area will do so in a culture that is mostly doing the opposite and these people are at risk of being disfavored and criticized because of their works and stance. Just by their righteous example, they expose the sinful. This is why the sinful prefer to include you in their deception.

This ignoring of scripture is used by many professing Christians. Somehow people are deceived into thinking if I turn my head and pretend it's not there it goes away and becomes ineffective. The refusal to deal with God's truth doesn't make it go away. The rejection of what God says about this subject doesn't make it disappear. It still will be standing there looking at you while you go to do your own thing. God's word doesn't shift or change because we don't like it, we don't want it, or we don't follow it.

Many Christian leaders past and present would not teach against fornication and adultery for the fear of a culture that would not support their ambitions. They would lose popularity and money. They don't want to offend others who want to stay in their sinful ways. Leaders in the churches are guilty of not only not teaching what God says about sexual relations but actually promoting others to do the opposite in secret. Many leaders involved in secret sexual sins themselves, know it would not look good if it was public knowledge. Since looking the part is more important than doing right, they find a way to still do what they really want behind closed doors.

The church in the community is guilty of sexual abuses and cover ups. My limited connections with men of the cloth thus far has uncovered many immoral issues. I can comment about several but I'll just choose a few.

On one of my initial visits to Liberia I met a woman minister who was on staff at one of the churches we regularly visited. I always noticed her quiet but seemingly somber demeanor. It was as if something had died inside her. She was definitely missing the joy of the Lord. During one of our visits to an orphanage our church was supporting there the following year, a team member took her aside and began to pray with her and she began to cry uncontrollably. God ministered to her. It was a few years later when she shared with me the pressures she was dealing with. There were many, but the one that stood out was the sexual harassment she worked under at the church she served.

In another situation, one of my Godsons in Liberia had contacted me that he was going to get married. He wanted me to perform the ceremony. He also wanted me to bring him a white tuxedo from the states and so on. If you know Africa, you know what I'm trying to say. Before I arrived, he and his fiancé had decided to delay the ceremony due to financial constraints.

When I arrived, I had the pleasure of meeting her at his house. She fixed us a great dinner, but when I first met her, she looked at me as if she had seen a ghost. I pretended to not notice how she looked at me. After she hurriedly left, I told my Godson there is something wrong. He didn't seem to notice anything wrong. That night we went to sleep. In the morning, he got up and told me he had a dream that his fiancée was sleeping with his pastor. I told him to confront her. She admitted it. He asked her why she would do this and she stated because she needed money and he was paying her. She also said he was paying other girls at the church and sleeping with them. I didn't realize it at this time, but this was more common than I realized.

Before I go any further, I think it is important that I mention, this is not an African church problem. This is a worldwide Christian church problem. I know it is happening in American churches as well. The goal here is to expose what is being covered up in secret and talk about it in the light. The greatest shame is not exposing it, but to keep doing it in hiding. God loves us and wants us to come clean. He wants to cleanse us from our sins and use us to build His kingdom and impact the nations of the earth for real.

We can't continue to ignore this issue and present ourselves as good. We must not cover up the shameful deeds done in the dark and pretend like nothing wrong is going on. We can't maintain falsehood where no one is to be made to feel ashamed, guilty, or wrong. This is especially true of leaders and people in position over others. This is truly what happens in many churches. Any one that is uncovered or is challenged to be accountable for their actions makes life miserable on those who expose them. Instead of the guilty correcting the behavior, the confronter is blamed for opening their mouth. Some are threatened and cursed. Scriptures are then used wrongly so leaders don't have to be accountable to God or others for their unrighteous actions. Scriptures like: *Touch not my anointed, do my prophet no harm* in Psalms 105:15. The actual context of this is God protecting His servants who were obedient to His will from evil men. This does not apply to you if you are confronted with known sin. Church leaders will use scriptures in the same way slave masters picked and chose scriptures to justify their actions of enslaving humans and treating them inhumanely.

The Christian church around the world and along with its leaders have made it comfortable for people to go in the church to have religious activity, but once outside to live their lives anyway they please. Scripture is very clear about God's view on sexual relations:

> *For **this is the will of God**, your sanctification: **that you should abstain from sexual immorality**; that each of you should know how **to possess his own vessel in sanctification and honor, not in passion of lust**, like the Gentiles who do not know God; that **no one should take advantage of and defraud his brother in this matter, because the Lord is the avenger of all such**, as we also forewarned you and testified. **For God did not call us to uncleanness, but in holiness**. Therefore, he who **rejects this does not reject man, but God, who has also given us His Holy Spirit**.*
> 1 Thessalonians 4:3-8

> *And now, dear brothers and sisters, **we give you this command in the name of our Lord Jesus Christ: Stay away from all believers who live idle lives and don't follow the tradition they received from us**.*
> 2 Thessalonians 3:6 (NLT)

Bad company corrupts good manners. One bad fruit or vegetable in a bag of good fruit and vegetables will make the good fruit become bad. One infested piece of fruit will contaminate the rest. There is what is called ethylene - a chemical – that comes out of the rotten piece to cause the others to ripen faster and even rot. In the right surrounding conditions and with time, the others will become bad. So, it is with people who stay around others who are involved in wrongdoing.

> ***Do not be deceived** it says, **Bad company corrupts good haracter**. Sober up as you ought, and **<u>stop sinning</u>**; for **some of you are ignorant of God. I say this to your shame**.*
> 1 Corinthians 15:33-34 (BSB)

To continue to sin is to be ignorant of God. Holiness living is not believed and taught much in many church organizations, so it is not practiced, yet it is the teaching of the Bible, the life of Christ, the command of God, and the character of the Holy Spirit. Everyone who refuses to seek after and live a holy life has not been born again, is not truly saved, and can't enter into the kingdom of God according to scripture. They are rather under God's wrath. This is what the Bible teaches. The Bible says you can't continue in sin if the seed of God remains in you. (1 John 3:9)

Sexual immoral behavior is one of the greatest tools and bait used in the kingdom of darkness. Satan understands the strong desire and lust of our flesh to feel good and have pleasure in this area. He knows that once we indulge in giving in to our feelings, it becomes very hard to stop. We become slaves to it and find it irresistible to give in to our sexual urges. These spiritually unclean spirits sent from him that cause temptation and then keeps anyone bound in the behavior, become attached through our willingness and appetite to experience more.

Satan watches in delight as we destroy the purity of what God created for His purpose. Our refusal to present our bodies as a living sacrifice misrepresents God to our world. It is an embarrassment to who He is and what He is all about. Satan sits back in mischievous laughter as our momentary delight destroys bodies, breaks hearts, sabotages intimacy, and produces children who will not have the security and support of their mother and father as they enter and grow up in this world. The perfect family unit, the foundation of any society's governmental order created by God himself, is now fragile, scattered, and being destroyed. If the foundations be destroyed, what can the righteous do. (Psalms 11:3) If the first and main cornerstone of what builds a nation and makes it strong is removed, missing, or broken then what can be done?

In my research, I found that transactional sex, which is sex given by women to men in exchange for money or favors, is a common practice. It is widely accepted, encouraged, and even celebrated by one's peers in certain circles. I found this happens a lot between young females and older more financially secure males to obtain cash, food, clothing, western commodities, pay school fees, and get possible employment.

It is not uncommon for males in power to use this power to have sex with females of their choosing. This can be found in every sector of society, including our schools. In one particular survey done, 20% of students say they have been abused by their teachers and 80% have reported sex for grades was a problem. One story shared how a male teacher held back a female student's grade until she had sex with him, while others received favorable grades in exchange for sex. Even some students are failed for not cooperating. One boy was failed because of a teacher's jealousy; the girl he liked was with this boy. This is not an uncommon practice nor does it seem to be frowned upon by many men and females alike. Almost everyone takes a blind eye, pretend they see nothing, and figure it is what it is, no big deal. Of course, all this is to be done and kept secret, without letting anybody know. The story goes on to reveal that the girl had to leave the school after exposing the teacher (through a taped voice recorder) because of the pressure from administrators and other teachers, male and female who blamed her for telling, while nothing was done to the abusing teacher.

The need for money at times has blinded what is really important and tricked some parents into encouraging their kids to exchange sex for money. How can young girls respect parents who do this? Even the tradition of giving a bride price shows that a woman is to be given some value.

I also found that it is covered up in some of our churches. It is encouraged by some of our church going parents and families and of course ignored by some who call themselves men of God. The bottom line for many ministers in our churches, I am ashamed to say, is not living to please God, but living for the money that goes in the offering box.

The moral accountability in the society is low, just like very few are held accountable or responsible at the judicial level, it is the same in our churches. Rape, underage prostitution, and sexual violence are all too common. Social pressure keeps people from holding people responsible and many don't have the fees that are created to process a complaint for prosecution. Those who have been accused usually are in power and have money, so they can get favors or pay their way out of trouble. Those in poverty are exploited with no way to defend themselves fairly and violators are able to get away. Peacekeepers and aid workers from outside of Liberia have been just as guilty of this behavior; taking advantage of the poor and vulnerable. They continue to exploit our women who give in due to their physical needs, not sexual needs. It becomes social interdependence, having several partners for resources to call on.

Can we see why this subject is so vital for the church community? Do we see the importance and affect we have in living right and representing the God of justice? Without us taking our role serious, people's lives are being ruined and our youth are victims of perpetrators who have taken advantage of their situation. Men of God, if we do not take the responsibility of taking care of our women, who will? These are our mothers, sisters, daughters, and aunts. They were created as weaker vessels not to be dominated by us but as helpers to walk along side of us. They are daughters of God and when you abuse a Father's daughter you will have to deal with the angry father. God tells us,

> *In the same way, you husbands* **must give honor to your wives. Treat your wife with understanding** *as you live together.* **She may be weaker than you are, but she is your equal partner in God's gift of new life.** *Treat her as you should* **so your prayers will not be hindered.**
>
> 1 Peter 3:7 (NLT)

Women believe they have scarcity and limited economic opportunities and are limited in access to financial freedom, social status, and power. They are looked at by many men as providing a commodity – sex. Something you buy or exchange for money. Though we try to keep these things in hiding, everyone knows though nobody talks about it. **God says the way that we treat our women, will affect whether He will hear our prayers or not.**

The prevailing culture has affected the majority of woman adversely in regards to how these women see themselves and their roles in society. The wrong mindset has been instilled and it is not seen as abuse. Some even believe it is good to have sex with an American or European; that in this lower role, there is privileges with being with these men that represent power. These guilty men are fearless while using this power to take advantage and exploit the vulnerable.

In support of some men around the world, there is a struggle with having a healthy relationship with a woman because they had no example. They may ask, "How do we have a good relationship with a woman when our mother and sisters have been raped before us?" When our fathers are nowhere around to show us? When we have never seen a Biblical example in real life to follow? We relate to others based off what we have been shown and taught. We can't do better if we don't know any better. This is real. However, we can't use this as an excuse, instead we must follow God's commands and know that He will never ask us to do anything without providing us with the ability to do it.

> ***Flee from sexual immorality***. *Every other sin a person commits is outside the body, but the **sexually immoral person sins** against his own body.*
> *1 Corinthians 6:18 (ESV)*

> *Now concerning the matters about which you wrote: "**It is good for a man not to have sexual relations with a woman**." But **because of the temptation to sexual immorality, each man should have his own wife and each woman her own husband.***
> *1 Corinthians 7:1-2 (ESV)*

> *For you may **be sure of this**, that **everyone who is sexually immoral** or impure, or who is covetous (that is, an idolater), **has no inheritance in the kingdom of Christ and God.***
> *Ephesians 5:5 (ESV)*

The scripture says we can be certain that no one who practices sexual immorality will inherit the kingdom of Christ and God. What is sexual immorality? It is the engaging or indulging in unlawful sexual intercourse. The Greek word used in the Bible is *pornos*. We get our word pornography - the viewing of sexual organs or activities with the intent to stimulate erotic feelings from it. The word means one, particularly a male, who prostitutes his body to another's lust. **Any kind of sex outside of a lawful committed marriage between an adult male and female is considered sin to God.**

Men don't see themselves as a prostitute when they have sex with different women, but this is what God calls you. When He refers to His church, He calls us His bride (male and female). Therefore, when we break the covenant we made with Him when we gave our life to Him as a Christian, by having sex with others and giving in to a lustful spirit, we commit spiritual adultery. We have taken on the role of a harlot, whore, fornicator, and idolater through unlawful sex. Anything you put before God is idolatry. Fornication (unlawful sex) is mentioned more than 40 times in the Bible and adultery (sex outside our marriage) is mentioned over 60 times, both as sinful and considered as evil in God's sight with a command to stop.

> Or **do you not know that your body is a temple of the Holy Spirit** within you, whom you have from God? **You are not your own, for you were bought with a price. So, glorify God in your body.**
> 1 Corinthians 6:19-20 (ESV)

God is not in favor of sexual intercourse between two people who do not have a covenant agreement with each other. He requires them to be held accountable to the promise they make. A promise that is not supposed to be broken unless there is an act of adultery. Sex is so important that a person is not considered fully married legally, even after the ceremony, until there is consummation (final act of bonding through sex). This would imply that everyone we have sex with, we become spiritually married to them, but it could not be honored physically because we spread ourselves too thin. The

Bible makes this plain to us when it says, "When you join yourself to a harlot, do you not realize you become ONE." (1 Corinthians 6:16) There are many things that happen in the spirit realm when you bond with a person sexually. I'm afraid we have underestimated what sex is, what sex is for, and what sex means to God.

God did not create us in the similitude of animals, but rather in His high image. With animals, such as dogs, they will mate with just about any other dog when they get in heat (have strong sexual urges). This happens to them for reproduction purposes. We are not to follow their example because we are better than dogs. Our image is God. Sex inside marriage represents a picture of commitment to God, His oneness, and His commitment to His bride (the church). He is faithful, loyal, and committed to us. He does not give His affection to another. He gives His affection to His bride. He is not intimate with those He does not have a covenant with, so why are we?

In Galatians 5:19-21, sexual behavior outside of marriage is called a work of the flesh. It is listed with murder and witchcraft. Flesh and the lust of it, war against the Spirit of God. They are on opposite sides. They battle against each other. It is not a work of God. It is a work of darkness. It is not a fruit or function of God's kingdom. This is why the scripture says that these things will not be allowed in His kingdom and those that practice these things will stay outside Heaven's gates.

God is serious about this sin. The worse thing the church can do and has done is to take sex outside of marriage lightly as no big deal. Many have fallen into the traps, some have met an untimely and painful death, and many others will find themselves after their death receiving eternal punishment. God have mercy on us. While there is still time, let us repent so that times of refreshing may come from the Lord.

LIE #11
ALL CHURCH LEADERS ARE GOD'S REPRESENTATIVES

Beware of false prophets who come disguised as harmless sheep but are really vicious wolves. You can identify them by their fruit, that is, by the way they act.
Matthew 7:15 -16 (NLT)

We have endangered species. This means that something is in danger of becoming extinct. It is the threat or risk of not finding a particular living thing anymore. It may seem silly of me to suggest that this is what our world is facing when it comes to men with integrity, morals, and Godly character. However, we are in a crisis when it comes to Godly representation on this earth.

Everything starts and ends with leadership. Churches, businesses, and nations rise and fall according to their leadership. Leadership is the leading of others to a designated goal and towards fulfilling an ultimate purpose. God's intention was for the purpose to benefit everyone and glorify God. In God's design, it must be done in a way that doesn't destroy the moral fiber or elements of truth that will build it correctly from the foundation up; otherwise it is unfruitful. There is a big difference between productive and fruitful. You can be productive and not beneficial. When one person or group wins and everyone else suffers, then it may be productive, but its purpose is unfruitful. Unfruitful is connected to the quality of life that affects all the people involved.

Bad leadership is hurting us. Bad leadership comes from sinful leaders. Leaders who fulfill their own lusts. Leaders whose goals are to take care of themselves. People end up following this leadership; learning and copying what to do from those who lead them. Their reference for what to do and be like comes from what they see and are taught from them. **Leadership always influences how the next generation will think and act.**

We see poor leadership all over our world. The world can be a very evil place. There are those with an agenda to have total control over all the major social systems of life; affecting transportation, food and water, education, law, health, religion, entertainment, and government. This is destroying people's livelihood. It is a dark, demonic attack. It's planned out strategically and is accomplished by controlling a population that has been duped into believing in a world government that is actually for the people. They have done a great job of deceiving many so that they can have the voluntary participation of their non critical thinking victims through lustful traps. When I think about how those, who control the money, treat those who are in need for basic things, it breaks my heart. Masses have fallen for a life of servitude, without realizing they have taken the bait that will lock them in and make it hard for them to ever get out.

We are tempted by our own lust. The lust of our flesh, the lust of the eyes, and the pride of this life (1 John 2:16). We give in to what our physical being desires, even at the expense of our own personal freedom. The fact is, our enemy needs our help to defeat us. **Every defeated nation is a result of its people's acceptance, not just government alone.** Most of this is done through fear. I believe it is seen greatest by the spiritual leaders first, followed by the spiritual condition of its people, and lastly, the evil hearts of its leaders in society. As the spiritual condition of the church goes, so goes the nation. Righteousness makes a nation great; sin is a disgrace to any nation (Proverbs 14:34). When the righteous follow the footsteps of the evil, instead of those in darkness being impacted by those who are children of the light, it is not good at all. It is like drinking bad water.

> *A righteous man who gives in to an evil man is like polluted waters or a spring that has been muddied.*
>
> *Proverbs 25:26*

God is in pursuit of people who are trustworthy. Everyone who says they are a Christian or a believer in Jesus Christ is not. Everyone who says they are an Apostle, Pastor, Evangelist, Prophet, and Teacher is not. Everyone who says you can trust them, you can't. Everyone who says they are telling you the truth, is not. So, it is never wise to go by what people say. It is wise to check out what people are doing. It is good to know God for yourself. **Do not depend on a preacher alone.**

We are told in scripture to test every spirit to see if it is from God. (1 John 4:1) Sometimes that takes time, so you must be patient because sooner or later you will know what you are dealing with. The Bible tells us a good tree can't produce bad fruit and a bad tree can't produce good fruit. You will know them by their fruit (Matthew 7:17-18). It doesn't mean that you won't find a bad piece from time to time on a good tree, but time will tell. No tree is perfect and no person is perfect, but if you keep getting bad fruit over and over. Take note that this is not a good tree.

> ***Do not believe every spirit, but test the spirits to see if they are from God,*** <u>because many false prophets have gone out into the world.</u>
>
> *1 John 4:1*

Why are there so many churches, so many religions, so many sects, so many denominations, so many organizations? This is a great question. The Bible teaches us that there are only two spirits; the Spirit of God and the spirit of the evil one. All of these operating entities on the earth through man is being led by either one or the other. Many have the spirit of the evil one because many operate through the spirit of error.

John responds with telling us in his book, *1 John chapter 5*, that there are three ways we can identify whether we are dealing with a spirit of truth or a spirit of error. We can know whether people truly belong to God or not. The spirit of truth versus the spirit of error can be tested and seen in these three ways:

#1

*There **must** be a confession and professing of Jesus as the Son of God. We **must** acknowledge Him as having come from God in heaven. He **must** be the **only** Savior of our sins and the **only** way to God.* (verse 1,5,10-12)

#2

*There **must** be **obedience** to His commands and **following** of **His teachings**.* <u>The greatest proof is seen in the way we love and treat other people.</u> *(verses 2-3)*

#3

*There **must never be practice or continuance in sin (wrongdoing). Those who belong to God, live righteous, pure, and holy lives.*** (verse 18)

    We must learn to love everybody, respect and honor every God given authority, but in God's name, **do not follow anybody who does not operate in the Spirit of Truth**. Paul said, "Follow me as I follow Christ." (1 Corinthians 11:1) The Good News translation says, "Imitate me as I imitate Christ" and the CEV says, "You must follow my example, as I follow the example of Christ." If you see leaders not practicing what the Bible teaches Christ would do, do not follow them. They are not walking in the truth. In Galatians chapter 1 Paul marveled that so many he had led to Christ were turning away because some had come to pervert the gospel. He said, "Even if an angel seemingly appeared from heaven to lead you away from Christ, don't go for it." We are to stay, far away from anything that would come to deceive us.

    This leads us to those leaders who are counterfeits. The Bible says many false and deceitful workers have disguised themselves as apostles of Christ. (2 Corinthians 11:13) How do we know the counterfeit from the real thing? We are able to tell false servants of God, not by their ability to speak, do miracles, or by what positions they hold. We are able to tell by the absence of the Spirit of God which can be confirmed in their character and actions.

> *Many will say to Me in that day, Lord, Lord, have we not prophesied in Your name, cast out demons in Your name, and done many wonders in Your name? And I will declare to them,* **I never knew you; depart from Me, <u>you who practice lawlessness.</u>**
>
> *Matthew 7:22-23*

The enemy is a liar, counterfeit, and disguiser. He would even appear to you as an angel of light. If he disguises himself, should we be surprised that his servants would not do the same? The anti-Christ himself, will work miraculous signs. Therefore, we must know Christ, the truth, to be able to tell the difference. My former pastor used to tell a story about the workers at the U.S. mint. The mint is where they make the money we use in our country. He said the workers are able to detect a counterfeit bill easily because they are so used to working with the real thing. In the same way, we should be so familiar with the truth; that we can spot a fake immediately.

People who are in a position of authority will be judged more harshly and held accountable for every deed done and every word spoken. Those who are teachers of God's word will be judged with a greater strictness (James 3:1). The Lord shall judge His people. It is a terrible thing to fall into the hands of an angry God. (Hebrews 10:31)

The goal here is not to scare people. The goal is for us to hear the ring of truth and let it resonate, causing those guilty to repent from their sins. We must keep praying for our leaders like God tells us to do. God will show us what to do in prayer. Some believe that Christian leaders who do evil will never pay. It sure seems that way. However, the workers of sin do not get away. Righteous men will not suffer forever while evil men are never brought to judgement or accountability. The Bible tells us:

> *Do not fret because of those who are evil or be envious of those who do wrong; for like the grass they will soon wither, like green plants they will soon die away.*
>
> *Psalm 37:1-2 (NIV)*

The position of a spiritual leader is a very respected and powerful position. There are many who want that power and pursue to be in that place. In Liberia, I have asked hundreds of children what they would like to be when they get older and at least one out of every five boys will say a pastor.

What are they seeing that is drawing them to this profession? I wish I could say it was the call of God alone. We have so many ministers who are using God as a means to fulfill their own agenda and dreams. They are in the ministry to do that which will bring glory to themselves. Too many are in power to serve themselves. Many get caught in this trap. It is part of the pride of life. We want to be great at God's expense. Full of the lust of our eyes, we want what we see. Since it's so important for us to have our desires, we put them before Him. Our churches have been infiltrated by false men who have turned from the truth and lead others from it. They change the gospel message to comply with their own personal desire.

People have been blinded and damaged by the institution of church and religious gatherings that follow man's tradition. They believe they know God when they only have a form of godliness without the true power. They have become entrenched in pride and miss the true reality of a life-giving spirit based on surrender and humility to God. Repentance from sins like lying, sexual immorality, and theft is never taught. Scriptures are read, but not applied to daily life. Having the Holy Spirit's guidance is not taught. Holiness for without which no one can see the Lord is not sought. (Hebrews 12:14)

There are always exceptions, but we also find the importance and need for the blood and sacrifice of Jesus is not mentioned. The true self-sacrificing love of God seen in our behavior to one another is not taught. Giving up our lives to God in everything is not taught. Complete surrender to His will and obedience to His commands is not taught. The importance of having faith in God and growing diligently in the faith of His Word is not taught. We have removed the purpose of being a church for just doing church.

God wants us as leaders to repent and do what is right. Righteousness builds a great people. He wants His people to be holy above anything else. **If a people who call themselves righteous, lived like they say they believed it, our country would change, we would change, and our circumstances would change.** We would stop lying, stop cheating, stop defrauding, stop committing sexual immorality, seek God, humble ourselves, truly love each other, forgive each other, and stop chasing money and material things.

If you are a leader and share the truths in this book with your congregation, it will have little power if you are not living it. Please stop trying to share with others what you yourself are not living. You don't have the power or authority for it to work. **People don't follow what you say, they transfer what you live.** Those who lead many, by their words to righteousness and holiness living, have the power and authority that come from their lifestyle. Words that are good, but don't match your life, have no conviction with you and hardly bring conviction to anybody else. Many of us are blowing hot air and that's all the people are feeling with no real meaning. Life style change where the fruit of God's spirit is seen is the proof of our life and effectiveness. **The attendance of our church, the amount of churches we oversee, our title, and our spiritual network is insignificant to God.** People honor people based on their position and how much power and influence they have, but God doesn't honor people based on this.

Jesus Christ is our Lord and Savior, the Son of God and Creator of everything. He was God taking on the form of man to save us. His greatest condemnation was not against sinners but against the religious leaders. The reason He was so upset at those that presented themselves as His representatives was because their hypocrisy not only caused them to be left out of the Kingdom of Heaven but it prevented those who were truly seeking God from entering. They were keeping innocent souls from finding God through their leadership. The leadership was leading all people astray and away from God. They taught the people to follow the traditions of men instead of the laws of God. They used religion as a position for power to make themselves important, gain money, and live good.

Jesus said many things about those who served as leaders in this religious system set up for church business. They used religion as an opportunity to take advantage of widows and exploit the poor among many other things. The religious leaders were in it for money and power. Jesus pronounced several woes upon them in Matthew chapter 23. Here is a summary: He called them hypocrites who would not enter the kingdom of God and prevented others from coming in. He said that they made followers worse than themselves. He called them the blind leading the blind. He said they neglected justice and mercy while nitpicking others about trivial matters. He said their outside image was clean, while their insides were rotten with greed and self-indulgence. Lastly, he referred to them as murderers.

God wants leaders to view His sheep as just as important as they are. They are to lead by example. They are to wash the feet of their members. They must sacrifice, respect, and serve people. When the leadership is corrupt, it affects the church and others give up and accept corruption as a way of life. My heart is saddened that the love of God is absent in so many that call themselves Christian leaders. It almost seems they have made a pact with the devil to become known and wealthy at the expense of the people of their own church and country.

The real shepherds who know their God, won't leave the sheep to be killed by the wolves, they lay down their life for the sheep. He doesn't leave his sheep, only the false shepherd does because he doesn't care about the sheep. He lets them get devoured.

> *I am the good shepherd. The good shepherd lays down his life for the sheep.* **The hired hand** *is not the shepherd and does not own the sheep. So, when he sees the wolf coming, he abandons the sheep and runs away. Then the wolf attacks the flock and scatters it.* <u>**The man runs away because he is a hired hand and cares nothing for the sheep.**</u>
>
> John 10:11-13

God says those who are HIRED run away. There is a difference between those who are called and those who are hired. The hireling is in it for the position and money mainly. The one who is truly called by God after His heart will love and sacrifice his life for the sheep. Many of our churches are being led by hirelings.

One of my biggest questions from reading about the civil war in Liberia was: Where were the fearless men of God during this time? Not the men and the children soldiers who lost their innocence and lives killing each other on the streets, but where were the men of God, the men of faith? While government leaders were fighting for position and people were running to churches for safety, the church leaders were where? The hirelings ran and those called of the Lord stayed, trusted God and protected the sheep. The righteous are supposed to be bold as lions. The righteous are not supposed to run from the enemy.

> *A wicked person flees when no one is chasing him, but **righteous people are as bold as lions**.*
> *Proverbs 28:1*

In my quest to find out the influence of the church and its leaders during this time, I found a few stories of men who were on a mission and assignment from God who refused to leave, but most so called men of God with high positions, big titles and growing churches were nowhere to be found. The highest religious officials of the land were gone. We have no reports of any male faith leaders coming together in the power of prayer and faith in God before, during, or after the war, but this is what it will take in order to change the tide for Liberia. **When the righteous men do nothing, evil men take control.**

We were given a picture of how the spiritual response of people can affect what happens in the political arena with the women of Liberia who came together to form daily intercessions to stop the war. They had prayer, sacrifice, and a plan of action. They cared more about the lives of their children than about winning a fight. When we love our children more than we love ourselves and our insistence to be right, we can drop our personal and individual wars so we can win the fight for our nation. This happens when we consider others as valuable as we see ourselves. **It is selflessness that builds a nation and selfishness that destroys it.**

Liberia was the first African nation to elect a woman as president. President Ellen Sirleaf Johnson ran with the appeal that the country needed a mother to nurture them back to health. I imagine this was accurate after hearing reports that up to 70% of women may have been raped during the war time. Still, it was a group of fearless women who prayed for five years and even put themselves in harm's way to see the end of the war that took so many human lives. They gathered and refused to be denied and I believe their influence turned the tide.

As it was in Judges, the prophetess Deborah was sent by God to a man named Barak to fight the enemies of God's people and bring true peace to the land. In fear, he refused to go unless the prophetess went. God's response was that the victory would come, but the glory would go to a woman. I pray that God would never have to use women again while Godly men are absent. It is His plan for the men to lead the way spiritually. Christian Liberian men should love and protect their woman and children from future abuses.

When all hell breaks loose, we find out if the Christian worker was sent by God or if he was in it for the money and power. We will find out if they were called by God or hired for the job. There is a judgment that awaits them when they stand before the Lord. Ezekiel 34 gives us a good idea of how God feels about bad shepherds and leaders of His people:

> *Then this message came to me **from the LORD**: "Son of man, **prophesy against the shepherds, the leaders** of Israel. **Give them this message** from the Sovereign LORD: **What sorrow awaits you shepherds who feed yourselves** instead of your flocks. **Shouldn't shepherds feed their sheep?** You drink the milk, wear the wool, and butcher the best animals, but **you let your flocks starve**. You have not taken care of the weak. You have not tended the sick or bound up the injured. You have not gone looking for those who have wandered away and are lost. Instead, **you have ruled them with harshness and cruelty**. So, **my sheep have been scattered** without a shepherd, and **they are easy prey** for any wild animal.*
>
> *Ezekiel 3:1-5*

Many Christians along with their Christian leaders today are powerless because they are disconnected from God and His son Jesus Christ. They are only associated with religion and church. A person praying who is not in right standing with God through Christ is never heard by God. God doesn't listen nor will He answer. The only prayer He will hear at this point is a prayer of confession and repentance from one's wrongdoings.

What many of us call prayer today is actually performance. It is being done for our and other peoples benefit. God is not involved. In this place of hypocrisy, when life becomes filled with great problems, in which there seems to be no solutions for it on the earth, we get to see what Christian leaders are really made out of. We get to see how powerful they really are in God.

Look at the condition of Liberia today with all the churches, men with positions and titles, and religious programs without the power of unity and change for a nation. We continue to have revivals, crusades, and prayer meetings without any major changes. **Revival without repentance is an unimpactful religious event.** It does nothing really. It is a waste of time. It just takes up space. It's a time filler that gives people in your community something to do. God does not attend. People attend in the name of God. The Holy Spirit can't be there because He won't dwell in an unholy environment.

I call out the church leaders to lead their churches by repenting of the sins we have committed against God and one another. I call them out to exchange looking good and looking out only for themselves to become God's spiritual shepherds who serve sacrificially, benefitting the sheep instead of getting fat off of them. God is disgusted by our sinful behavior and His mercy is asking us to please change before it is too late. We must stop lying to ourselves. We must stop ignoring His correction. We must stop making excuses. We must stop sleeping with women in and out of the church. We must stop directly disobeying the scriptures we swear we follow. God is waiting for us to return to Him and repent of doing things our way.

God does not recognize authority from men and organizations. He only recognizes the authority that comes from Him. We can be a success in man's eyes, but a failure in God's eyes. If you are a church leader and you are guilty of not following the Biblical mandate for Christ like leadership and you want to repent, be forgiven, and make things right please pray this prayer:

Father God,

Please forgive me for my pride. Please forgive me for making money my focus instead of making you the focus. Please forgive me for using my power and position to influence others in an ungodly way. Please forgive me Lord for selfishly fulfilling my lustful passions including having sexual affairs with people I am not married to. I have lowered myself to a place of shame and dishonor before the Most-High God. My guilt remains when I refuse to stop these ungodly practices and do not turn away from these behaviors. My heart has been in the wrong place. I have not been completely loyal to you Lord. I need your mercy. I repent and change my ways and direction today. In Jesus Name, Amen.

LIE #12
FATHERLESSNESS IS JUST ANOTHER PROBLEM

He will turn the hearts of the fathers to their children, and the hearts of the children to their fathers; or else I will come and strike the land with total destruction."
Malachi 4:6

Today, as I visited the post office to mail letters, I couldn't help but notice a man waiting outside holding his seven-year old son. The man was kissing his son and his son was hugged closely to his dad. I could feel the love they had for one another. It caught my attention because it was so out of the ordinary. This was not a baby, but a big boy. I commented to the man that this was beautiful to see and how important this was for our boys and girls. They really need it.

Everyone loves to be loved. I have never met anyone who hated to be loved on. Everyone loves to be shown love. Don't be deceived, even those who are grumpy and push you away want this. They may be uncomfortable with showing affection because they are not used to it, but trust me they want it and truly need it. It is universal to want to be loved and be held by someone. God created us this way.

We have a problem that is not outside of our ability to fix. The answer to this problem is within our capability of solving to help transform our communities and world. Fatherlessness is more than a big deal. It is actually one of the biggest problems we face. If you were to ask me, "What is the number one problem in our world today?" I would say, "*Fatherlessness.*" This one issue affects so many of the other issues that plague our nations and world. This one problem unsolved is responsible for keeping whole nations from being able to move forward.

Everything starts with a Father. He is the first and beginning of everything. We refer to God our Creator as our Father. Everything starts with God who is the Father. The Father is the foundation for everything. Everything was made by Him and everything came from Him. Everything in Heaven started with a Father. Everything on the earth started with a father. Every church and community started with a family and every family started with a father. Every marriage starts with a father figure who leaves his family to connect with a woman to begin a family of his own. At the beginning and foundation of heaven and earth, there was a Father and at the end of life on earth in heaven, there will be the union of a Heavenly Father with His children.

We are adversely affected by missing fathers. The father brings too many irreplaceable benefits to our life. A father gives definition in life. He gives purpose. His blessing is needed for the children to carry on their purpose. His absence causes insecurity, many questions, and fear.

If we understand this, how can we just easily ignore the significance a father's role has on everything that happens on the earth. If we dismiss his necessity and contribution, we are completely left without hope. If the father is not represented or has been removed, how can justice, morality, and righteousness stand or function properly. These attributes all come from the Heavenly Father and is given to fathers on the earth for its salvation.

> *When the foundations are being destroyed, what can the righteous do?*
>
> *Psalms 11:3*

The father, as the foundation piece of the family structure, is the key to unlocking the destiny of God for generations to come. The family was the very first institution ordained by God on the face of the earth. The others are church and government. These next two are made up by families and were created to serve the purpose of the families.

Everyone needs a father just like everyone needs a mother. The mother is the feminine expression of the father. Mothers are an extension of the fathers. They are not a replacement for them. Mothers can never be fathers, just like fathers can never be mothers. Each has been given certain characteristics by God necessary for the perfection of the union and the benefit of the family.

Children are scattered all over the world with many different women by many different men because people don't understand the importance of family and fatherhood. They don't know their purpose. When free sex between people who have no permanent commitment with each other replaces God's love and responsibility, then you have human lives that come into the world affected negatively. I like what Myles Munroe says, "Anything you don't understand the purpose for, you will inevitably misuse and abuse." Everything and everybody has been given purpose. Many fathers don't know their purpose. This purpose was given to them by God before they were even born. To fulfill this purpose, they must follow God's instructions.

We have so many children without fathers. We need our fathers involved in the life of their children up to the time they leave this earth. Unfortunately, the seriousness is not seen yet, but the earth will forever be cursed unless the spirit of the Father is fulfilled and seen. (Malachi 4:6)

One way for the enemy of our souls to steal, kill, and destroy lives is to begin early in a child's life to get them to believe lies about God and the world He created. When a father is removed, children are uncovered and the enemy has access and influence in their lives. He uses many different ways to defeat our children. They don't have protection and they are never told who they are. This is the father's job. He was given the responsibility of naming the child in earlier times. The names were always connected to the purpose. Many times, the names were given by God himself.

There has been a purposeful fight to remove God's image of a father and replace it with a secular image. If the correct image is distorted, how can we do anything? What do we have that works better? What can we build on if the unshakable foundation has been replaced with a perishable, makeshift one? How can one stand up or build without a base? No one has ever found a substitute for the father or a family because nothing will ever be able to replace it.

As we discuss this issue, we are actually tracking where the enemy has begun to plant his seeds of low esteem, fear, insecurity, loneliness, feelings of being incapable, and not trusting. These are seen in depression, falsehood, anger, self-destructive addictions, abuse, greed, and selfishness. This whole process starts with a distortion or removal of the Father image. The way we see our earthly father affects the way we see any father, including our Heavenly Father. Until another righteous example is seen and experienced, we can't possibly know and understand how it has changed us.

We are supposed to love people and use things, but we love things and use people. We have been infected by this world's evil system. People are so weary of others including family because they are the people who many times have hurt them the most. I believe that is part of the unexplainable increase in pet owners. Many people love pets and treat them as humans. They get attention, loyalty, and unconditional love from their dog and cat when they can't seem to find it in a cruel, inhumane world from another human being.

We must be careful of believing all psychological reasoning that may suggest a father's absence is not a main factor of our world's basic problems. Don't believe the lie. There is a huge connection in most cases. I believe you can trace almost any societal illness back to the lack of fathers and dysfunctional families.

Now, since everything starts with a father and we acknowledge our need for one, that we were created to have one and to receive from one; what happens if we don't have one or we are not fathered; meaning we do not get what we truly need?

We will have minus, lack, be missing things, be deprived of something that is essential and a necessity. We will be deficient, short of everything we needed, be in the negative, and have a void. It will be seen and played out in our life in some way. We will see it perhaps in our relationships, fears, insecurities, loneliness, handicaps, trust issues, and low confidence. These issues keep coming up in our life and we keep struggling with them.

We must be honest enough with ourselves to admit when we did not get everything we needed and as a result we were impacted negatively. Every solution starts with identifying the problem and dealing with it. The goal is not to blame others, but to assess what has happened to get the correct answers that will lead us to recovery and full health in spirit, soul, and body. The truth is not always easy to deal with, but **what is never admitted, can never be fixed.**

I reflect today on what it must be like for a man to never have known or had his earthly father. In truth, I can't relate because I have always had and known mine. I know that it is very important and without one, there are things that are affected inside and outside of you just by virtue of his absence. This absence could be emotional as well as physical. Some fathers are present, but so far detached from their children, that it is as if they are not there at all. Too many sons and daughters are still looking for a father.

I can remember as a little boy not having my father around at times. This was when he and my mom separated. I never knew where he was or when I would see him again. Sometimes I would lay in my bed at night with an aching heart just wanting my daddy. I didn't know how to verbalize to him how much I wanted him around and how much I needed him to be there. I needed someone to talk to and ask questions, someone to guide me, someone to hold me and tell me it's going to be alright, someone to tell me I was valuable, accepted, and fine and that I had what it took and I could make it. Having a dad involved in your life makes you feel safe and not so fearful. He helps you feel supported and not so alone. There is an assurance and security that is inside you when you experience the support of a loving father.

Figuring out life all alone is hard and scary. You hate having to do everything without guidance or someone teaching you. You experience the feelings of being abandoned, rejected, and neglected. You may even come to expect others to treat you the same way. The worst is you grow up closing up your heart and feelings to everyone as a way to protect yourself. You may subconsciously expect to be left and abandoned by others. You may feel you are not worthy to be loved. You may try to send others away, pushing them to move on, when in secret you want them to stay close. We act this way because we have too much pride now as a man and we never want another man to think that we really need them. It takes a humble man to recognize when he needs someone else. This is not necessarily for livelihood, but for mental and emotional support.

So many men today are so afraid to let another man know how they really feel. I believe it's because they don't know how to have an emotionally bonding relationship with a man because they never grew up with one as a child. How does a man relate to a father as an adult when he never had one as a kid? It's a journey, he has to figure it out. Men taking on the role of a father have to be patient with them.

When I look across the globe today, I count my blessings for having my father in my life. I had somebody to watch and learn from. I believe manhood is caught more than it is taught.

A FATHER'S HEART

I was named after my grandfather. I don't know much about my family history before him. He had two brothers and one sister. I'm not sure what their mother and father were like but they seemed to be a close-knit, hardworking family. They appeared to love and get along with each other. One thing I noticed however, was the absence of personal attention, personal interest, and personal touch given to his children. My grandfather was a great provider. However, words of affirmation and affection was almost nonexistent. This was passed down to the next generation as I'm sure he received it from the previous generation.

Although I knew my dad loved me, there was very little verbal expression or affection of it shown. It was passed down from his dad. When I had my first son and daughter, I followed this same format. By the time my next two sons were born, God had taught me the importance of fatherhood and what my children needed. I did better in some areas because I learned from the best Father there was. I had to pray and surrender my heart in order to get His heart so I could pass that heart on to my children. This is how generations begin to change. It starts with humility and being loved by a God who gives you a love for others.

I remember hearing a story about a news interview. The news reporter was interviewing a guy from a tribe that was in a very long war with another tribe. Many people were being killed. The reporter asked the man, "When did he think the war would end? I never forgot the answer this man gave. He said, "I guess when we love our children more than we love ourselves it will end." It is time for us men to stop fighting for our own selves and start thinking about our children. As I said before, selfishness is killing us, our families, and our nation.

In Malachi 4:6, the fathers are sent forth to break the curse on the earth. They are being challenged by the spirit of the Lord, through his messengers like Elijah, to turn their hearts where God's heart is – children. The earth will forever see destruction until there is a reunion between fathers and their children. Our Heavenly Father broke the spiritual curse over mankind by loving His own son and using Him to show His love for all of His creation. We must follow His example.

NEED FOR LOVE

The number one need in humanity is love. There is no greater love than God's. His love is shown by Him giving us His best gifts. **These are not physical things**. The love of a real father provides three things that are needed in the life of every person:

- *Love is affirmed with a voice*

God tells us He loves us. He left us His words that we might read them and He places them in our heart when we receive Him. He reveals the importance of this characteristic of speaking love through his relationship with His own son, our Savior Jesus Christ. When Jesus was being baptized on the earth, after coming out of the water, God said, "This is my son, whom I love, with Him I am well pleased." We all need to hear our fathers tell us they love us and they are pleased with us; even Jesus received this from His own Father. Please don't miss this powerful example.

The reason it is so hard for us to tell our children we love them and we are pleased with them men, is not just because we are not used to it, but there is a spiritual fight against us from principalities and powers of spiritual wickedness over our countries that will be broken when we begin to do this. It will break chains of bondage that the enemy has had over our sons and daughters in the earth. The enemy will use the spirit of pride in us to keep us from allowing this to happen. We must be broken by God and break this curse.

- *Love is seen in fellowship*

God shows us He loves us by desiring to be with us. He has given the life of His only begotten son to save us from sin and bring us to Him. The Holy Spirit represents God's presence that is with us today. God's best gift is Himself. Little children understand this very well. They would rather have a loving father be with them, then for them to work all the time and bring them material gifts. The relationship is the most treasured gift you can have in this life. It is what our children need and desire. Let us stop buying into the lies of this world, where we put our emphasis on our self, work, and giving material things. We must understand what is really needed and not leave our children alone.

- *Love is felt with touch*

God allows us to feel His presence through His Holy Spirit. If you then, being evil, know how to give good gifts to your children, how much more will your Heavenly Father give the Holy Spirit to those who ask Him!" (Luke 11:13) It is our fathers desire to touch us. Jesus picked up children and held them in His arms. Jesus touched the lepers, who nobody else would touch. He allowed the disciple John to lay his head on His chest. He allowed a woman to wash His feet and wipe it with her hair. He put His hands on the blind eyes, on the deaf ears, and the mute tongue. He told Thomas to touch His hands, feet, and side. He washed all His disciple's feet. God is now waiting to hold you in His arms when He sees you. In the meantime, His Holy Spirit is here so you can experience His touch. What are we waiting for to hold our own children in our arms?

God spoke to me many years ago and said, "I have called you to be a father." Today God sends me to the nations so that people can receive the Father they so desperately need. I am not Him. I just express Him so that they can receive Him. The more children I reach out to, the more father wounds I can help heal and father's I can raise up.

As a father called by God with many children around the world, the greatest responsibility I have is to let them know how uniquely valuable they are: for they need to be constantly reminded. They need to know that it's alright to get close because their Father will never leave. I pray that God will continue to work His fathering spirit through many more willing vessels.

WOUNDED

You may find that by not having a father, you have control issues. A person needs to be in control because they feel they have to become their own security since they had no control over the things that made them insecure. They will now do their best to control everything that gives them security in life. We may even feel threatened and reject all the people and things we can't control.

The things that one can try to control are natural things, but they are unable to control God and the spiritual things that bring real fulfillment. This is why sometimes there is a struggle to submit to God. Submission to God's authority and His designated authority through man becomes an issue. We want to be our own man without any man telling us what to do. The man that God wants is a man that surrenders all control to Him.

Some jobs have done a study and found that men who have had a bad relationship with their earthly fathers tend to not be the best employees. Some screen how they hire based on this. I believe this supports the belief of how men are still affected by a father. A person's relationship with their father affects their attitude about life.

Remember, God's love fixes everything because He is all righteous with absolutely no defects. His perfect love cast out any fears we may have. There is no greater love in the world. God's love is expressed by fathers and mothers who follow in His footsteps. It is the Father who gives us our purpose and identity. Every one of us need the Father's love expressed to us. If we ask, I believe He will even give us His example in the flesh. He will use Godly father figures on the earth. In the meantime, He wants us to know for sure about His Fatherly love.

> *And I will be a Father to you and you will be my sons and daughters, says the Lord Almighty.*
> *2 Corinthians 6:18 (NIV)*

> *Though even if my father and mother forsake and abandon me, the Father Lord will receive me.*
> *Psalm 27:10*

> *Father of the fatherless and defender of widows - this is God, whose dwelling is holy.*
> *Psalms 68:5 (NLT)*

What He is saying is, we need a Father. In order to get the Father, He understands we need, we must first let go of everything we have been using to medicate ourselves in the absence of the Father's love. This may be boyfriends, girlfriends, drugs and alcohol, entertainment, finding fulfillment in food, work, and achievements. All of these momentary pleasures and more are just temporary fixes to fill the Father void. We just need the daddy relationship to give our life true meaning. We just need the Father's love; for Him to grab us in His arms and tell us how much we are loved. This will cause all our fears to go away. We can find a place to rest and get comfort.

Think how much the Father loves us. He loves us so much that he lets us be called his children, as we truly are. But since the people of this world did not know who Christ is, they don't know who we are.

1 John 3:1 (CEV)

He loves us so much that He adopted us. Why? Just because He wanted us. There was no performance, no work, no beauty, or actions needed on our part. We did not have to earn His love either. Our own family members who are not walking with the Lord, don't really know who we are and how valuable we are. They are in the dark. They don't get it. Your natural dad may not have understood this. He may have been ignorant and disconnected from the Heavenly Father, so he couldn't do what God wanted. He may have been saved, but may have not allowed God to rule in many areas of his life. FORGIVE HIM. We must now leave behind the earthly father for the Heavenly Father. **You will find your true destiny in the Father you came from, not came through.** If you were negatively affected by a mother, family member, or anyone else in your community growing up, you can apply this forgiving process to them as well.

Most importantly, we must purge our being of all poison that is inside us from holding on to what other people did to us. God says, if you forgive others, I will forgive you, but if you don't understand how much undeserved mercy I have toward you and you choose not to forgive those who wronged you, then I can't forgive you. (Matthew 6:14-15) This is part of the healing and repentance needed to change the destiny of a person, family, and nation. Let's get clean. Say these words that apply to you and mean it from your heart, giving everything to God:

- *I forgive my earthly father for not being present*
- *I forgive my earthly father for not thinking about me*
- *I forgive my earthly father for not protecting me*
- *I forgive my earthly father for not being there*

- *I forgive my earthly father for not giving me counsel and guidance*
- *I forgive my earthly father for not showing me love*
- *I forgive my earthly father for not giving me attention*
- *I forgive my earthly father for not showing me affection*
- *I forgive my earthly father for not giving me affirmation*
- *I forgive my earthly father for not praying for me*
- *I forgive my earthly father for not blessing me*
- *I forgive my earthly father for not standing up for me*
- *I forgive my earthly father for not apologizing when he was wrong*
- *I forgive my earthly father for not considering my feelings*
- *I forgive my earthly father for not accepting me for me.*

These are all the things that are supposed to be given to a child from his father. We must receive this from our Heavenly Father and trust Him to meet these needs in our life.

HOW THE FATHER'S LOVE WORKS

The most challenging part of our Father's love is understanding how it operates fully. We as human beings have a very superficial idea and humanistic definition of what love is, what it is supposed to do, and what it is not. What it won't, what it will allow, what it can't let happen and so on. We say if it is really love than it ought to do this and it shouldn't do this, but God is love and His love which is real love is not limited to or operates according to our feelings and opinions about how love should work, instead He gets to define it.

As we look in His word, I believe He gives us a great indicator or description of love in the New Testament:

> *Love is patient and kind. Love is not jealous or boastful or proud or rude. It does not demand its own way. It is not irritable, and it keeps no record of being wronged. It does not rejoice about injustice but rejoices whenever the truth wins out. Love*

never gives up, never loses faith, is always hopeful, and endures through every circumstance.

1 Corinthians 13:4-7 (NLT)

Now when we see how God defines love, there are some things we can conclude: Real love does not cause pain or hurt, it does not kill, and it does not cause problems, trouble, or discomfort. However, real love does not prevent it from happening to us or allowing us to experience all these things in this fallen, evil world we live in. When God tells us something we don't want to hear, or allow us to go through something we don't want to feel, or experience something we don't like, do we recognize that He still loves us?

Part of growing up and becoming mature is dealing with things that don't feel good but we understand it was good for us even when it is not good to us. I am not saying God wants bad things to happen to us to teach us. **God's allowance is not God's initiation.** He is not the giver of bad things, but He is the giver of free choice and He knew that would mean we may experience some bad things. He didn't stop them because of free choice and He knew He was greater and would still bring out the best of whatever the enemy and humanity would try to do.

GOD'S DISCIPLINE

Discipline is good for me. I need discipline. God knows this so He in His love disciplines us as well. You can't have real love without discipline. God disciplines those He loves:

> *For whom the LORD loves He chastens, and scourges every son whom He receives."*
>
> *Hebrews 12:6*

> *For whom the LORD loves He corrects, just as a father the son in whom he delights.*
>
> *Proverbs 3:12*

If God does not discipline us then we are not really His child. The proof we belong to Him is He handles us when we need handling. It is a sign of love. No chastening feels good at the moment but it will benefit us in the end. When He stops correcting us when we are wrong, we better start worrying because that means we may be illegitimate. We may be a fake family member, what we called growing up - a play sister or play brother.

> *Now no chastening seems to be joyful for the present, but painful; nevertheless, afterward it yields the peaceable fruit of righteousness to those who have been trained by it.*
> *Hebrews 12:11*

Our wonderful end is the goal. Our loving Father is looking at the end. We are looking at the moment. This is why we fight and struggle many times with understanding what God is doing in our life because our view is different. We want now and He is doing what is best for us in the long run. He loves us too much to give us what we want now. He knows giving us what we want now will cause lasting pain later. He is looking at us from a different perspective than we are looking at. Thank God. We need somebody who has our back and who can see what we can't. He will get us where we need to be without us coming up short.

Since His view is different, His plans are different. His movement in our lives is a process of constructing and removing things. We must trust Him. We trust His love for us. His discipline has to do with guidance, leading, training, and correcting. He desires to bring us into eternal life. He wants to give us an expected end and what will be most beneficial for us. He is thinking about permanent blessings. Therefore, it is necessary to perfect our character through patience and suffering. It is His will that we produce much fruit.

This is why we are not commanded to make Christian converts but disciples. You can't do this without discipline. The goal of the Father's love, is for us as His children to be like Him and be with Him. We can't live in harmony with the Father unless we share the same characteristics and desires.

Our struggle is we have been taught in life and sometime erroneously from the church that God's goal is to make us feel good, bless us, and give us everything we like and want. Instead, it's to make sure we have what we really need, His presence and His character. Therefore, the loving Father will put us on His potter's wheel as a child in the hands of a loving father. He will keep us there to form, mold, and make us. In order to start this process of making vessels, a piece of clay must be soft and moldable. This means we have to be broken. Many of us come to him already molded and hardened by the external world we grew up in and our shape has already been formed. Our image looks nothing like what He had planned. He has to break and grind and take us down to a palpable state.

We don't always want to be broken down. We still like what we have already become many times. However, it interferes with God's plan and purpose for our lives. Everything must be broken down to the wet mold and He starts all over again. This is the forming process he's working out in us and the more powerful He is making us, the more process and work that is needed.

According to His use of us, determines how long and how much is needed. Our time of molding is also determined by the cooperation of the clay in His hands; which is us. Every time we jump out because it is getting uncomfortable, the longer it will take. Let us let the loving Father discipline us and let Him get the most He can out of us. He loves us too much not to do what is best.

MOVING FORWARD

God wants us to get the heart of the Father and pass it on. Our children need fathers to train them. The church has to be in the presence of God to do this. We must also be in the presence of our children to share this.

I have been a part of many churches with many female single parents who were crying out to find some Godly men that would play the role of mentor for their growing sons. I've seen coaches, teachers, and youth pastors take on some of these added responsibilities because of their love and concern for the youth. In the church we have an overwhelming amount of disinterested so-called Christians who love themselves, only their own families, and have time for no one or nothing else. This is extremely concerning since I believe the church should lead in reaching others and looking after orphans. The people that are most vulnerable are the people God is most concerned with. We are supposed to be God's representatives but we are least concerned many times or involved in what is happening with children in need.

I never understood how churches could focus on getting money for new buildings, offices, schools, transportation, and crusades while the orphans and widows in the community around them go without. Our priorities are not God's. I see many with more than enough clothing and shoes, but others in the church without hardly anything. They buy even more new clothing for themselves when they know others have hardly anything. What kind of Christianity is this? In the book of James, we are told pure religion is looking after the orphans and widows. Our involvement in nurturing our children makes an incredible difference. God is waiting for us to do His work in this area.

We must choose this day if we are going to do something about this subject. The enemy is out to distort the image of the father and kill our sons and daughters. He lies to our children and tells them while they are holding their broken hearts, "you don't need him," "you can do better without him." The truth is we need our fathers. The children help bring to pass the purpose of the father. God the Father had his purpose accomplished through His son, Jesus Christ. The enemy knows this is how God works, so he fights against this so it will not come to pass.

TRAINING

David is known as a man after God's own heart. David had several sons the Bible tells us. He loved all his sons but he wasn't involved much in all of their training. This ended up coming back to hurt him. His own son Absalom, whom he didn't train or correct as a youth, grew up and tried to kill him and take his throne away.

His son Amnon raped his sister, David's daughter from another wife. When David had his son Solomon, he spent much time with him. He trained him and prepared him to take his place on the throne. He surpassed his father as one of the most honored, wisest, and richest kings ever to live. This is the legacy we can have from investing in our children like God had determined from the beginning. **Remember, our children will not become what we tell them but what we show them.** If we leave them to themselves, what steps will they follow? If our life is crooked and deceptive, we will reproduce that in them. As the saying goes, "The apple doesn't fall far from the tree." In other words, you can usually see what the tree is like from looking at what it produced.

In Luke chapter 16, a loving father lost his son to selfishness, arrogance, and discontentment after being trained in his house. The son went out on his own to find his way before he was ready. He ended up losing everything including his future inheritance that had been given to him. At his lowest moment, he came to his senses and said I will go back and apologize to God the Father and my earthly father for what I have done. I will humble myself to a lower position since I don't feel worthy to be his son anymore. The scripture further tells us, his father was looking out for his return while he was still far away. His father was so excited to see his son return. He ran to him, kissed him, put some new clothes on him, gave him a ring, had a servant prepare plenty of good food, and prepared a festive party on his behalf. Why? This is what a loving father does.

There is nothing better than the relationship between a father and his children. This is how God feels. When a child comes to Him, the Bible says there is rejoicing in Heaven over one soul who turns from his sins. (Luke 15:10) If God is excited about all His children, not wanting to lose even one, what is our problem? Today we need the Father's love. We need the right example to see and receive the expression of the love of the Father. We need His love expressed by fathers who follow in His footsteps.

Father God,

Please help us to get our act together and see where your heart is at. Let our hearts be one together with you in love. Let us demonstrate this love to our children. In Jesus Name. Amen

LIE #13
WE UNDERSTAND BLESSINGS AND CURSES

"See, I am setting before you today a blessing and a curse...
Deuteronomy 11:26

God told me one day, "You need to be extremely careful of the words that come out of your mouth." He then brought a scripture to my remembrance: "But I tell you that every careless word that people speak, they shall give an accounting for it in the day of judgment." (Matthew 12:36 NASB) When I took a moment to really ponder what God was telling me, I immediately started thinking about the way I let words flow freely out of my mouth without even thinking too much sometimes. I thought about the words that I had spoken which were not positive or edifying. The words that were critical, accusatory, and judgmental. I began to ask the Lord to forgive me for every word that I allowed to come out of my mouth that is not in agreement with His will. I asked Him to please make a note on His accounting book when He calls me into account, that this day I repented from speaking these words, so I would not stand before Him ashamed.

This was just the beginning for me in this journey of understanding how much our words impact our life. You see, at first, I was only concerned about making sure I won't be held accountable for all the useless words that I speak, until I realized that these words won't just hurt me at the judgement seat, but are hurting my life here and now.

What you say can preserve life or destroy it; so, you must accept the consequences of your words.
Proverbs 18:21 (GNT)

Life and death are surely in the power of the tongue. What happens to you in this life is directly tied to what is going on with your tongue. God set it up this way. We were created in His image and likeness. God speaks what is on His mind and heart and brings it to pass with His voice. He spoke the world into existence. He gave man authority on earth to do the same thing; speak things into existence. He allowed the first man, Adam, to name all the animals. His words framed his environment and as long as he spoke the words of life from God, he was fine. When he disobeyed God and followed the words of Satan, mankind became lost and everything around him changed for the worse.

We are told Jesus appeared to destroy the works of the devil (1 John 3:8). He came to show us the power we have in our words. He demonstrated this when He spoke to the fig tree and told it not to produce anymore and it withered and died. (Mark 11:14-21) He says, "Whatever we bind on earth, will be bound in heaven and whatever we loose on earth, will be loosed in heaven." (Matthew 18:18) This is of course, according to His will. He said, "If you have faith and do not doubt, you can say to a mountain be removed and cast into the sea and it will be done." (Matthew 21:21) This again is having faith in what He has said, not what we think and want alone. The tongue is a very small part of our body, but can cause the whole course of one's life to change. (James 3:6) There are many scriptures that we can share that reiterate the power of our words affecting our daily life.

What we need to understand is our words were given to us to accomplish God's purpose, not our own. When our words match His will and purpose, they are being used for the reason He created them. When our words are otherwise, they go against what He intended. The words that we speak out of our mouths, come from the things we process in our mind and download to our heart. That's why we are told, "Be diligent to guard your heart, for everything you do flows from it." (Proverbs 4:23) For out of the heart the mouth speaks. (Luke 6:45) Listen to someone long enough and you can get a good idea what they are all about.

God's words are synonymous with blessings. The word bless is to speak well of, favor, and give an inheritance. A blessing is freely given. It's not something you have to work for or work to retain. It only requires you to trust and obey for complete access. Blessings are initiated by God, not by man. They are only received by man. Like everything else with God, the blessing starts as an intangible thing but always ends tangible. Blessings are things you can't see first because they are based on God's promises. Blessings are the receiving of God's promise. It is like knowing you have an inheritance and coming into it. We as His children are recipients of these blessings and are given the ability to bless others as He desires.

There are spiritual blessings and physical blessings. Both are involved when God mentions blessing. If we receive a blessing from Him that is physical, it is a result of a spiritual blessing. One is a prelude to the other. It is a prerequisite. This means in order for something to happen, another thing is required to take place before it. For example: 3 John 1:2 says, "I wish that you would prosper and be in health even as your soul prospers." As John sent greetings to the church, he desired and prayed the will of God for them. It was God's will that they would enjoy good health and receive material blessings in this life. However, it was always to follow after how well their soul was doing. **Our physical blessings are a result of our soul condition which is a result of our spiritual condition.**

Our soul consist of our mind, will, and emotions. We have been blessed as children of God with all spiritual blessings in Christ Jesus. This means God has given us spiritual authority so we can attain in this life all that is connected to Godliness in every area. Our spirit man who should be leading the way, helps us to transform our mind to the way God wants us to think, conform our will to want and desire what God wants, and mold our heart to affectionately chase with passion those things that please God. It is in this place that God hears our prayers and answers them in the natural, because we are really connected to Him and we are asking according to His will and not our own desires. Any purpose and plan we embark on outside of His, is not His responsibility and do not have His blessing.

I had made up my mind, when I entered college after high school, that I was going into business. I had already received my call to ministry, but I saw it as a side thing. It was not something I wanted to focus and give myself fully to. I started taking business courses at school and I had started my own business and found a little success. However, I noticed when I would reach a certain level, no matter how hard I seemed to work, things would go down again. Being a dedicated believer, I cried out to God asking Him what more could I do. I told Him, He promised to bless His people who followed Him and I was not experiencing this. When I finally got quiet from all my noisemaking, I heard a voice within me say, "You want me to bless your thing, but I don't just bless anything - I only bless my thing. He then said, "What did I tell you to do?" It was that night, that I made the commitment to trust God fully and go to Bible school to engage in full time ministry.

When we look at the story of Balaam, Balak, and Israel in Numbers chapter 22, we will see further that blessings and curses are designed to work within the framework of what comes out of God's mouth. So many ministers of God have this wrong. They don't speak for God and they definitely don't say what is on His mind, rather they speak what is on their mind. As we are His people, we are also His mouthpiece in the earth. Where we get in trouble is when we use our mouths for our own benefit and we agree with the enemy instead of God.

In this story, God's people are traveling, ultimately to take possession of the lands He has given them as an inheritance. They are moving forward and it doesn't appear they can be stopped. They have whipped the Amorites and are camped next to Moab. King Balak of Moab, along with his people, are afraid and the king decides to hire a prophet, turned sorcerer, to curse God's people in an attempt to stop them. Balaam, the prophet/sorcerer, wants to get paid for his services by this king, but is having trouble getting permission from God who warns him not to go because these people belong to Him and are blessed. As He puts it, "You can't curse what I have already blessed." King Balak is insistent that he comes and Balaam continues to try to convince God to let him go. Finally, God relents, telling him he can go but must only speak His words. While on his way, God in His anger is ready to kill Balaam, but the donkey is used by God to speak and rebuke the mad prophet turned sorcerer. He gets there but is only allowed to bless Israel four times. We find out later, because he is unable to curse God's people, he teaches the king of Moab how to get Israel to curse themselves through sexual immorality and idol worship.

There is much we can learn here about blessings and curses. First, if God calls you blessed and you are in right fellowship with Him, it doesn't matter what someone else does; they can't change it. Next, God will frustrate the plans of your enemies and in their attempt to curse you, you will receive more blessings. Lastly, the only way blessings give way to curses for God's people is if they live in disobedience to God's commands.

Blessings and curses work in our life based on conditions. Our actions and behaviors determine which one is currently working in our life. In Deuteronomy chapter 11, God told His people He was giving them two options. They could either love Him with everything, being careful to obey all He commanded and receive His blessings or not obey Him and turn to worship other gods, receiving a curse. We must understand that curses are a result of not having the blessings at work. The blessings include one being covered and kept from experiencing what comes with being under a curse. In other words, we don't have to curse to be cursed, the absence of blessing puts us in that place. We are now susceptible to everything that is not protected under a blessing. We only have two choices. There is no gray area or in between place. I always tell people that we never stay in the same place spiritually. We are either growing or we are dying. We are either moving forward or taking steps backward. Life and the world we live in, forces us daily to make a choice that either takes us closer or moves us further away from God.

MYTHS ABOUT BLESSINGS

Many professing Christians don't study God's word or spend enough time with Him to really know Him and His ways. The danger is they come to their own conclusions based on what they imagine, what somebody told them, or using the limited knowledge they have. We are quick to make assumptions about how things work, instead of seeking the answers in God's word to find out His truth. Hosea 4:6 says, "My people are destroyed for a lack of knowledge." Here are some false beliefs we have about the subject of blessing and cursing:

Myth #1
Everything good that happens to humans
is a blessing from God.

There is a difference between God's blessings and God's goodness and mercy. God's blessings are God's approval on us. They are tied to obedience and they result in God receiving the greatest glory in that particular situation. The favor of God is seen because of our obedience to Him. However, God's goodness and mercy is shown to all despite our disobedience. It may appear that God is silent about it and therefore it is not important to Him, but God knows exactly what He is doing.

There are people who are killing and stealing every day. They are making a lot of money dishonestly. They may be eating good, visually living good, and doing whatever they want in this life that makes them feel good. They may even be saying God has blessed them, but we know that God does not bless or put His approval on sinners or the work of sin. So, how is it that they are doing exceedingly wicked but enjoying the best of this world without suffering any consequences right now? Is God fair? Where is justice?

There are a few things I have come to learn about life and God. **First, we are all God's creation, but we are not all God's children.** He extends mercy to all His creation. There are laws at work in the earth regardless of whether a man fears God. The law of sowing and reaping where every action has a consequence, good or bad, is one example. God made a promise about the earth after the flood that as long as the earth remains, there will be seedtime and harvest, night and day, hot and cold, summer and winter. (Genesis 8:22) He also says,

…...he causes his sun to rise on the evil and the good, and sends rain on the righteous and the unrighteous.
Matthew 5:45 (NASB)

These are God's promises to mankind. This is his mercy at work. This is God's goodness demonstrated to the righteous and unrighteous alike. God is fair and just and also loving, merciful, and full of compassion. He does not want anyone to perish. (2 Peter 3:9) He demonstrates His mercy to man for a time, hoping they will respond to His appeal and change. If we don't ever change, we are judged, condemned, and will ultimately reap the total punishment we rightly deserve.

Since God is still merciful, not wanting anyone to die and be eternally condemned, it will appear He is doing nothing. In actuality He is doing everything through His servants on the earth to get a sinner's attention. He knows if they don't get right, this will be all the good they can experience. His compassion gives opportunity for them to change. There are many so called blessings that these sinners enjoy that are actually curses, they just take time to manifest. To insure we will not wake up one day, finding we have reaped negative consequences from something received, we better make sure, we are in God and it came from God. Let us ask the question, "Did God do this and do it His way? Otherwise it may very well have a curse attached to it.

When we look at this, we understand that just because we receive good things does not mean God was the one who blessed us. His blessings are extended only to all His children. Are sinners not blessed? Isn't everyone blessed? I submit to you my answer would be NO. Blessings only come from God. Yes, and every GOOD and PERFECT gift comes from God. However, we must understand that **Satan can reward his servants.**

This has nothing to do with God. Satan can act and cause things to happen as god of this world through man's submission to him and God's permission. Satan promised Jesus all the things of the world if He would bow down and worship Him. Many have received the riches of this world by selling their souls for wealth, fame, and power; in doing this they have surrendered to the devil's will. The children of the devil are rewarded by the devil temporarily. In the end, the deceptive bait of his so-called blessing given to them, will leave them hopeless for the rest of eternity.

Myth #2
When good things happen to Christians,
it means God is pleased with them.

The scripture tells us, "The blessings of the Lord makes one rich and no sorrow is added to it." (Proverbs 10:22) These are the positive results from God's blessing on our life. His blessings are different from what the world considers blessings. We know they are from God because He distinguishes by insuring there is absolutely no ill will or pain, hurt, stress, or punishment or curse connected.

Many have come to believe God approves of your lifestyle based on what you have and your life *comfortability*. A false message has been preached with the focus being on attaining things and having nice things in this world. People get a new car, new house, new church building and we call it a blessing. This is not necessarily a blessing. Did God provide it His way? Or did we manipulate, cheat people, steal funds or accomplish it wrongly by our own hands? Was God really involved in the process or was it the work of the hands of man? We must be careful not to assume when something good happens, we are pleasing God and everything is fine. This is not the way our effectiveness is determined. For it to be God, His fingerprints must be all over it.

Anything that has God's blessing on it, is beyond our effort and represents His presence and He gets all glory. He is completely involved and it has His touch and supernatural provision. There is absolutely no sorrow attached to it. (Proverbs 10:22) God's blessings always bring about glory to God, not to man. Did God get any glory from this happening? Did this situation cause people who witnessed it to praise and worship God? If the focus is more on the thing we got, than on Him, without proof of His provision beyond our human effort, we shouldn't be quick to attach that blessing to God. We also should not ignore how we live our life, thinking it doesn't matter what I am doing because of the good things I am receiving.

Myth #3
When bad things happen to me,
this means I am under a curse.

Some believe it is the physical outward signs of what is happening that determine whether you are blessed or cursed. If bad things are going on in my life, this means I'm not blessed versus when good things happen, now I'm blessed. This is just false. First, God is not like man, where He is constantly changing His mind. He doesn't give and take constantly from His children. His promises are yes and amen. When God blesses His children, they are blessed. Being blessed is a state of being. Being blessed is who I am, not based on what is being done. It is not dependent on what is happening or not happening in my life externally. I'm blessed because I am in Him and I know that whatever is happening, my Father is always in control. Whether things are seemingly going my way or not, whether I have trouble and adversity or not, I am still blessed as someone in right standing with God.

When we look at Jesus and what He went through, was there ever a time that He wasn't blessed? He fed five thousand, healed the blind, the lame, the deaf, turned water into wine and we say He was blessed. He was also attacked by a mob in the garden, He was spit on, hit, beat, and crucified; now Is He no longer blessed? Do you see how ridiculous this is? Look at the fathers of the faith: When David was running from Absalom, he was still blessed. When Naomi lost her husband and sons to death, she was still blessed. When Abraham and Sarah were old with no children, they were still blessed. When Daniel was in the lion's den nothing changed, and when the disciple Stephen was being stoned, God received His spirit. We could go on and on. Paul said he was shipwrecked, was hungry, thirsty, bit by a snake, imprisoned, beaten, stoned, and whipped many times; at any of these times, did he cease from being blessed?

In Matthew chapter 5 Jesus said, "We are blessed when we are persecuted for righteousness sake and when people insult us and tell lies on us because of our faith in Him."

We must stop equating blessings with physical comfort. God does not guarantee as a child of God we will not have many trials. His only guarantee for His blessed children is He will never leave us or forsake us. (Hebrews 13:5) Jesus told His disciples, "In this world, you will have trouble, but be of good cheer because I have overcome the world." (John 16:33) We will always have access to Him. When we have Him, we are blessed and have everything we need. He gave us eternal life and nothing can take that away and nothing can separate us from Him. The joy, peace, love, and rest that He gives us remains. Since the world didn't give it to us, the world can't take it away.

Myth #4
God's goal for me in this life
is to be physically blessed.

Our life in Christ is about the relationship we have with our Lord; our journey and walk with Him. The blessing is not the focus, as much as the relationship. The benefits of the relationship are His promise, blessings, and reward. If we are only looking for the blessings, then we missed what the Christian life is all about. The blessings and benefits are the added things. God Himself is the real joy.

I am just now learning to enjoy the journey of walking and trusting God. His presence becomes the most important part of the journey. The presents are not as much. As you walk with Him, you come to the place where you rather have Him than what's in His hands.

Blessings are not about what we get but who we are. What kind of person we are determines if we are blessed? When Jacob asked God to bless him, he was asking God to change his character. This is why God asked him his name, then changed it to Israel. Jacob was already rich when he asked. There is so much more to blessings than the riches in this world. I pray we don't miss this. I am a receiver of who I am. I am a recipient of my own character. It has always been about who we are, not what we have. If the world's materials brought about the destruction of evil and the salvation of souls, we would have witnessed it by now. However, on the contrary, they seem to distract and get in the way of most professing Christians witness of the real answer our world needs. Look at what the scripture says:

> *The seeds that fell among the thorn bush are also people who hear the message.* ***But they start worrying about the needs of this life. They are fooled by the desire to get rich and to have all kinds of other things. So, the message gets choked out, and they never produce anything.***
> *Mark 4:18-19 CEV*

We are to be salt with taste to this world and light in the darkness of this world. We don't need all the comforts of this life to accomplish our purpose, nor is this God's focus. We have much more important things to give and do. We have the answer for the world about eternal life.

UNDERSTANDING CURSES

In our effort to understand how curses work, we find that curses are words used to invoke supernatural harm. Jesus came to remove the curse brought through man's disobedience and agreement with the enemy. This is sin and it is a curse. Christ became sin (curse) on the cross to defeat it. (Galatians 3:13) Through His blood and in His name, we gain victory over every curse. We are set free from it and no longer align ourselves to it.

We as believers in Christ are not to condemn sinners. We follow our Lord who does not condemn sinners in the world. (John 3:17) The Bible says they condemn themselves by not believing God's testimony. We also don't curse those who sin, they are under a curse already unless they accept God's way. Our job is to bring them to God. We want them saved, delivered, and blessed because this is our Father's will.

Spiritual authority is given to us to bring about the will of God in the area He has given to us. We are responsible for what happens when we are given authority over our house, children, church, business, nation, or other territories. All those who operate within the territory God has given to us, look to us for spiritual leadership. Our authority is not given to us to speak anything against anyone. Remember, we are only to speak for God, not according to our own feelings and thoughts. Any words spoken that do not come from God are lies and illegitimate. They work in cooperation with Satan. **God NEVER gives spiritual leaders the authority or permission to curse other people**.

> *And so, blessing and cursing come pouring out of the same mouth. Surely, my brothers and sisters, this is not right.*
> *James 3:10 (NLT)*

This is especially true of fellow believers who God has determined to bless. Anytime someone says: "I will pray something negative or bad happens to you," they are operating in the sin of witchcraft. Anytime you try to control or force your will upon someone else, you are doing the same thing witches, warlocks, and soothsayers do with their spells. If a spiritual leader threatens you and says, "You will regret it if you don't leave or if you don't stay." This is once again witchcraft. Satan is the accuser of the brethren. So, you are following the footsteps of Satan when you do this. Words like, "you will die" or "rot in hell" or "you will never be nothing." All of these type of negative pronouncements over another person's life is the work of evil. The one who does this is now acting in God's place. They are condemning and making something permanent that God never did. This is not the will of God.

> *But I say, **if you are even angry with someone, you are subject to judgment! If you call someone an idiot, you are in danger** of being brought before the court. And **if you curse someone you are in danger of the fires of hell.***
> *Matt 5:22 (NLT)*

This scripture admonishes us about what we are pronouncing over people. It is not focused just on the name you call them, but the meaning behind the name. You are telling them they are a fool, which is giving them a permanent identity God never gave them. This word means you are calling a person made in God's image worthless and not valuable, but God thought they were worth dying for. You are saying they have no worth. This is dangerous. God takes this seriously. We can't make that call because we did not create them, God did. We also don't know everything like God does. We must be very careful how we treat each other and speak to each other and what we say about each other.

The Judge of all tell us in 1 Corinthians 4:5, "Judge nothing before the appointed time, and wait for God who will reveal everything." Could we be condemning someone forever based on a temporary character flaw? God is in the business of redeeming and saving, not condemning. How can we truly be His servants, if we are working against Him?

God's word instructs us to bless our brethren and our enemies with our mouth. Yet, I see and hear my dear Liberian pastors and brothers speaking curses on other people with their mouths; people putting curses on other people. This practice is from the enemy, not of God.

> *With the tongue we bless our Lord and Father, and with it we curse men, who have been made in God's likeness.*
>
> *James 3:9*

James is telling us what we are doing and continues by telling us this is not good. When we speak curses over others, we are doing the very thing the ruler of darkness does. We are copying Satan, who is the adversary of men and the accuser of the brethren. He uses his tongue to stand before the Lord and speak against them day and night (Revelations 12:10).

Christians are not his children. We as believers do the exact opposite of this. We bless those who curse us. This means we don't predict or speak evil, doom, or death over others. We speak well over those who speak evil against us. We are told in scripture that we are to repay hate with good and persecution with prayer. God has mercy on the unbeliever like He has on the believer. It also tells us we would be just like the ungodly, if we only loved those that loved us. We are to follow the example of our Father in heaven and be like He is (Matthew 5:43-48). Are we acting like our Father in heaven? Are we speaking life and blessings over all of God's creation, no matter who they are or what they have done?

> ***Bless those who curse you***, and pray for those who mistreat you.
> Luke 6:28 (NIV)

The Bible further helps us to understand this principle when we look in the book of Jude and it tells us that angelic beings refuse to slander one another. They also honor authority among themselves. They follow order and do not correct any authorities that were placed over them even if fallen. They await God's instructions and speak only His words. This is why they say to Satan, who was higher in order than they were before his fall, "Satan, the Lord rebuke you." (Jude 1:9) They know one must submit to the word of a greater authority than themselves. They understand military rank. They understand we must do things in order.

In the same way, all accusations we have against others should be brought to God and when our heart is right, God will show us what to do. He always wants us to trust Him to deal with any issue. God is above any authority we are under and He knows how to deal with those He has allowed to be in that place.

OVERCOMING CURSES

God's people can't be touched by curses by any enemy, unless we are not covered by God. The curses will only affect us if we align ourselves with the curser by our own decisions and actions. As long as we are obedient and following God, they are ineffective. We have been given the authority to speak God's word, condemning any words spoken against us. (Isaiah 54:17) What do you do about the words that are spoken against you? What defense do you have? We take authority over them with our mouth by saying what God is saying. For example: No weapon shall work against me according to God's word. We have to know what God's word says. This is why a believer should know the scripture. The Psalms says,

> *I have hidden your word in my heart, that I might not sin against you.*
> *Psalms 119:11*

The word has to be in your heart, not just in your head through memorization. The word will keep you from sin, which will keep you from being impacted by the curse. Israel was told to obey God and carefully follow all the commands given so that they will not be affected and overtaken by the curses that other nations received from their wickedness. (Deuteronomy 28:15)

In my study of scriptures, I don't recall God cursing man. Some will say I have read where God says to man you are cursed. Let's understand that **God never tells a man he is a curse.** And the meaning of being cursed was always conditional upon a person's actions. God cursed the ground and Jesus cursed a fig tree. There was also the pain that came with child bearing, the ability to win a war, and loss of possessions because of the robbing of God through non-tithing in the book of Malachi. It appears people can be under a curse, but not cursed themselves. **God cursed things not people.** They were things done and said that affected man. When God says someone is accursed, He is saying someone through their own will have allowed the curses that come from sin to operate in their life. This is just like death. Death impacted mankind only when they sinned. Death had no power or impact on a human life until it was activated by sin. No person is a curse, but by their actions can activate a curse on their life.

God told Joshua, "Be careful to obey all the commands so that no curses will be upon you. (Joshua 1:8) Things are cursed because of people's actions, not the people themselves. It means what a man does will not be fruitful or favorable. The man himself can't be a curse, but can live under a curse. Curses are things that happen to us as a result of our disobedience. It is our disobedience to God that brings about a curse. God told Moses,

> *He said, "If you will obey me completely by doing what I consider right and by keeping my commands,* **I will not punish you with any of the diseases** *that I brought on the Egyptians. I am the LORD,* **the one who heals you.***"*
> *Exodus 15:26 (GNT)*

The people were under a curse when they sinned. They cursed themselves by their own disobedience. This was the result of the power of a set word put in action until someone breaks the curse by the power and blood of Jesus, using His name and following His command. If someone was cursed themselves, how would you remove it? It would seem that it was a part of them and permanent, but this is not true. God took on himself the curse that was connected to sin, so that we would no longer have to live with it.

BLESSED TO BE A BLESSING

We as children of God are not cursed, but blessed and we have received all spiritual blessings in the heavenly realm. We have access to all the blessings of God. We are blessed to be a blessing to others. We are always receiving from God so that we can share it with others. Please let us think higher than what man has a tendency to think about. We are not referring to material things for these are not the true blessings given to us by God. I call what we receive from God here on the earth *benefits*. These come with the promise of God to take care of us; giving us what we need while we do His kingdom work here on the earth.

The true blessings we have been given from being a part of the Kingdom of Heaven are God's love, peace, and joy. (Romans 14:17) The kingdom of God is a kingdom of power. (1 Corinthians 4:20) This power is demonstrated in the destruction of evil. The greatest gift you can have as a believer is not a car, house, or high position; it is the Holy Spirit. This is received by the one God has blessed. He has blessed us with blessings that far surpass anything this earth could offer us. God's children on the earth have received spiritual blessings that can also be seen in the natural.

People who understand the true blessings don't focus on the benefits; the natural things we are given. People who understand real blessings, don't even give to get natural things in return. They give because they are motivated by the God of love who leads them.

Blessings from God are out of man's ability to control. It's only in man's ability to obey God and expect His results. We have no control over how, when, or where the blessing will come. This is the part God does. This is besides what we do. My focus is not on the blessings that come as a result of the relationship, but on the relationship itself. **God does not need our help to bless us, He only needs our obedience**. A life of obedience means we have fellowship with the Master and in knowing His will and hearing His voice, we are then able to do in this earth what He would want us to do for Him.

Dear God,

Where I have been misinformed about blessings and curses, I thank you for helping me today. I don't want to be destroyed from lack of knowledge about you. Forgive me for curses that came out of my mouth against others. Forgive me for seeking physical blessings instead of you alone. In Jesus Name, Amen.

LIE #14
WE ARE HEALED FROM OUR PAST

He heals the broken-hearted and bandages their wounds.
Psalms 147:3 (NLT)

We are all broken in some way. We all need Jesus to fix us whether we choose to admit it or not. Broken people are many times the most defensive and sensitive people in the world. No matter how delicate you are in dealing with them, they still tend to feel hurt and attacked. If you begin to confront the layers of issues that have become their protective covering, they may fight you. The defensive and survival mechanisms we wear, I will call fig leaves.

I first learned this idea from a pastor in the USA. Fig leaves are what the Bible says the first man, Adam, used to cover him and his wife after they realized they were naked. They disobeyed God and lost their innocence. (Genesis 3) These fig leaf coverings are symbolic to how humans use false layers to cover their shame, guilt, and sin. We become used to our coverings even though they are not comfortable, preferable, or beneficial in the long run. When we've had them on for such a long time, trying to get us to exchange it for what is better can be really hard. The better option, we will call soft wool.

This wool from the sheep became available through death. This blood of a lamb was later replaced by Jesus, the Son of God, who came in human form. He was the sacrificial lamb slain for us. It was He who clothed Adam and his wife Himself in the beginning using this animal skin. He did this to demonstrate in picture, what it would take in years to come with His own death on a cross, to cover mankind from his broken state. It is He who desires to clothe and make Liberia whole along with every other nation.

We have been brain washed in this world to believe that image is everything. This believed lie has cost so many of us, keeping us from experiencing freedom in our lives. The truth is, **image is important, but it is not everything**. Unfortunately for many Liberians image is still everything. We are willing to pretend everything is good and fine with us when it is not the case. We are willing to look good on the outside regardless of the pain we have on the inside. Looking good is the way to feel good about ourselves temporarily and to feel like we have some value. We don't realize our value should never come from things like clothing, houses, jewelry, positions, and diplomas. Our value comes from God who created us. We are valuable just because we are made in His image. We are to find our value in God, the source. Any other way and any other thing we use to make ourselves valuable is a falsehood and cover up.

Insecurity still prevails in our life, but it's rarely admitted. When a person is really ashamed, they will fight for any pride that remains. That's why people will fight one another over the most minimal things. They feel to give in, is to lose the little remaining pride they have left. Deep inside the man is a broken boy hiding in a prideful man's body and inside the woman, a shattered girl suppressing feelings that come from being abused. We mirror a boy or girl who was abandoned, never able to cry, to feel the pain or emotions of the moment, to share their real feelings, to ask anyone for help and ask why, but to suck it up and take the abuse and survive anyway possible, dealing quietly with hunger and abuse, and never letting people see us be weak. We are still broken and not healed. Those coming from this experience soon come to the conclusion in their own mind that no one cares, has compassion for them, or wants to help them. They are convinced that reaching out will only end in rejection anyway. What do you do when you have been pretending for so long that the things you went through have not affected you deeply? We have become adept at hiding our feelings, emotions, secrets, pains, and hurts.

How many of us have been made to believe that we should not cry over it or dwell on it, because it's over now? We have been told that we made it. However, the reality is, there was so much trauma and it is still affecting our life today. If we don't truthfully deal with it, not only will we suffer a low-quality existence, but we will pass this on to our children as well.

The church does a great job of using God and religion to cover and hide things. We say we have God and we are alright, but we don't deal truthfully with the horrible things that were part of our growing up and have impacted our minds, thoughts, feelings, and behaviors. The things that have left an imprint on our life still shows up in how we act and treat ourselves, family, and others. It impacts how we see ourselves, family life, and our world. Our trust issues, our anger issues, our addictive behavior whether sexual, alcohol, food, control, lying, greed for material, and abusive parenting can all be traced to thought patterns gained from our experiences.

Many Liberians I personally know, don't deal with the truth. They hide it. They ignore it. They conceal what is really going on. It's like pretending you don't see it. It's tough because acting this way has become a part of us, because it is a part of our culture. It's what has been taught through modeling and experience; it's how people have always dealt with it.

I believe there are a few reasons for this. **The first is: I think it's a way of dealing with the atrocities of evil all around that conflict one's soul.** There is a feeling of helplessness and we can't see how anything can change. There is the thought that this is the way it is, has been, and there is nothing that can be done to change it. We feel we have to find a way to live around it. The most often quoted phrase I hear from people is, "THIS IS LIBERIA." They are saying to me, this is what you should expect. This is how we operate here. People have accepted what Liberia has become and now participate in the lifestyle most live, many times against their own conscious. Dysfunction has become the norm for too many.

The second reason is: we want the appearance of looking and feeling good without the sacrifice of actually being good. The goal is to look good socially at all cost even though we know the shameful things that are happening behind closed doors. Using people and exploiting the vulnerable while getting all you can get, becomes part of how many survive. Looking out for ourselves first and foremost is what we seem to do. This supersedes walking with purity and being right with God and man. We would rather pay the cost of appearing good because it matters so much to us. We exchange it for character, integrity, and discipline. We pay no attention to the idea of delayed gratification (waiting patiently for better results).

I didn't quite understand why this was like this so much with Africans and Black Americans alike. One of my regular sayings when addressing this is "BLACK PEOPLE ONLY SEEM TO CARE ABOUT LOOKING GOOD AND EATING GOOD." Perhaps having been deprived of such basic psychological needs for so long, we prioritize the need to feel good about ourselves immediately. Perhaps, it is a sense of low self-worth and needing to feel important anyway we can. It wasn't until I went through an experience with someone of African background, living in a Caribbean country, that I got an idea of how important appearance is to us in everything.

In this experience, I had known this particular person for several years. We have a mutual love and respect for each other and I consider him as my own son. He had never dealt deceitfully with me before. One day, it came to my attention that he was given some money by a donor. His secretary was to deliver the money to him for children we were helping. Despite her promise, she never did. One of his advisors, upon hearing about this, told him she would replace the stolen money. When the donor had asked him if he had received the money, he told them he had. When I asked him if he had received the money, he said No, but he had the money. Unable to understand this, I inferred more and he told me what happened. He did not want to tell the donor what happened because his advisor, who replaced the money, said it would make their people look bad.

As I reflected on what happened, I realized I saw this subtle mindset in other dealings with others. Some call it saving face. Keep the appearance clean so someone won't think less of you or your people. We have been taught to conceal and cover at every opportunity. It is the hiding game. We feel we must present ourselves in a positive light even if we have to lie. We must protect ourselves from all shame and guilt. We will do whatever it takes to make sure we appear good.

We have been told never to expose the secret deeds of evil. Although, we all fail at times, we are supposed to not allow it to be known.

Any evil is not to be exposed, talked about, or discussed is the philosophy many have. We say everyone does it; but if everyone does it, WHY ARE WE HIDING IT? I think I get it. We don't want other people to think we are doing it too. Liberia, just like anybody else, sees exposure as shame. The shame and guilt of wrongdoing must never be admitted to the world. This is what one psychologist deems as a broken ego. When all you have in your eyes is your self-respect and nothing else, you will do whatever you must do to protect it. To lose your self-respect is to lose everything. When you are broken already, that is the last break to a state of non-recovery. To be broken all the way down is to lose everything and we feel our self-respect is all we have left, so we must protect it. So, we continue to pretend, ignore, and forget about the truth. The harm that is done is never fixed. For Liberia to continue to function like this, keeps a cycle of abuse and lies continuing from one generation to the next.

The most damaging thing is the unspoken code. This behavior of silence and secrecy seems to be followed by almost everyone. Everything must stay as secret as possible. We don't want to endure public shame for our secret shameful deeds. What we do in the dark must never come to the light. Anyone who exposes anyone else in our family, church, or community must be discredited, disgraced, and slandered. Everyone must see what happens to anyone that tries to make us look bad.

Since all this behavior is accepted and seen as normal, nobody believes it is wrong. Nobody acknowledges any wrong. If they do, they keep it to themselves for fear. Things resume the same and nothing ever changes. This is the very opposite of what Jesus said we should do, "Have nothing to do with the worthless things that people do, things that belong to the darkness. Instead, **bring them out to the light**." (Eph 5:11)

> *This is how the judgment works; the light has come into the world, but people love the darkness rather than the light, because their deeds are evil.* ***Those who do evil things hate***

*light and will not come to the light, because they do not want their evil deeds to be shown up. But **those who do what is true come to the light*** in order that the light may show that what they did was in obedience to God.
John 3:19-21 (GNT)

I believe the third reason that people struggle to deal with ugly truth is because they don't know how. They don't really know what to do about it. I consider myself a patient person. I will try to figure anything out. I do not like to throw anything good away. I just hate wasting things when I know there is a good use for it. However, there is one thing that I give up on immediately: any string like things that are all knotted up. I throw it away. The entanglement is way too much for me. If it's a few, maybe two through ten entangled things together, no problem. But if it is too many, forming a knot, in my mind it's almost impossible for anyone to untangle. I don't have that much time to try to straighten it out and I know my frustration level will rise during the attempt.

We can look at our lives sometimes and envision it like that. It is one great big knot. How in the world will we ever get everything untangled and straightened out with some order? What steps does one take to try to fix what seems to be such a tattered life? How do you undo what has already been done? How do we go back and get what we needed and missed as a child? The answer to the question is WE CAN'T. There is only one person who can take the broken, shattered pieces of our life and somehow make some sense out of it and bring us into wholeness again. His name is Jesus.

We must allow Him to do His work. We must first get out of His way. We can't deal with our hurt and broken souls, that are full of deep pain, through avoidance. We can't block it out by immersing ourselves in worldly activities to fill our mind, thoughts, and time; trying to drown out bad memories and voices that come from our past. We can't use money, materials, food, relationships, or anything else in this world as a substitute to make our soul feel better. God is the only one that can truly fill the hole in our soul. True joy, peace, love, and rest will never come unless we abandon all else realizing He is the only answer and more than capable Himself of repairing us once and for all.

As I look through the scriptures, I notice that the way God approaches us with our sin, shame, guilt, or the negative events, that have happened in our life, is to ask questions. The reason why God asks man questions is to get to the truth. Look at the questions He asked people before He resolved their issues:

- He asked Adam, "Where are you?" when he was hiding.
- He asked the lame man laying at the pool, "Do you want to get well?" as he had been in the same condition for many years.
- He asked Moses, "Who gave man his mouth?" when Moses said he couldn't speak well enough to represent God.
- He asked Sarah, "Why did you laugh? Is there anything too hard for God?" when God promised to give her a child in her old age.
- He asked Cain, "Why are you angry?" when God would not receive his disrespectful offering.
- He asked Jacob, "What is your name?" when Jacob wanted God to bless him.
- He asked Peter, "Who do you say I am?" when others were calling him just another good man.
- He asked Paul, "Why are you persecuting me?" when Paul was persecuting His church.

He already knows the truth, but we need to be able to see this truth. He wants us to answer His questions so we can come to the truth in every situation. Without this truth, we can't be healed and move forward. If we go on with our life without the truth, we will never be healed inside. It will be like living with a broken leg or broken heart for the rest of our life, anytime something happens that touches it, we will hurt all over again.

We can no longer use the name of God and the appearance of being spiritual to cover up our dysfunction. God calls us to relationship and in relationship He wants us to deal with the truth. He wants to expose the darkness and bring healing. He wants us to be fixed and not to hide.

> *He who covers his sins will not prosper, but whoever confesses and forsakes them will have mercy.*
> *Proverbs 28:13 (NKJV)*

God's goal is for us to get well, become better, and be fruitful. Let us start making some progress to see positive change. We can accomplish this with God's help, true repentance, and a commitment to living a righteous life. Where do we start?

- **Have a real prayer session. This is honest communication between yourself and God.**

The key is to tell the truth about yourself, the person that hurt you, the situation that happened, how that made you feel, how that hurt you, what you wanted and needed, how that has affected you. What struggles do you have today because of it? What mindset do you have today about God? about authority? about life, security, and your ability? Do you see yourself as valuable? How do you see love, family, and how to treat others? What broke your heart? What wounded you? You must work through the pain to resolve it with the help of the Holy Spirit. Look at the ugliness of what happened and give it to God. Forgive yourself and forgive others. Deal with your suppressed emotions. You have to allow yourself to be broken.

> *The sacrifice pleasing to God is a broken spirit. You will not despise a broken and humbled heart, God.*
> *Psalms 51:17*

Many of my fellow Liberians can show lots of emotion when it comes to arguing a point, fussing over things, and protesting, but I have rarely seen them cry, express heartfelt love, and give affection.

God is looking for us to allow Him to take our hardened and broken heart with broken dreams and trust Him with it. He is looking for the passion from our heart towards Him instead of everything and everyone else.

This is not the time to blame other people, other things, and God. Though it is important to let God know if you are disappointed in Him. He won't get mad at your truth. This is what He wants, so He can address it. This is not a feeling sorry for ourselves or blaming ourselves session. This is acknowledging our mistakes and receiving God's love, forgiveness, and healing so we can move forward and never beat ourselves up again.

> *For the kind of sorrow God wants us to experience leads us away from sin and results in salvation. There's no regret for that kind of sorrow. But worldly sorrow, which lacks repentance, results in spiritual death.*
>
> 2 Corinthians 7:10 (NLT)

We can't do anything about what others did or what they do. We have to set our heart to love and forgive them. We can only take full responsibility for ourselves. **Change your mindset. Change your habits. Change your company. Change how you speak.** Don't live in fear and take action to fulfill your God given destiny.

- **Get Godly counsel from a mentor - spiritually mature person - who can pray with you and walk with you through your healing process.**

The reason we as believers of Christ are called the body of Christ, is because we are many members. These members of the body are there to support each other. This works much like our physical body works together so we can live our life well. I always suggest making sure men are counseling men and women walking with women. We want to prevent the enemy from trying to come in. We are well aware of his schemes. The Bible tells us:

Two are better than one because they have a good return for their labor, for if one falls down, his companion can lift him up; but pity the one who falls without another to help him up!
Ecclesiastes 4:9 (BSB)

A person's thoughts are like water in a deep well, but someone with insight can draw them out.
Proverbs 20:5(GNT)

Many are afraid of the perceived shame that may come when someone else knows the truth about what has happened to us. Nobody likes being judged by another or feeling judged. I don't want people judging my actions either. However, I must not fear man and seek man's approval above God's. **We will never be free to live our best life as long as we are fearful and too concerned about what man thinks of us.** You will notice that I made a distinction between you and your actions. The focus is on judging the actions. This is what people need to do because this is what they see. We can't always know someone's heart, but God knows it. So, God's judgement about the actual person is most important.

I can remember going through my own personal struggle with a particular issue. I knew what I was doing was not pleasing to God, but no matter how much I prayed, read my Bible, and repented, I still found myself constantly falling. I took the chance of sharing with a brother in the Lord because I did not want to keep hiding in the darkness and I knew I needed to expose this thing and have someone keep me accountable for my actions. It was a monumental step in my becoming whole, keeping my integrity, and being more empowered by God. What the scripture says about this is very true:

Confess your faults one to another, and pray one for another, that ye may be healed. *The effectual fervent prayer of a righteous man has much power.*
James 5:16

Let's make sure other people's judgement of us can't matter so much that we will disobey God. The only people that have a right to judge our actions are those that have authority over us and fellow believers for righteous living; even then, their judgment must be righteous. Righteous judgement is in accordance with the way God would judge us. God is the ultimate judge. When someone judges you un-righteously, they are bringing that same judgement on themselves because none of us are completely innocent of sin. God says, we should never fear man's opinion, judgement, or actions against us because He has the final say.

> *Do not fear them, for the LORD your God is the one fighting for you.*
> *Deuteronomy 3:22 (NASB)*

> *Don't be afraid of them who can only destroy your body and nothing else, but fear him who is able to destroy your body and soul in hell.*
> *Matthew 10:28*

- **Expect God to completely heal you.**

In the gospel of John chapter 11, the Bible shares with us the story of a lady named Mary who was very expressive in her worship to our Lord. She loved Jesus with everything, as seen by the way she stayed at His side when He taught. One day she even washed His feet with oil and her own hair. One particular event happened that would challenge her greatly. Her brother Lazarus was sick and she sent word to Jesus that the one He loved was sick. Jesus response was to show up after he had been dead in the tomb for four days. When Mary was told Jesus was finally almost there, she didn't even go out to greet Him like she normally would. She was still in mourning for her brother and my guess is, probably a little hurt and angry at Jesus for not coming a lot sooner. Jesus requested for Mary to come to Him. When she finally came, she just kneeled before Him. Being overwhelmed with sorrow and absent of a proper greeting, she blurted out with tears rolling down her face, "If you would have been here, my brother would not have died." Immediately after this, with her wailing loudly, Jesus could not take any more as he was deeply troubled by her hurt and pain. He himself about to cry asked her, "Where have you laid him?"

Why would He ask this question? I believe Jesus asked her because He always wants for us to show Him the source of our pain, so He can do something about it. If we don't give Him the root of our pain, how will He be able to permanently remove it from our life so it never comes back again. God doesn't want us to give Him symptoms. He doesn't deal with symptoms. He deals with roots. If we give symptoms, we will wonder why years later we are still dealing with the same problems. It is not our government, neighbors, spouse, or God that is our struggle, usually it is our disobedience, rebellion, generational curses, broken childhood, hearts of unforgiveness, and prideful arrogance that are our real problem.

We know in the end of the story, that He raises Lazarus from the grave. God was showing them that it is never over, until He says it is done. He has power even over death. There is nothing that He can't do. There is no problem or situation that He can't change. He is the God of the impossible. If you show Him your pain, He will heal it. We must believe and let Him speak and pronounce life over the dead places in our life. Our ending will always be most glorious if we let Him work in it.

Ruth, the Moabitess, was daughter in law to Naomi. Naomi was a descendant of the children of Israel, God's people. Naomi left her people with her husband and sons to live in another place for a short time during a famine. In this temporary place, her husband and both her sons who had married, died. Now all alone, Naomi decided to return to her country. Her daughter in law Ruth, refused to let her go back alone. Ruth abandons her own heritage to join Naomi, her people, and her God. In short, God provides a kinsmen redeemer to marry Ruth, giving Naomi a grandson that would bring forth the worshipper King David and later Jesus Christ, the Savior of the world. Just like Ruth and Naomi, nothing we have had to go through or deal with was to completely defeat or destroy us. It was rather to bring us into seeing God's greatest triumphant victory in our life.

In February 2020, while visiting Liberia, I was praying in the early morning hours at my hotel and the Lord told me He was going to transform Liberia. God said He was going to get the glory out of it. God will do it by His mighty hand. Let God redeem your situation. He will bring back the value to something that seems worthless. If you were left empty, it was so that God could fill you up with what He wants you to have.

I pray you will use the three ways I just mentioned to help in your recovery and restoration for spirit, soul, and body. We don't have to live a life of pretend and make believe leading to a life of survival and temporary happiness. Never forget, **GOD CAN'T HEAL WHAT YOU WON'T GIVE HIM.**

As I have said before, the major barrier to healing is getting people to deal with the truth. I believe many mental hospitals would be almost empty if people were willing to deal with truth. When the truth is too hard, people resort to creating another world in their mind to cope. Some people turn to drug and alcohol use. Suicide also becomes an option people consider when they feel they are unable to fix a problem in this life. They feel things can't or won't be fixed in their mind and they would rather die than to live with it. For as many people, who thankfully don't choose that option, there are many who live daily in a depressed state; hating life and wishing they were not here. This seems to be just as bad.

Remember, God is here to turn your mourning and sorrow into joy and gladness. Jesus said:

> *If you are tired from carrying heavy burdens, come to me and I will give you rest. Take the yoke I give you. Put it on your shoulders and learn from me. I am gentle and humble, and you will find rest.*
>
> Matthew 11:28-29 (CEV)

I knew a young man I used to mentor that was a habitual liar. He came from a broken family with lots of dysfunction and he would tell the most grand stories about his father and his family. His stories would seem to be unbelievable but why would I question him. When the truth was actually found out, it was nothing close to what he shared. He had created and imagined this in his mind until he believed it. His reality was so bad, he created a false reality that was good. He felt he couldn't be honest with what was really true. He wanted everyone to believe he was important, so he told a story that he thought would give that impression.

I told him one day, he didn't have to lie to be important and worthy. He was already created valuable and that could never be taken away no matter what he went through in life. He didn't need to say he was something he was not to prove how valuable he was. However, he had formed this habit and didn't stop. It continued up to the day his life was cut short early when he was the victim in a shooting by his neighbor. His mentality and mouth, while trying to establish an image that was not real, helped lead to his demise.

This is a great example in many ways of the result of one's own sinful and broken state. We have two choices; one to cover ourselves as best as humanly possible or to come to God completely broken admitting all and asking him to fix it because we can't. My mentee had been pretending so long, it had become a way of life and he was now unable to find his true self. Our identity and purpose can be found in God, not in man's idea or this world's idea of success. Until we stop looking to this world for validation, we will never be secure in who God made us to be.

It has been almost 20 years since the end of the civil war in Liberia and many people have learned to live with trauma. **Time doesn't heal what you have never properly dealt with.** The deception we find ourselves in, is the belief that we are ready to move on from the past when we are not. Until properly dealt with, we will carry poison into our future and self-inflict ourselves while hurting others. We can't get over the past without confession and healing. God will bring glory out of the worst situations. Will you allow Him to do it for you?

Healing is not only physical

Many think that healing is only physical. So, people will ask for prayer for sickness and disease in their body. The preacher may in turn place some oil on the head and attempt to pray the sickness away. However, we just can't lay hands on people in every situation. Growing up in church, it appeared to me that the majority of the people that received prayer never got it answered. I now realize that many outward forms of illness are a result of mental and emotional disease as well as disobedience. It is a common understanding in science and medicine that many diseases can be connected to stress, fear, and one's own emotional state.

When Christ did His ministry, He preached the kingdom, healed the sick, and cast out demons. We know that demonic spirits can cause sickness as well. It is referred to in scripture as a spirit of infirmity (Luke 13:11). However, there are more regular church attenders that are bound by the spirit of fear, deception, and unforgiveness I believe. All these and more, allow the enemy to affect their health.

Churches need more teaching, understanding, and focus in these areas. There would be more services of complete deliverance if that were the case. In order for true deliverance to happen, people have to open up their mouths and make confessions about the areas they are bound in and speak what God's word says. We must open up our mouth and speak Gods truth in order to receive our own healing. If I want you to be healed and you want to be healed, but you won't do your part, my words won't overtake your non-action. If I pray for you to stop sinning and you don't want to stop sinning, my prayer will not overcome your will. Your change and miracles happen, when you really want it and you are willing to declare it with your mouth. Your words bring forth your reality. The only way someone else's words bring about your reality is if you agree with it, speak it, and allow it to happen in your own life.

When a person agrees from their heart with a particular word, change will happen. The man in the tomb possessed by devils wanted to be free and Jesus set him free inside and outside. (Mark 5:5-6)

Healing is a process

Healing is not an overnight occurrence all the time. Healing is a process many times. God is definitely able to do an immediate healing in one's emotions, but some healing is gradual. When we have lost a loved one, it takes time to grieve that person not being with us anymore. When we have been taken advantage of for a long time and we are frustrated; when we have been manipulated and lied to and are now dealing with the real truth, we may need to work through it. There may be other traumatic things we have experienced, that could be heartbreaking. We will probably need some time in experiencing our complete healing.

We are healed at the moment of our confession spiritually. The stripes of Jesus were already received so we can appropriate what God has done for us already in our lives today. However, sometimes the full complete physical showing in our body, mind, and actions may take a minute. For example: I can get a cut on my arm and it can look really bad, bleeding with flesh showing and broken skin. I can apply ointment right away and cover it. If I use what is necessary for the healing, will it look fine immediately? Probably not. When looking at it twenty-four hours later, it may not look that much better. In another month, I'm positive you will see it in a much better condition. You may only be able to detect a small scar of where there was once a really bad cut. The healing process begins immediately but the results may not be seen right away. Time must be given to close the wound. Medical care must be applied without further initial damage. The sore can never fully heal if it is constantly being reopened, picked, or reinjured during the healing process.

Some things we receive by faith but while we are waiting to see the physical manifestation, we must be diligent in keeping the prescription given by the doctor. The Great Physician, our Lord and Savior, commands that we continually speak words of life, separate from others who can reinjure it, and remove ourselves from any activity that could cause more problems.

God want's us as His children to be clean, pure, holy, uncorrupted, and undefiled by this world's negativity and abuse.

God wants us to be healed from the inside out. He wants us to be completely whole in our spirit, soul, and body. Then and only then, can we shine like lights in our world.

Heavenly Father,

I come to you broken. I have been through so many things in my life as you know. I didn't know how to properly deal with them and I didn't have anyone who knew how to help me. Today, I realize that I can give all my hurts, pain, and burdens past and present to you. I need your healing touch in my heart and my mind. I take authority to remove every spirit that has been at work in my life that is not from you and I release your Holy Spirit of love, joy, peace, and rest in its place. In Jesus Name. Amen

LIE #15
SOME PEOPLE ARE BETTER THAN OTHERS

For God shows no partiality [no arbitrary favoritism; with Him one person is not more important than another].
Romans 2:11 (Amplified)

A brother in the Lord recently shared with me that while he was working at a hospital treating his patient, this particular man treated him really bad. The man called him a nigger and told him that black people were created to serve white people amongst other things. This man delighted in the fact that he was a racist and saw white supremacy as a God given right. He even attempted to use the Bible to support his views. My dear brother in the Lord responded to him with nothing but love and even offered to pray for him. My brother even left him a beautiful note on his board before his shift ended. The more he expressed love for this man, the more insults that were hurled at him. Although this is very un-fortunate, I said to myself, "At least this man is open and honest about how he really feels." I seem to have more respect for people who don't have a problem letting me see who they really are. I rather deal with these people, than those who secretly do me wrong behind my back.

This chapter was added at the end of writing most of this book. I just couldn't print this book without dealing with this subject matter. This belief that some humans are better than others, has been around since time began; in fact, before the earth was even created. God created an angel named Lucifer and gave him one of the highest positions in the heavenly realm; right next to Him. Lucifer begin to see himself more than what he was created to be. He made a decision to try to overthrow Almighty God and become Him. The thought is unbelievable, but I guess those who get caught in the pride trap, need no good reason and have no boundary in an attempt to accomplish their goal of being on top.

After man disobeyed God, sin came into the world infecting everything starting with man's heart. The spirit of pride was activated. Men immediately began to fight, compete, and rival one another. Our selfish nature took over and instead of peace, unity, and harmony, we felt entitled to dominate each other. Man began to focus on their surroundings and live for their selfish desires instead of living for the purpose God gave them. Hate replaced love, taking replaced giving, having dominion over the earth included taking dominion over each other. God never created man to dominate other men. He is the only Lord over all of us. He calls His children, kings and priests.

Man is supposed to love the unique assignment God has given him to accomplish, but instead he wants to compare himself to others and what they are doing and top it. So, God is no longer man's standard of what is good, right, and successful. Now, they look to what everybody else is doing in the world in determining their worth and value.

Each man has inside of them a desire to be great. This is not a bad thing. In fact, I believe it is God given. God is great and He created each of us with greatness. We should want that greatness to come out and benefit the world we live in. This is why it was given. It is when we take pride in our own greatness that we have truly lost our way. First, we fail to understand that nothing we have came from us; it is a gift from God. In Him we live, move, and have our being. (Acts 17:28) We were never supposed to use the gifts He gave us for our own purpose. This is what Satan did.

Man wants to be worshipped when he follows the ways of Lucifer, the fallen angel, who wanted to be worshipped. He wanted the position of the Most-High God. He wanted the attention to be directed to him. He was created by God with so much beauty, talent, and gifts that the very thing God gave him, he used it to become proud and place it above the one who gave it to him.

King Nebuchadnezzar's story (Daniel chapter 4) reminds us also of what can happen when we don't see ourselves correctly. He was warned that he should give glory to God for everything God gave him. He disregarded the warning and lost his mind for seven years. He afterward gave God glory.

King Herod Agrippa died immediately when he accepted the worship of people who called him a god. (Acts 12:21-23) When we start believing in our own mind that we are something special or great, God will ultimately show us who we really are and who He really is. Since it all came from God, all the glory belongs to God. He doesn't share His glory, worship, or praise with anyone. We don't deserve it. How dare we put ourselves on a level to have people worship us.

JEALOUSY, ENVY, AND DIVISION

Jealousy and envy are a result of sin. Jealousy has more to do with one's emotions that target another person. Envy has to do with desiring the possessions that belong to another. They both occur when man stops looking to God and he begins to look at others. When man operates at a natural level instead of the spiritual level he was created to operate in, there will always be problems. Our flesh counts for nothing at all. The flesh stinks and is decaying because of sin. The flesh is rotten and doesn't give or bring life to anything. In other words, we stink apart from the Lord.

> *However, **if you have biter jealousy and selfish ambition in your heart**, then **stop bragging and living in ways that deny the truth**. This is not the wisdom that comes down from above. Instead **it is from the earth, natural and demonic. Wherever there is jealousy and selfish ambition, there is disorder and everything that is evil.***
>
> *James 3:14-16 (CEB)*

People are jealous because man is naturally selfish. They see what someone else has and they want that for themselves and are mad when they can't have it or get it. It is rooted in selfishness. They must allow God to deal with that fleshly evil spirit operating in their life. "For you are still of the flesh. For while there is jealousy and strife among you are you not of the flesh and behaving only in a human way?" (1 Corinthians 3:3)

Man's flesh wants to be seen by others because he likes to be the focus. He likes the light to shine on Him instead of on God. He does everything to make himself look good before making sure God is pleased. This is what happens when we are led by our flesh instead of God's spirit.

> *What is causing the quarrels and fights among you? Don't they come from the evil desires at war within you? You want what you don't have so you scheme and kill to get. You are jealous of what others have,* but you can't get it so ***you fight and wage war to take it away*** *from them. Yet **you don't have what you want because you don't ask God for it**. And even **when you ask**, you don't get it because **your motives are all wrong** – you want only what will give you pleasure.*
>
> James 4:1-3 (NLT)

We are jealous because of our sin nature. This sin nature has been played out in history from the very beginning. **Jealousy is the fearfulness of superiority.** It was the root for white supremacy, the idea that white people are better than other people. This belief did not initially come from truth, it came from fear. This whole desire to position oneself on a level above other human beings and pronounce yourself as superior, comes from the evil one. He starts with jealous thoughts that are suspicious lies and a desire to want what rightfully belongs to someone else. When men look at each other or when one nation looks at another, what do they see? In the case of the Europeans, they saw a blessed, prosperous land and strong people. They feared them and wanted what they had. This is the backdrop of a superiority complex. It is birthed by fear and insecurity. The Europeans past, present, and future who functioned accordingly were actually afraid of blacks. Let me take you back in history a moment.

> *But the people of Israel were fruitful and increased greatly; they multiplied and grew exceedingly strong, so that the land was filled with them. The new king said to his people, "Behold,* **the people of Israel are too many and too mighty for us.** *Come,* **let us deal shrewdly** *with them,* **lest they multiply, and,** *if war breaks out,* **they join our enemies and fight against us and escape** *from the land.*
> Exodus 1:7,9-10 (ESV)

The reason God's people were enslaved by the Egyptians was FEAR. False Evidence Appearing Real is what some have powerfully defined fear as. This fear led to lies of superiority to justify evil behavior. In order to keep control, trickery must be used. This is what is meant by dealing shrewdly with others. The main mode of operation is to divide. An enemy can take what he wants by keeping disorder, disunity, and division going. The enemy has used whatever he could to bring division through lies and fear to the human race. This includes white versus black, male versus female, Jew versus Gentile, Protestant versus Catholic, natives versus explorers, one tribe versus another tribe, and one nation against another nation. The wealthy versus poor, light skinned versus dark skinned, and educated versus uneducated. All of this is the work of the enemy.

When we are confronted with this truth and we don't do anything about it, we are not the peacemakers God created us to be. If we believe we are better than someone else for ANY reason at all, we have been deceived by the evil one. If we believe we are more worthy and more valuable than others, we have been deceived by the evil one. If we believe we deserve more than other people because of our position, title, education, gender, or anything else, we have believed a lie.

> ***Faith in Christ Jesus is what makes each of you equal with each other***, *whether you are a Jew or a Greek, a slave or a free person, a man or a woman.*
>
> *Galatians 3:28 (CEV)*

In the book of Acts, Peter visits Cornelius. This was significant because a Jew was in the house of a Gentile. This was forbidden. Jews saw Gentiles as unclean, but God told Peter not to call anything unclean that He made clean. When Peter saw how God visited the household of Cornelius like He did with the apostles at Pentecost, he said surely God is no respecter of persons but accepts all who genuinely seek Him.

We have been given a few examples in scripture of how the early church had to overcome showing partiality and practicing discrimination. James corrected the church after noticing when someone came into the church with stature, nice clothing, and jewelry, they were given a great seat and treated with reverence as opposed to those who came in dirty and poorly dressed. The poor were told to sit on the floor or stand. (James 2:2-4). The hearts of men are always shown by their actions. God would never treat us this way, yet we justify why we show preferences.

Paul had to confront and correct some of the disciples for their hypocrisy. They had acted differently around the non-circumcised when other circumcised believers were around. They would eat with Gentile Christians when no one was around, but stopped when Jewish Christians were around.

The scriptures let us know, "For there is no respect of persons with God." (Romans 2:11) God judges everybody by the same standard. God sees people in only two groups - those who are righteous and those who are ungodly. There are those who obey truth and disobey God, sheep and goats, the saved and the unsaved. His children and the devil's children, the lost and the found, the holy and unholy, those in darkness and those in the light. There are those who accept Him and those who reject Him. There is no advantage outside of that no matter who you think you might be. God doesn't have favorites among His children. The same rules apply, the same truth. He loves none greater or less, this includes man that has rejected Him.

KNOWLEDGE WITHOUT LOVE

I am reminded of a story I heard about some Americans who came to a village in Africa to show them how to plant particular crops and harvest them for their food supply. During the time of growing, certain animals destroyed all their work. As they surveyed the damage, the villagers told them we could have told you this would happen if you had asked us. This is what happens when we think we know it all and don't consider others and their experiences because we believe they don't know anything. We believe we are so much smarter and that nobody we see as below us is able to teach us anything.

So many times, people come with their knowledge they have gained to show somebody else what to do without involving them in the process. These are what I call dumb experts. Knowledge puffs up, but love builds up. (1 Corinthians 8:1) Knowledge makes people feel like they are special. I don't minimize honor for hard work and completion of programs, but we need to put them into perspective. Hopefully we learned more to serve our fellowmen, instead of pridefully seeing ourselves as better than another.

Learning seems to make people boast and walk around like they are better than others. Because they know something someone else doesn't. This is foolishness. Somebody, no matter how uneducated they may be, will know something you don't know; no matter how educated you may think you are.

Years ago, I helped a young man in Liberia to go to college. I only asked in return that he turn around and use his gifts to help other young people in his country. After completing his initial college education, in a conversation about some other people I was dealing with and helping in Liberia; he commented that he couldn't understand why I was placing faith in them. I should have looked to him because he was better than they were. In his eyes, they were uneducated. He now saw himself as educated and in a different group and spoke with disgust when referring to them. I'm sure this happens a lot and is unavoidable when you forget God and you buy into the social system based on wealth, education, and association. These are created by a society that doesn't fear God and value people. I told him don't ever say that to me. Don't ever say you are better than someone else. I don't care who you think you are and I don't care who you think they are. This rivalry, envy, and attitude of being better with each other, especially in the church of Jesus Christ, must end.

BEING GREAT

An argument started among the disciples as to which of them would be the greatest. Jesus, knowing their thoughts, took a little child and had him stand beside him. Then he said to them, "Whoever welcomes this little child in my name welcomes me; and whoever welcomes me welcomes the one who sent me. For it is the one who is least among you all who is the greatest." (Luke 9:46-48)

Let us take a five-year boy and stand him next to a man who has a church of a thousand people and the title of bishop. This man travels around the world and is involved in many good endeavors that help others and make his country better. He even gives counsel to government officials. If we were to ask God which person was more valuable to Him? What do you suppose God would say? They both have the same value to Him. They are both His children. One can't be compared to the other. Some people will have more responsibility and be accountable for more. These people are not more worthy to God than others who have less responsibility or notoriety.

If this is how God determines worth, why do we have a church that doesn't follow God's way, but instead operates according to a bias. Pastors have placed themselves as lord over the people instead of servant leader. The leadership has placed themselves as accounted more worthy. Women are used as servants to men. Many times, children and their needs are considered least and last. Our churches expect and receive much from its people, but give back little in return.

I am reminded of a story I heard about someone's vision of heaven where rewards were being given out to the righteous. This person said they recognized great men of faith from the earth and crowns were placed on their heads, but he noticed a really large crown and was wondering who that one could be for. He said when the Lord took that bigger crown in His hand, He placed it on the head of a lady nobody recognized from the earth. The Lord said, "She was an intercessor and her ministry made it possible for His great servants on the earth to be successful; leading many souls to the Kingdom." We can't determine someone's value based off of looks and our personal thoughts. God sees each one's heart and He knows what He has called each one of us to do.

Another time in Jesus ministry, He placed a child among them. This humble and innocent child was referred to Jesus as the greatest in the Kingdom of Heaven. (Matthew 18:2-3) We must become like one of them to be great. We must serve and put everyone else first. We must wash everyone else feet if we want to be great. Most people won't humble themselves enough to apologize when they are wrong, let alone wash another's feet. The easiest thing is for people to be full of pride and the hardest thing is for people to be humble. **Pride is the absence of humility. I would say the absence of this character trait is most responsible for the dying, ineffective churches in Liberia.** We will never experience His glory as long as there is an unwillingness by church leaders everywhere to practice this one trait God requires from us. The church will remain active, but powerless without humility. God resists the proud and gives his grace to the humble. Humble yourselves under Gods mighty hand so in due time He can lift you up. (1 Peter 5:5-6)

God only lifts those up who lift Him up. We can only lift Him up when we have humbled ourselves. Most of the humility we see today in our churches is false humility. It is like the religious leaders of Jesus day where they appeared to humble themselves with disfigured faces during fasting and long great sounding prayers, but their intentions and behavior revealed the truth. They loved the greatest seats in the high places and to be saluted by men. They wore clothing that set them apart as a special group.

Today, you see men in robes, hats, chains, kingly chairs, big rings, and you see people treat them as gods. I was watching not too long ago a video from an African nation that held a rally at a stadium for a clergyman who made a name for himself throughout the world. The celebration supported by government and the church society appeared to be more about national pride since he was a native from there. I did not see any worship to the one true God during the whole program.

Why is it that man, who wants to be worshiped, finds it easier to worship someone just like him more than God who created them both? I believe that it is preferred by prideful man to take turns worshiping each other as they receive worship from the masses. This is opposed to seeking God. The enemy loves this. It is following in his footsteps of self-worship.

LOVE WALK

The scriptures make it very clear we are not to love ourselves above God and others, yet many in the church that supposedly represent Jesus do not follow in His footsteps nor obey His commands concerning this. This means they don't really belong to Him. You can't belong to the Light and walk in darkness.

> *If someone says, "I love God," but hates a fellow believer, that person is a liar; for if we don't love people we can see, how can we love God, whom we cannot see? And he has given us this command: Those who love God must also love their fellow brothers.*
>
> *1 John 4:20-21(NLT)*

The early disciples in the beginning of the church were together and had all in common. They sold their goods to meet each other's needs. They were of one heart and of one soul. They considered all their possessions as belonging to everyone. There was no lack. The money given to the disciples were given away to all the followers so that everyone's need was met.

Why do we look down on other people? Why do we believe other people are not worth our time or day? Why do we not care what happens to them good or bad? Why are we not concerned about where they will spend eternity? Why are we so willing not to give, love, or pray for others as if it was us in need? The second to the greatest command is just as important to God for us to follow: "Love your neighbor, as yourself." Another scripture says "Do unto others as you would want done unto you." (Matthew 7:12) If everyone who claimed to be a Christian actually lived according to this command, everything would change overnight in our world.

The problem is many who lead and govern nations have been corrupted by the deception of believing they are better than everyone else and more deserving. They withhold good, resources, and decisions that would be in everyone's best interest because of this false belief. They govern according to what is in the best interest of themselves and everyone like them.

Everyone else seems to be at the mercy of these leaders. They are exploited, excluded, and oppressed. Their life becomes expendable to evil leaders because of their lower roles in society's class structure. It is disturbing when we hear words like de-population, doctor assisted suicides, abortion, organ harvesting, trial vaccine experiments, and other things that are happening that devalue human life.

When you consider evidences that suggest diseases like Aids, Ebola, and Covid-19 were created as biological germ warfare used against mankind, it makes one sick to their stomach of how evil man can be. The unnecessary loss of life all over the world that is presented to us as one thing when in reality it is something totally different and based on greed, control, and this idea of superiority of a small percent of the world, shows us what can happen when this errant philosophy is at work.

It is not limited to people at the top, it can be seen in the poorest communities amongst those who are considered the undesirables. The way people can treat people, it doesn't take much for them to find something about themselves where they feel they are better and can mistreat others.

Christ said we should love as He has loved us. He tells us to honor one another. Where is the brotherly affection? Let us please his neighbor for his good, to build him up. We are to have a unity of mind, be sympathetic to one another with a tender heart. We are never to repay evil for evil or exchange insults. We do not rejoice when our brother fails or be happy to see him fall. We were called to love everyone as much as we love ourselves. We are instructed to do everything in love. "Therefore, as God's chosen people, holy and dearly loved, clothe yourselves with compassion, kindness, humility, gentleness, and patience." (Colossians 3:12)

THE ROLE OF GREATNESS

In Mark chapter 10, we are told that James and John secretly asked their mother to request from Jesus a seat for them next to Him in His kingdom. When the other disciples found out, there was anger and arguing. Jesus disciples were just like us today. It was not good enough just to be one of His followers, there was ambition on the part of most of them to attain the highest position of authority as possible. They craved honor and respect. They thought this was a good thing. Jesus explained to all of them that His kingdom does not operate like the worlds. The way up is down. The cup of suffering and sacrifice is what you have to drink to be great. They didn't get it at that moment and many of us still don't get it today.

The way to greatness in God's eyes is to see how low you can go to serve others. Great people are servants who give up their life and serve with sacrifice and unselfishness. On another day, Jesus disciples were arguing again about who is the greatest. (Luke 22:24) Jesus told them that earthly leader's rule over others, but His leaders in His kingdom always take on the role of a lower status where they serve instead of being served. God's desire is to save and use as many people as possible to reach even more.

In the story found in Matthew chapter 20, God is shown as an employer providing opportunities for all to work and be rewarded. We find that He rewarded those who worked at the last minute the same way, He rewarded those who had been working all day. The workers who started much earlier were upset. His response was, "Are you angry because I am generous?" He said, "The first shall be last and the last first." He wanted them to understand that their focus should be on serving Him, not how he deals with others. Our focus must be on the mission He has given being completed. We can't see ourselves as greater than the vision and mission of our Lord. Our focus must be on Him. He is the author and finisher of our faith.

After Peter was told by the Lord what kind of death he would die to bring God glory, he asked our Lord what about John. The Lord responded, "If I want him to stay until I return, what does that have to do with you, you follow and obey me." Like runners at a track meet, we have all been given a lane to run in. We are disqualified if we get in someone else lane. We must be careful not to interfere with another's progress or kill them through comparison. Liberia is waiting for leaders who understand greatness doesn't lift itself above others. We are our brother's keeper and God's love is the greatest tool we have.

DO YOU WANT TO GET WELL?

This was the question Jesus asked the impotent man laying by the pool of Bethesda. He had been laying there for thirty-eight years. Instead of answering Jesus question, he proceeded to tell Him about all the problems he faced that kept him from getting well. He told Jesus he had no one to help him and that someone always got in front of him in his effort to get to his miracle. Jesus never asked him these things. It was only a simple question that needed a simple answer. You may be thinking like the man thought, "It's not as simple as that, if it was, I would not still be in this place." However, it is as simple as Jesus made it. A simple answer would be YES, I want to get well. Jesus response would be to you, the same as it was to this man, "Get up, take up your mat, and walk."

He challenged him to do what he could never see himself doing physically. In order to get up, he had to look up. He had to stop looking at himself laying there and look at the one who could empower him to get up. He had to get out of the posture he was in. If you want to walk, you shouldn't be in a lay back position. He had to grab hold of what was holding him back. He had to overrule the bed that was carrying him, by carrying it. He had more power over the situation he was laying in, but couldn't see it without Christ command. He had to attempt to move forward on his feet in faith on what Christ spoke, instead of waiting for his friends or some luck to come his way.

The goal of life is not to survive, but to live out the purpose you were created for no matter what is happening around you and to you. You have moments where you have to fight to keep living, but it's not for you to just exist and stay in the same place. You were not meant to die there. We should always be expecting something more than what we had before. We are trusting God as we change our mindset and our actions.

It is time for us as leaders to take responsibility; we have been honoring ourselves long enough.

It is time to allow God to teach us through His Holy Spirit; man has taught us long enough.

It is time to know God and His Word; the enemy has fooled us long enough.

It is time to worship from our heart; we have memorized what to say and do long enough.

It is time to be an original; we have copied others long enough.

It is time to think for ourselves; we have let others think for us long enough.

It is time to believe in what God has given us; we have believed more in others long enough.

It is time for us to get God's wisdom; we have been learning from man long enough.

It is time for us to live; we have been surviving long enough.

It is time for us to pay our debts; we have been borrowing long enough.

It is time to provide for ourselves; we have asked others for money long enough.

It is time for us to invest in ourselves; we have been spending our money elsewhere long enough.

It is time to activate our faith in God; we have depended on others long enough.

It is time to actually be the church; we have done church long enough.

Those who think righteous living doesn't work are wrong. I am a living example. I also have many witnesses I know who demonstrate the blessing of living a righteous life. You have to believe God and you have to commit your life and submit your total will to Him to find out. **WE HAVE TO STOP JUST PRAYING AND WE HAVE TO START REPENTING AND OBEYING.**

The cost has been heavy; too many people are suffering and too many lives are being destroyed unnecessarily. All in the name of looking as good as we can, ignoring the needs of each other, and looking out for ourselves. The hypocrisy and games with God and against the innocent must cease.

My former pastor says, "If you throw a rock at a pack of dogs, the one that barks is usually the one that got hit." The content of this book hits us and forces us to look at ourselves and be honest about where we came from, where we are at, and where we are going. We spend our life trying to avoid problems and conflict instead of dealing with them. We must not run from conflict, but fight for our God given destiny and future heritage.

It is in our nature to not like anything that doesn't stroke us or make us feel and look good. However, there is no real growth that comes from that. There is a scripture that says, "Faithful are the wounds of a friend; but the kisses of an enemy are deceitful." (Proverbs 27:6) I speak to you as a friend. Even Jesus says no one enjoys discipline at the moment, but it produces fruit in the end, if it is taken. God's love disciplines.

If we do not listen to the Word of God and we don't repent, we will not see God's blessings, yet we will be held accountable for what we heard. If we listen with our ears, but do not open our heart and mind to the Spirit of God, instead allowing pride and stubbornness to keep us from obedience, then we truly do not belong to Him. He said, "My sheep hear my voice and another they will not follow." (John 10:27) If we follow a voice that is not His, then we prove we are not His sheep.

The church is not powerful enough to deal with disobedient spirits from those outside until it has been obedient to God in dealing with itself. It remains powerless to do anything in the meantime. We must no longer be fooled. We must no longer stay divided. The greatest and only weapon against darkness and evil in the world, is the real church of Jesus Christ; those that make up His Spirit filled body. Without His church and their influence, there is no hope for one's country and the world. He is the ONLY answer to our problems. **LIBERIA's destiny is left in its own citizen's hands.**

If one person reads this book and makes a decision to commit to repenting from sins, changing their mind, acknowledging lies they have believed, and begin to agree with God instead and live differently, then my purpose was done and this writing was worth it. You are one person, but can affect many people by your behavior. As a leader, you can powerfully change the course of your church and ultimately the society at large by bringing God's truth into every area of life.

The church has not been doing what it is called to do: WIN SOULS. It has lost this purpose and has reduced itself into an organized religious activity which is dead to God. It is an exchange of people's time and talents. God is hardly benefitted by anything and God is not there to do anything, except revealing himself to those truly looking for Him outside of man's ritualistic services. It might as well be called tomb worship. There is nothing but dead dry bones there.

Like Ezekiel asked the Lord, "Can these bones live?" This was my question about Liberia's churches. The Lord's response to me about Liberia is the same as it was to Ezekiel, "Speak to the dry bones and command them to live." I prophesy into the atmosphere and I call forth the remnant of God's people in Liberia and I say, "You shall live and not die!" You shall be changed! You shall see the salvation of the Lord! You shall come to life and help transform your nation! I declare the breath of God to blow on you! I decree the Holy Spirit will empower you for great works of service!

God has called me to speak to this nation. I pray you take all of what He has given me for you. Remember you can expect the winds of true revival after you have repented to God in every area and allow His word and spirit to lead your life. It is only then that He is able to bring His word to pass. He said if **HIS PEOPLE** humble themselves, turn from wickedness, and seek a real relationship with Him, He would *hear* them, *forgive* their sins, and *heal their land*. **THAT IS HIS ONLY WAY AND THAT IS OUR ONLY HOPE.**

Here are the missing ingredients needed for anyone who wants to experience the blessing of God in their life and country:

1. Make a commitment to prayer. Communicate daily with God and let him communicate with you.
2. Make a commitment to love God with ALL your heart, mind, soul, and strength. Put Him before everything and be willing to suffer for Him.
3. Make a commitment to live righteously as Christ lived. Do not make excuses for doing wrong. Repent and change your mind.
4. Make a commitment to love your fellow man – including your enemies. Love as God loved you.

BIBLIOGRAPHY

Boge, Paul. *Father to the Fatherless: The Charles Mulli Story.* Canada: Castle Quay Books 2005

Ciment, James. *Another America: The Story of Liberia and the Former Slaves Who Ruled It.* New York: Hill and Wang, 2013.

Johnson, Sirleaf Ellen (2011, August 12) *How America Aid is Lifting Liberia.* The Washington Post. Retrieved from https:// www.washingtonpost.com/opinions/how-america-aid-is-lifting-liberia/2011/08/12/glQAASLxBJ_story.html

Mensah, Wisdom. University of West Florida. Oct 29, 2018 https://theconversation.com/girls-in-west-Africa-offered-into-sexual slavery-as-wives-of-gods-105400

Merriam- Webster.com, *Merriam Webster*, 2019 retrieved March - June 2020 from https://www.merriamwebster.com/dictionary

Reef, Catherine. *This is our Dark Country: The American Settlers of Liberia.* New York: Clarion Books, 2002.

Strong, James. *Strong's Exhaustive Concordance of the Bible.* Abingdon Press, 1890

US Relations with Liberia: Bilateral Relations fact sheet Bureau of African Affairs August 2, 2019 www.state.gov/us-rlations -with- Liberia Accessed: 6/1/2020

Kamkwamba, William, *The Boy Who Harnessed the Wind: Creating Currents of Electricity and Hope.* New York: Harper Perennial, 2010

Vulnerable Child Youth Studies 2017 www.ncbi.nlm.nih.gov the impact of transactional sex with teachers on public school students in Monrovia Liberia – a brief report

OTHER BOOKS BY THIS AUTHOR

TIME FOR A NEW KING

Everyone is impacted by a king, either one you chose or one you are not familiar with. Man believes he is the ultimate answer to solving his own problems; in a way he is, but in another way he is not. As he rules his and other men's lives, the world progresses materially while regressing in the areas of life that matter most. In a world plagued with so much evil and pain, there is only one king who can truly help mankind. In order for this to happen, man must be willing to give up sitting on his own throne allowing another to take his place.

ISBN: 978-0-9729904-1-7 SOFTCOVER 133 PAGES
Published in 2019

www.ingramcontent.com/pod-product-compliance
Lightning Source LLC
Chambersburg PA
CBHW052013290426
44112CB00014B/2226